Raising
Adopted
Children

Raising
Adopted
Children

Practical Reassuring Advice
for Every Adoptive Parent
Revised Edition

Lois Ruskai Melina

Quill
An Imprint of HarperCollins*Publishers*

RAISING ADOPTED CHILDREN (Revised Edition). Copyright © 1998 by Lois Ruskai Melina. All rights reserved. Printed in the United States of America. No part of this book may be used or reproduced in any manner whatsoever without written permission except in the case of brief quotations embodied in critical articles and reviews. For information address HarperCollins Publishers Inc., 10 East 53rd Street, New York, NY 10022.

HarperCollins books may be purchased for educational, business, or sales promotional use. For information please write: Special Markets Department, HarperCollins Publishers Inc., 10 East 53rd Street, New York, NY 10022.

Reprinted in Quill 2002.

Designed by Helene Wald Berinsky

Library of Congress Cataloging-in-Publication Data

Melina, Lois Ruskai.
    Raising adopted children : practical reassuring advice for every adoptive parent / Lois Ruskai Melina.—1st ed.
        p. cm.
    Includes bibliographical references (p.   ) and index.
    ISBN 0-06-095717-4
    1. Adopted children—United States. 2. Parenting—United States.
I. Title.
HV875.55.M44 1998   98-11880

05 06   RRD   30 29 28 27 26 25 24 23 22

To my daughter, Emily, and my son, Galen

Contents

ༀ *Part II:* AT HOME WITH ADOPTION

ༀ *Part III:* SPECIAL ISSUES IN ADOPTION

Preface

⁊❧　Being an adoptive parent is immensely satisfying, as I know from personal experience. In addition to the other joys parents know, we who have adopted sometimes marvel at the serendipitous creation of our family—adults and children who probably would never have known each other have become a family with deep attachments to one another.

I believe our enjoyment is enhanced, though, by greater insight into our children's thoughts, feelings, fears and experiences, as well as into our own psychological development as adoptive parents.

This book is intended as both a look at life in the adoptive family and as an ongoing source of information—a book parents will pick up again and again as their family progresses from adjustment to attachment to adolescence and to adulthood.

The need for a book like *Raising Adopted Children* was demonstrated more than thirty years ago by sociologist H. David Kirk. Surveying adoptive parents in the 1950s, Kirk found that some adoptive parents tried to view themselves as "just parents" and did not want to recognize the ways the adoptive family is different from the biologic family.

But there are differences. The primary difference is that our children have another set of parents. This is not typical in our culture, and children must struggle to understand what it means for them in their family and in society.

Just as our children grow up with the knowledge that most children live with the parents they were born to, we probably grew up thinking we would live with the children born to us. For most of us—fertile as well as infertile—the role-playing and fantasizing we engaged in about parenthood did not include adoption. As a result, we are functioning in a role we did not expect to have.

Kirk's research also showed that many people outside the adoptive family view adoption as a "second-best" way of becoming a family and even believe infertile parents are less "naturally" effective as parents. As false as these attitudes are, our awareness of them influences how we function as parents.

In his books *Shared Fate* and *Adoptive Kinship*, Kirk suggests it is vital for adoptive parents to acknowledge lovingly the differences between the adoptive family and the biologic family—including acknowledging our own pain and loss. By doing so, we can become more sesnsitive to the feelings of our children, more open to their questions, and, consequently, more able to meet their needs.

Kirk was nearly alone in the 1950s in studying adpotive familes. But in recent years, new research has given us more insight into adoptive parents and adoptees. Some of this research grew out of a genuine interest in the dynamics of the adoptive family, while other researchers, particularly those involved with heredity and environment issues, found adoptive families a convenient research sample. Whatever the motivation, we now know far more about adoptive families than we did even a few years ago.

This book provides adoptive parents with a comprehensive source of practical, reassuring advice, firmly founded on the available research as well as on the experiences of those involved with adoption.

Parents who adopt infants, older children, children of their own race, children of other races and ethnic backgrounds, disabled children, or children with serious behavior problems, will find the assistance they have long needed in recognizing and dealing with the special situations that arise when children are adopted.

While directed at the adoptive parent, this book is also useful for professionals such as social workers, psychologists, healthcare personnel, and teachers, who all need specific knowledge about the workings of adoptive families to serve them well. In addition, it is hoped that the adoptees who read this book will develop an understanding of the many factors influencing adoptive parents.

I have many people to thank for their contributions to this book. At the top of the list are the adoptees, adoptive parents, and birthparents who have shared their stories with me over the years, giving me a greater understanding of the universality of adoption as well as the unique experiences of individual familes. Their stories are in this book, unchanged except for minor details such as gender and age. But to protect their privacy, with few exceptions, their names have been changed.

I am also grateful to a few individuals who have repeatedly shared their remarkable knowledge of adoption with me and who have been supportive of my work: David Kirk, Ruben Pannor, and Barbara Tremitiere. David Kirk's work has profoundly influenced my thinking about adoption. I have also learned to count on him for thoughtful analysis of my work, which he provided after reviewing the manuscript of this book. Reuben Pannor has shared with me his years of experience in adoption, and has given me valuable feedback both on my writing in *Adopted Child* newsletter and on this book. I particularly appreciate the enthusiasm he showed for this project from the beginning. Barbara Tremitiere has made herself available to me whenever I needed information about special needs adoptions. She read parts of this manuscript and offered her thoughful comments.

One cannot overstate Claudia Jewett's influence on contemporary adoption thought and practice. Her work on helping children deal with grief, helping children understand why they left one family to move to another, and her most recent ideas on how to help adolescents leave home in responsible ways are major influences on this book, and I thank her for her comments on those sections of the manuscript.

I appreciate Judith Schaffer's willingness to read this book in manuscript form and offer suggestions. Individual sections were read by Josephine Anderson, Robert Bilenker, Frank Bolton, Jr., David Brodzinsky, Dirck Brown, Remi J. Cadoret, Kathryn Donley, William Feigelman, Jim Forderer, James Mahoney, and James McLoughlin. I appreciate the time and care they took with it.

Thanks must also go to Sue Smith and her co-workers at Adoptions in Idaho, as well as to the staff of Holt Children's Services, who are always no more than a phone call away when I have questions, and who provided me with some of the information on children from the Philippines, Latin America, and Korea. Sue Smith has also been a helpful source of information on large adoptive families. Nancy Boucneau of International Mission of Hope detailed the experiences of children from India. Hyun Sook Han gave me a personal interview on the adjustment of Korean children. Dennis L. Murray offered helpful comments on the transmission of hepatitis B. Jim Forderer shared with me his insights into single parent adoption as well as the adoption of disabled children.

While I am grateful for all the help I received, I should make it clear that there are controversial issues in adoption as well as differing philosophies. Unless otherwise indicated, the views in this book are mine, and are not necessarily shared by all those who played a part in the book's development.

In Patricia Hart I found the thorough and demanding editor I always hoped to work with someday, as well as a friend who could be called upon for help with child care and other necessary support. I would also like to thank Ivar Nelson at Solstice Press who has been a valuable sounding board for ideas since the conception of the book, and Janet Goldstein at Harper & Row who understood the need for this book.

Final thanks are saved for my husband, Carl, who showed in ways both big and small that this book is as important to him as it is to me.

Lois Ruskai Melina
January 1986
Moscow, Idaho

Preface to Revised Edition

When I wrote the first edition of this book twelve years ago, my two children were preschoolers, just becoming aware that they had been adopted into our family. As I finish this revised edition, my daughter is in her senior year of high school, becoming increasingly sure of who she is and getting ready to leave home, and my son is fourteen and in the midst of exploring his identity. When I wrote the first edition, I was looking for answers as a relatively new adoptive parent. Now I feel I can reassure new adoptive parents that the satisfaction of raising adopted children continues and the deep love we feel for our children grows. Although my journey as an adoptive parent is not over, and never will be, I believe that I am coming to a significant transition as my children approach adulthood and start to leave home. It is natural to look back at this time, and as I do I realize how much I have grown and learned as a parent, particularly as an infertile, adoptive parent. Infertility and adoption turned my world upside down, but the new perspective has been fascinating. The knowledge that our children came into our family by chance, but have become the core of our daily lives, is truly awesome and has confirmed my belief in a higher power. The process of getting to know them as they have grown and developed has been exciting and humbling. Exploring the complex dimensions of adoptive families has been stimulating, but has left me far more comfortable with unresolved paradox than I thought I could ever be. And I am sure more growth and discovery are ahead.

I am struck by other changes also as I write this new edition. When the first edition of *Raising Adopted Children* was published, there were few resources for adoptive parents. We had little to guide us. Today, there are books on every topic, from designing rituals for adoptive families to helping severely troubled children, demonstrating a recognition by publishers that adoptive families not only have unique needs, but that there are enough of us to be considered a significant audience. If there is an issue presented in this book that you want to read more about, chances are that more information is available. I have made every effort to list those resources in the back of this book. I am also struck by the change in the public awareness of adoptive families. Since the publication of the first edition, legislation has been passed granting adoptive families tax credits for adoption expenses; guaranteeing that our children are covered by health insurance; and ensuring that if we take time off from work to care for them, our jobs will be safe. We are being recognized, and our needs are being addressed.

I cannot possibly list all the people who have increased my knowledge of adoption issues over the past twelve years, but I would like to thank Jerri Ann Jenista, M.D., and Dana Johnson, M.D., for their ongoing commitment to learning more about the health issues of internationally adopted children; Ira Chasnoff, M.D., and Dan Griffith, Ph.D., for their work on children prenatally exposed to drugs and alcohol; Kay Johnson, for sharing her knowledge of the social, economic, and political conditions in China; Victor Groza, Elinor Ames, and others, for their work on children from Eastern European orphanages; Joseph Crumbley, William Cross, Jr., James Mahoney, Thomas Parham, Felix Padilla, and many others who have helped me better understand what racial identity is and its importance to children adopted transracially; and the many professionals, adoptive parents, adoptees, and birth parents who have shared their stories and their concerns with me over the years. I would also like to thank David Brodzinsky, Joyce Maguire Pavao, James Gritter, Vera Fahlberg, and Sharon Kaplan Roszia for their friendship and readiness to share their knowledge and perspectives with me. I have also been privileged to know H. David Kirk and to call him a friend. Though he is now in his eighties, he continues to make important contributions to the field of adoption. Some of these people read portions of this book and made useful suggestions.

Mary Schierman, who typeset the original edition, has been an incredibly capable and helpful assistant. My children continue to be an inspiration to me, and my husband, Carl, was as always supportive and enthusiastic as I worked on this project.

Lois Ruskai Melina
Moscow, Idaho
April 1998

Part I

Instant Family

1

The Transition to Adoptive Parenthood

Adoptive parents are often told that they got their children "the easy way." Those who say that know little about the decisions and adjustments children and parents must make when they become "instant families" through adoption. Whether it is furnishing a nursery, buying school clothes for an older child, suddenly asking for a leave from work, dealing with parasites a child acquired before he left his country or grief experienced because he left his home, adoptive parents are hit with the full force of parenthood at once.

Although adoptive parents have often waited a long time to become parents, they are not always prepared psychologically or physically for the arrival of a child. The unpredictability of the adoption process sometimes keeps prospective adoptive parents from getting ready for the child's arrival. A fully furnished nursery is a symbol of hope to some, but a reminder to others of what is missing in their lives, so they put off preparing a space for the child in their home.

More important, they may not be emotionally ready for the significant new roles they will be assuming. In their efforts to protect themselves from the pain they will feel if the adoption does not proceed as planned, some prospective adoptive parents inadvertently fail to prepare themselves psychologically and spiritually for the likelihood that they will soon become mothers or fathers. Although pregnant women may be equally worried about the outcome of their pregnancies, they have a difficult time ignoring their impending motherhood. Waiting adoptive parents have nothing to remind them to slow down, to start making changes in their lifestyles, or to take care of themselves during what is a physically and emotionally stressful time.

I was one of those waiting adoptive parents who kept myself from thinking about our daughter's arrival by keeping busy. I was a bit put off when a friend arrived one day packing a used crib. "It's time to get the baby's room ready," she said as she marched into the house with the furniture, even though we still had no idea when our daughter would be arriving. I let her put up the crib, but made no effort to decorate the bedroom we had set aside for our daughter to turn it into a nursery. However, I found myself wandering into the room, standing by the crib, and imagining a baby there. The physical presence of the crib allowed me to believe that it would be occupied one day and started me on the psychological process of becoming a mother.

Adoptive Parenting

The first Sunday after our daughter arrived, we proudly took her to church with us, eager to share our joy with our friends. At the same time, I was somewhat reluctant to show her to people. I wanted everyone to see how beautiful she was, but she had begun to develop a rash on her face and scalp that we thought was probably an allergy to something new in her diet. Nevertheless, I was pleased to be sitting in the church "crying room" surrounded by other families—a mother at last. Later that day, our daughter spiked a high fever, and in another day it was clear she had the measles. My husband, a family physician, gave gamma globulin injections to all the children who had been exposed to the measles and had not yet been immunized, and our daughter recovered rapidly. Still, we were struck by the fact that within a week we had become not only parents, but parents of a sick baby who could have started an epidemic. Being unprepared for a baby who contracted a disease that is practically nonexistent in the United States was our first indication that traditional sources of child care information are often inadequate for adoptive parents. The majority of these manuals assume that the child was born into the family. They advocate breastfeeding, but fail to mention how adoptive mothers can stimulate lactation. They tell parents the symptoms of teething, but not how malnutrition can affect a child's teeth. They talk about the awareness of sexuality that develops in adolescence, but not about the fear some parents have that their child may be at a special risk of teenage pregnancy. They give advice for handling a child's nightmares, but do not address the real fears of a child who was abused in another family. They provide ways to build a child's self-esteem, but offer no guidance for helping a child who thinks he was "given away" because he wasn't "good enough." They talk about the importance of a good birth experience for bonding and attachment, but do not address the fundamental fear of adoptive parents that their child will not love them as much as he would had he been born to them and the corresponding fear of the child that he has been shortchanged when it comes to parental love because he was not born to these parents.

Parents can feel overwhelmed when they realize they have taken on not just *parenting*, but *adoptive parenting*, with these additional challenges. Sometimes when we feel overwhelmed, we minimize what we are facing. It isn't unusual for adoptive parents to believe that once their child is home, their family life will be no different from what it would have been if the child had been born to them. But just as it isn't realistic to approach adoptive parenting with the idea that *every* interaction will be influenced by the way the child joined the family, it isn't realistic to discount it either. Our experiences as adoptive families are colored by many factors, including the journey that we took to become families. Some of the experiences may have increased our sense of vulnerability, while others may have made us stronger. The patience and persistence we develop to get through the often frustrating process of adopting and the trying process of resolving infertility are qualities that we can use as parents. People come to adoption having had their decision to raise children tested and affirmed. Couples often grow from the stress placed on their marriages by infertility. They learn how to identify their needs and solve problems together. The decisions they must make along the way cannot be made without good communication skills.

Adoptive parents, particularly infertile ones, also have experienced the need to reconcile their expectations with reality. All parents have some fantasies about parenthood that are quickly dashed when they are faced with the real situation, and adoptive parents are no exception. But adoptive parents, particularly those who are infertile, have already learned that parenting can still be rewarding, though their original expectations of the role have changed.

Perhaps what is most important, adoptive parents have had to look at their notions of *mother, father,* and *family* to see if they embrace relationships formed arbitrarily, albeit deliberately and legally. We have not rushed into parenting with vague ideas of family based on our single experience growing up. Most likely, we've had to expand that model. In proceeding with adoption, we have embraced new interpretations of mother, father, and family that contain many of the traditional ideas embodied in those terms, but take into account broader ideas of what makes a family a family. We have come to realize that family is as much about relationships as it is about biology. Although we are undoubtedly nervous about whether the love we will share will be as deep and satisfying as in other families, we also do not take that love for granted, but enter our new role dedicated to building those relationships.

Becoming parents in a way that is different from the norm can help prepare people for future adjustments, but can also be confusing. Sociologist H. David Kirk, in his books *Shared Fate* and *Adoptive Kinship,* says that when there is a contradiction between the way people have been culturally prepared for an expected event—such as parenthood—and the way it really happens, people experience a "role handicap." As adoptive parents, we experience a role handicap not only because we expected to become parents in a different way, but because our culture does not necessarily provide support for nontraditional ways of becoming parents. Although this situation appears to be changing, it has not always been easy for adoptive parents to find baby announcements or baby books suitable for our circumstances, employee benefits that recognize adoption, or ceremonies to celebrate occasions unique to adoptive families. Having arrived at our role in a different manner, we may not be sure that the role is the same. Without adequate role models, we may wonder if adoptive parents are different from biological parents. And if we are unsure about our role, we may not perform it well.

In many respects, being an adoptive parent is no different from being a biological parent, but situations arise in raising an adopted child than are influenced by the child's history prior to joining the family, the parents' infertility (when that is the case), information about the child that is missing, or the need in an open adoption to maintain relationships with members of the child's biological family. Looking back on some of these situations, I can see that although they were challenging at the time, and I sometimes wished parenting was simpler, the unique perspective of adoptive parenting has provided me with opportunities for growth and enrichment that I would not have otherwise had. For example, by having children of a different race, I have become more conscious of subtle forms of racism—both in myself and in others. Being on the receiving end of hurtful comments by people who were not malicious but merely unthinking has made me more alert to times when I may inadvertently offend someone whose choices are different from those I've made.

Getting Ready

Before a child arrives, there are several ways for waiting adoptive parents to prepare themselves for their new role as parents while acknowledging the unique way their family is being formed or expanded:

Have faith. Adoption is so uncertain that it sometimes seems that *expecting* it to happen will certainly doom it to failure. Furthermore, infertile couples have already experienced the pain of pinning their hopes on the arrival of a child who doesn't arrive. Some prospective adoptive parents have had adoptions fall through, and all have heard of situations in which others have expected to adopt particular children only to have the birth mothers decide to parent. When our bodies aren't cooperating and something that seems so fundamental—creating a family—seems out of our control, it isn't surprising that we have difficulty believing that we will ever be parents. Nonetheless, adoptive parents-to-be must have faith that they will someday have children.

One way to start believing something that is difficult to believe is to hear it repeatedly. Prospective parents can write *I believe I will be a parent someday* on a piece of paper, tape it to the bathroom mirror, and read it aloud the first thing every morning and the last thing at night. Furthermore, because we sometimes get the impression that we must be "perfect" to be selected as adoptive parents, it may be necessary to add an additional affirmation—that we *deserve* to be parents. Since psychologists tell us that "feelings follow actions," another way for prospective adopters to start believing they will become parents is to start behaving as expectant parents and to encourage others to treat them as such.

Be expectant. Rest. Eat properly. Take care of yourself physically and emotionally. Slow down. Change habits, like smoking, that you don't want to model for your children. Explain to others that you are taking special care of yourself because the process of getting ready for a child is emotionally and physically exhausting. Refer to yourself as expectant; for example, celebrate Mother's Day or Father's Day as any expectant parent might do. Once others begin to think of you as parents-to-be, the informal system used to pass on parenting information from experienced parents to new parents will begin, which will be affirming in itself.

Nest. Prepare a space for the child by accumulating necessary clothing, supplies, and furniture. Earlier in this chapter I explained that for me, setting up a crib seemed like more than I could handle, but led me to start thinking of myself as a mother. While parents must decide for themselves when to ready the nursery, consider that you will feel the pain of waiting—and possibly the pain of disappointment—whether the nursery is ready or not. The nursery may be a symbol of that pain, bringing those emotions to the surface, but such pain can be cathartic. At least be aware of the need to prepare for the child's arrival.

When my husband and I were waiting for our daughter to arrive, we joked about the "nesting instinct" pregnant women have that can cause them to clean the house thoroughly shortly before they go into labor. "Do adoptive parents nest?" we asked each other. One day, weeks after my friend had insisted on setting up the crib in the nursery, I found myself sitting on the floor of the kitchen, putting together the high chair we had recently purchased. My friend arrived to pick me up for an appointment we had, and when she found me in the kitchen, not quite ready to go because I was still trying to interpret the instructions for assembling the high chair, she was sure we had received word of our daughter's arrival. I was embarrassed to explain that I was making us late even though there didn't seem to be any rush to set up the high chair. Less than a week later, our daughter was home with us.

Take classes. Learn how to care for a baby. Routine tasks, such as diapering and feeding, are communicated informally to a pregnant woman or during prenatal visits to her physician. Adoptive parents sometimes find they are all thumbs because they haven't had the same opportunities to learn the skills necessary for caring for a baby. Check into instruction at your local hospital or through childbirth preparation classes. Some communities offer special classes for adoptive parents, who may feel uncomfortable in a room filled with pregnant women. You can also make your own arrangements with a nurse or childbirth educator or get a group of adoptive parents-to-be to start their own series of classes.

If you are adopting internationally, use this time to learn about the adjustment of children whose situations are similar to your child's (see Chapter 2). Learn child care customs. Find out about the experiences of other parents. Learn important phrases in the child's language, such as, "Do you need to use the toilet?"

If you are adopting an older child, learn about attachment with older children (see Chapter 3). Learn parenting techniques for children who have been abused or who have attachment difficulties.

Explore parenting issues. If you have a spouse or partner, discuss your approach to raising children—how you plan to discipline, handle money questions, give the child a religious education, and other issues. These questions may be asked in your home study, but you may be reluctant to explore major differences in parenting styles or philosophies with a social worker present.

Choose a family physician or pediatrician. In addition to finding a competent physician to care for your child after placement, you will also want to find a physician who is supportive of adoption. Most professionals outside the field of adoption do not have any particular training in adoption issues. They bring to an interaction with an adoptive family as many of their own prejudices, misconceptions, and attitudes as any other member of society. It is unfortunate, but they cannot be expected to be any more sensitive to adoption issues than are teachers, grandparents, or other individuals who have not been educated on the subject. As a result, some physicians have diagnosed serious medical conditions in adopted children and counseled the parents to send the children "back to the agency." There have been occasions in which a nurse commented about an adoptive mother who was staying in the hospital room with her ill son, "She's just like a real mother." While you wait to adopt, get recommendations for physicians from other adoptive parents in your area and make an appointment to talk to the physicians. By engaging a physician in conversation about adoption, you will be able to ascertain attitudes that may later be a source of conflict or discomfort. If your child has particular medical needs, such as a missing medical history, a history of prenatal drug exposure, or an illness not commonly found in the United States, you will want to ask the physician how he or she will deal with that situation. (For more on medical issues of internationally adopted children, see Chapter 10. For a discussion of children without known medical histories, see Chapter 7.)

Look for adoption announcements or record books. Adoptive parents sometimes have a difficult time finding adoption announcements or "baby books" suitable for adoptive families. Fortunately, desktop publishing has made it much easier for parents to create their own announcements. Furthermore, there are a number of cottage industries developed by adoptive parents to meet the need for announcements and baby books in adoptive families. (Sources of announcements and record books are listed in the Merchandise section of Selected References and Resources.)

Nurture your relationship. A couple can use the waiting period to nurture their relationship, which may have been stressed by the frustration and demands of both infertility and the adoption process. It's easy for a couple to move from focusing all their energy on conceiving a baby to focusing on adopting a baby to focusing on taking care of the long-awaited baby. A couple needs to get back in the habit of nurturing themselves and their relationship, for if the marital relationship is neglected, it will eventually need critical attention, leaving them with little energy with which to nurture their child.

Keep a journal. Journal writing is recognized as a beneficial way for people to get in touch with their emotions. By writing about your experiences, you can explore everything, from your feelings about having an ongoing relationship with the child's birth parents to other people's reactions to your plans to adopt. Although many adoptive parents plan to keep a journal to give to the child, some find that they are able to fully express themselves in a journal only if they consider it a private document. Those who want to have a record of the waiting period may want to keep two journals—one for their child and one for themselves. Though they are not actually journals, the books *In Search of Motherhood* by Barbara Shulgold and Lynne Sipiora and and *Secret Thoughts of an Adoptive Mother* by Jana Wolff are good examples of the emotional catharsis that can come from writing about infertility and adoption. There are also numerous books available to guide you in journaling if you have never kept a journal; check your local bookstore or public library.

Transition to Adoptive Parenting

During the time that we are waiting for our child to arrive, most of us have an idea of how we will feel the moment we are handed our child or take our child home. We think there will be an overwhelming feeling of joy, and for many people there is. Often, however, that joy is mixed with other emotions or even overwhelmed by them. Parents who have met and developed a relationship with the birth mother before the child's birth often feel torn between their joy and the unbearable grief of the woman whom they have come to care about. Others find that their joy is mixed with the fear that they may lose their child to a birth mother who changes her mind. Some may feel almost numb, as though the shock of finally becoming a parent is so great that they can't even identify the emotions it arouses.

There are other reasons adoptive parents feel emotionally confused. Our role as parents begins when the child is physically in our care, and we often (though not always) begin to love the child then. However, we may not yet have legal recognition of what is in our hearts. Certainly, when a birth parent reclaims a child after he has been with the adoptive parents for weeks or months, the adoptive parents still feel like the parents even though they do not have physical or legal custody. The birth parents—especially the birth mother—may have similar conflicts. The birth mother may have signed away her parental rights and given up physical custody, but may still feel like the child's mother. In fact, early in the placement, although the adoptive parents have physical custody of the child, the birth mother may feel a more emotional tie to him. This overlapping of roles can be confusing and even lead to tension between the birth parents and the adoptive parents. (For more on this topic, see *The Open Adoption Experience* by Lois Ruskai Melina and Sharon Kaplan Roszia.)

An increasing number of adoption professionals are finding that both adoptive parents and birth parents are helped with their role transition at this time through a ritual called an "entrustment ceremony." In an entrustment ceremony, the birth mother (or another member of the birth family or even someone representing the birth family) formally entrusts the child being adopted to the care of the adoptive parents, and the adoptive parents formally accept that responsibility. In contrast to the offhand way that children are sometimes placed with adoptive parents—in a hospital parking lot or attorney's office—an entrustment ritual helps the adoptive parents take on their new role and helps the birth parents let go of theirs. Though it lacks legal standing, it is a commitment, and when witnessed by relatives or even close friends, it provides the community support that is so often lacking to both adoptive parents and birth parents. Furthermore, like all ceremonies—from weddings to funerals—it gives the participants a chance to express their feelings about the significant change that is being marked by the ritual. This ceremony can also be an effective way for children in the birth or adoptive families who are too young for verbal explanations to gain an understanding of what is happening.

Claiming

One of the first ways parents think of themselves as a mother or father is by identifying the ways their child is like them. Family members stand around a tiny, wrinkled baby expressing certainty that the baby's nose is just like Dad's. Even though adopted children have no genetic link to their adoptive parents, mothers and fathers find similarities between themselves and their children in mannerisms and personality characteristics and sometimes even in physical appearance. This is an essential step in "claiming" a child as one's own. A study in Great Britain, reported in *The Adopted Child Comes of Age*, actually found a connection between the degree to which adoptees and adoptive parents perceive themselves as similar and how satisfied they are with the adoptions. (Another study, reported in *Behavior Genetics*, found that biologically related families *perceive* more similarities than adoptive families do, but that their perceptions do not correlate with actual similarities.)

When Kara saw a photograph of the one-month-old girl who would be her daughter, she immediately thought how much the baby looked like her younger sister at birth. She dismissed the impression, thinking it ridiculous that a Latina baby would look like her sister of Irish ancestry. But her sister's reaction to the photograph was the same. Chances are that the two babies' expressions were more alike than their appearance, but noticing the similarity was an important way of saying "You're one of us."

Entitlement

Developing a sense that a child "belongs" in the family, even though he wasn't born into it, is a crucial task for adoptive parents. Unless parents develop a sense that the child is really theirs, they will have difficulty accepting their right to act as parents. In his book *The Realities of Adoption,* Jerome Smith, Ph.D., suggests that the question is usually not whether adoptive parents feel entitled to raise their child, but to what *degree* they feel entitled. In *How They Fared in Adoption: A Follow-up Study,* Benson Jaffee and David Fanshel note that the amount of entitlement parents feel can be determined by looking at the extent to which they take risks with their children, deal with separation, handle discipline, and discuss adoption with their children and others. Extreme behavior in these areas may indicate that the parents do not feel "worthy" to act as parents. Parents who either overprotect their children or neglect their children's safety may not have come to grips with the risks and responsibilities inherent in parenting. Those who cannot bear to be away from their children may feel insecure about whether their affection (or their children's) is able to withstand separation, while excessive use of child care can indicate a lack of affection. Parents without a sense of entitlement may have difficulty disciplining a child, either believing they do not have the right to do so or fearing their relationship is so tentative that discipline will alienate the child. Excessive talking about adoption, either to the child or to those outside the family, or excessive attempts to hide the fact that the child was adopted may also be signs of impaired entitlement.

The question of whether adoptive parents are entitled to be a child's parents is obviously a result of the child having been born to another set of parents. However, the issue is more complicated.

Infertile couples may wonder if they are going against some kind of "heavenly plan" by adopting. They may wonder if infertility is a "sign" that they weren't meant to have children. Consequently, these couples may have a hard time believing that it is OK for them to be

a family and to function as a family. Feelings of inadequacy are usually fleeting, but when a couple believes their infertility was sent by
God or fate, they may not have the confidence to act as parents. A
couple with a true sense of entitlement may still believe in a heavenly plan, but they believe that God or fate sent them their child.

If parents feel guilty that their above-average income, occupational status, or "good connections" to a physician or attorney
enabled them to adopt while other parents continued to wait, their
sense of entitlement may be impared.

External factors may also influence the development of entitlement in adoptive parents. Although some adoptions are finalized
shortly after placement, there is sometimes a waiting period after a
child is placed with a family before the adoption can be finalized.
Sometimes the birth parents can legally "reclaim" the child during
all or part of this period. Although it happens rarely, adoptive parents are painfully aware that the agency or state overseeing the
adoption could have the child removed from their home during the
waiting period. Even though highly publicized adoption custody
cases are unusual circumstances, they have heightened the anxiety
of adoptive parents about when they can truly consider the child
"theirs" and may cause some parents to "hold back" emotionally so
it will be less painful if the child is reclaimed or removed.

Even when adoptive parents develop a sense of entitlement, it
can be undermined by those outside the family. When strangers at
a grocery store or park comment on the striking dissimilarity in
appearance between us and our children, they are saying, in effect,
"You don't *look* like you belong together." Sometimes their language
reflects other people's questions about our entitlement: "Do you
have any children *of your own?*" "What do you know about her *real*
mother?" I've even had people who know my children were adopted
express surprise when my parenting behavior is consistent with
basic parenting behavior. The implication is that because our family
was formed differently, I would feel differently and consequently
behave differently toward my children.

Sometimes I think adoptive parents are unusually sensitive to any remark or implication that calls into question their authenticity as a family. I also suspect that as we develop a deeper sense of entitlement, that sensitivity diminishes. I was much more offended years ago than I am today when someone asks me about my children's *real* parents. I know that I'm the mother who has driven through snowdrifts to get my children to ski hills while pondering the balance between recreation and the rest of their lives, who has tacked their art to the refrigerator and talked to teachers about their strengths and weaknesses, who has cleaned up after sleepovers and watched to see how my children deal with peer pressure, and who has celebrated my daughter's new driver's license and stayed awake nights worrying. Like every adoptive parent's, my authenticity—my entitlement to be their parent—is not derived from biology. It is not even derived from the legal document that says I'm their mother. It comes from the relationships we have built as a family, from functioning as their mother even when I wasn't sure I knew what I was doing.

If there is one question that people have about open adoption, in which the birth family and the adoptive family have contact with each other, it is whether this situation affects the entitlement of adoptive parents. Usually it isn't stated that way. More often people question whether the adoptee will be confused about who her parents are, or whether the authority of the adoptive parents will be diminished if the birth parents are accessible. The underlying issue, though, is whether adoptive parents can fully function as a child's parents if the birth parents are around. Some adoptive parents have said that being in an open adoption has helped them develop a sense of entitlement. Having been selected by the birth parents, they feel they have the blessing of the birth parents to be the child's parents. Rather than the birth parents interfering in the child's upbringing, their presence in the child's life in ways other than parenting seems to affirm the adoptive parents' parenting role. Although more information is needed in this area, research by Ruth

McRoy and Harold Grotevant indicates that adoptive parents who have direct contact with their child's birth parents are less anxious than are those who have no contact or who have contact through a confidential intermediary.

In *You're Our Child: A Social/Psychological Approach to Adoption,* social worker and educator Jerome Smith and attorney Franklin I. Miroff say that a sense of entitlement can be developed by recognizing and accepting the differences between adoptive families and families formed in other ways, by resolving feelings of inadequacy resulting from infertility, and by learning to handle the remarks of family members and friends that betray a view that biological parenthood is superior to adoptive parenthood. *Supporting an Adoption*, by Pat Holmes, is an excellent booklet for parents to give friends and relatives that tells them how to support the adoptive family through the adjustment period.

Postadoption Feelings

Occasionally an adoptive parent, particularly the mother, becomes depressed after the child arrives. Postpartum depression in biological mothers is caused by hormonal changes associated with pregnancy and birth, and although adoptive mothers do not go through those physiological changes, they, too, may feel letdown after their children arrive. Postadoption blues may occur because the adoptive parents, who were excited about the arrival of the child, feel discouraged when faced with the daily tasks involved in parenting a new child.

In addition, the parents may be grieving for the loss of an idealized version of the child they expected would arrive. One of the tasks that should be accomplished prior to adopting is grieving for the biological child who will not be born. A couple who look forward to a little red-haired boy with freckles because that's what the husband looked like when he was young must let go of that image before adopting to accept the adopted child as he is. But even then, they may replace this wish with a fantasy about the adopted child. Perhaps they were offered a boy when they had been expecting and wanting a girl. Grieving for that girl is an important step in ultimately accepting the boy as their son.

Even when the adopted child does fulfill the parents' fantasies, the adoptive parents may feel sad that they couldn't produce the child of their dreams, says California therapist Deborah Silverstein. The fact that there is no biological connection between the adoptive parents and the child can also leave parents feeling sad that they did not make a genetic contribution to *this* wonderful child, that they will not achieve immortality through *this* child. They may feel this way even if they have biological children as well. Although we wouldn't change anything about our children, we can still be sad that we do not have every possible connection to them or that we didn't share their lives from the moment of their existence. That loss can be particularly poignant for parents of children who were abused or neglected. *They* would not have used drugs or alcohol during the pregnancy, neglected the children's welfare, or hurt the children.

It can be difficult for adoptive parents to express their feelings of loss without sounding dissatisfied, so adoptive parents often keep their feelings to themselves. This is especially true if friends or relatives "warned" them against adopting a child with special needs or were not supportive about adoption in general. Parents may think that expressing their wish that they could have kept their child safe or that they had given birth to him could be interpreted as wishing they had made a different choice.

In addition, in the early days following the placement, adoptive parents may find that seemingly supportive comments from relatives, coworkers, or friends leave them feeling uncomfortable. Having expected finally to be recognized as a mother or a father, adoptive parents may be taken aback when someone predicts that a pregnancy will soon follow the adoption—with the implication that the adoptive parents will then have what they really want. They may be further distressed to find some people predicting problems as the adoptee grows up. Adoptive parents may feel reluctant to express the kind of frustration or exhaustion that is normal for any parent because they don't want others to interpret it as dissatisfaction or regret.

Social worker Sharon Kaplan Roszia says that a major dilemma for adoptive parents is thinking that by acknowledging the loss or expressing sadness they are somehow giving up the right also to express joy and satisfaction. As a result, they either deny their feelings of loss or feel compelled to counter any expression of loss with a corresponding positive statement. We can have more than one feeling at a time about a given situation. We can, for example, wish that we had given birth to the child we love, even though if we had done so, the child would be genetically different from the child whose unique qualities we cherish.

At these times, a support group of adoptive parents can be a godsend. Adoptive parents may have an easier time expressing their mixed or complex feelings about their adoption to people who have had similar experiences. This healthy expression of loss is essential if people are to move beyond it and grow from the experience. By working through our feelings at this time, we can come to a greater understanding of what it will be like for our children later on. Our children may also have conflicting emotions about themselves, about their family, and about their adoption. They, too, will feel sad about not having been born to us, not sharing early times, or not having their fantasy adoptive parents. This doesn't mean that they don't love us or that they wish they hadn't been adopted by us. Our better understanding of these mixed feelings will enable us to help them work through theirs.

Naming and Renaming

In Western cultures, choosing a name for a child is an important parental function. Giving a child a name is a way of saying, "This is my child." As a result, adoptive parents often want to select names for their children, even if the children already have names. As important as this claiming task is they should be cautious about changing the first name of even a young child. Furthermore, because naming is a parental function, both the birth parents and the adoptive parents may correctly believe they have the right to choose the child's name. Adoptive parents who will be having contact with the birth parents as the child grows up should discuss with the birth parents how the child will be named. Sometimes adoptive parents name the child, and sometimes they name the child in consultation with the birth mother. Sometimes the birth mother names the child, and the adoptive parents use her chosen name as the child's middle name. Sometimes the birth mother names the child, and the adoptive parents honor her by keeping that name. All these methods of naming are fine. What is most important is that the adoptive parents and birth parents have the same understanding of how the child will be named. If they don't, it could be a source of conflict as the adoption proceeds (for more on this topic, see *The Open Adoption Experience* by Lois Ruskai Melina and Sharon Kaplan Roszia).

It is important to many adoptees to know the names their birth parents gave them. If the birth parent gives the child a name, the adoptive parents should make every attempt to keep that name in some way. Doing so acknowledges the importance of the birth parents to the child. If the original name is not kept, the adoptive parents should at least write it down and keep it in a safe place so it can be given to the adoptee when appropriate. It is amazing how details like this, which we think we will always remember, are eventually forgotten.

Adoptive parents who plan to name their child after a relative should consider their motives for doing so and the message that it gives the child. For example, naming a child "Junior" may be a way of pretending that the child was born to them. More likely, the parents are trying to show how much a part of the family the child is.

They may want to consider other ways to communicate that idea, such as by giving the child a family heirloom. In an extreme reaction to claiming by naming, one adoptee, whose family traced its ancestors to the Mayflower, felt that being named for those ancestors was dishonest. He felt that adoption attached him to a family, but not to a heritage that he had no claim to.

Pediatrician Vera Fahlberg cautions against giving a new first name to a child who already has learned to respond to a name—a task normally accomplished before the age of one. Although an infant will learn to respond to a new name quickly, it is just one more new thing for the child to adjust to at a time of many major adjustments.

A preschooler may have a particularly difficult time adjusting to a new first name. A young child's identity is so closely tied to his first name that changing it during the preschool years can cause a child to think he is not really the same person or that one name goes with being a good person and one name with being a bad person. A name change can make it more difficult for the child to integrate his past life into his present one.

Even internationally adopted children do not necessarily have to be given an anglicized first name, particularly if the family is living in a multiethnic or international community. My daughter attended school with children who had Arabic, Spanish, and Japanese first names. Keeping her Korean name would not have made her an oddity in the classroom.

Parents who want to change the foreign-sounding name of a school-age child because they think it will help her assimilate her new culture more quickly and be accepted more readily by her peers should discuss the proposed name change, perhaps with the aid of an interpreter. The child may prefer teasing to giving up what may be the last tangible remnant of her life in her country of birth. Adoptive mother Joyce Kaser wrote about the naming dilemma she and her husband R. Kent Boesdorfer faced when adopting a six-year-old Colombian boy—a problem complicated by the fact that

Kaser and her husband have different last names. They found that the boy wanted to keep his full name, and so became Christopher Jorge Cruz Kaser Boesdorfer.

Most parents recognize that a school-age child has lived with his first name for so long that it would be difficult for him to give it up. This is something that should be discussed with the child with care. Some children may want to change their names when they are adopted as a way of trying to get rid of their past. This wish may indicate that a child has unrealistic expectations about adoption. The child needs to be helped to understand that his past is part of him and that even if it was unpleasant, it doesn't make him bad. He is not a "new person" because he has been adopted.

Sometimes the adoptive parents are the ones who seek a name change as a way to leave the child's past behind. However, the past is always part of the child's history, and parents shouldn't pretend otherwise. Even if the child was named for a parent who abused him, the effects of the abuse will not disappear with a new name.

Parents who want to choose a name for their child may consider selecting a new middle name, incorporating any family or religious naming traditions into their choice. Still, it is important to call the child by the name that he identifies as his "self."

When a Change Is Necessary

While adoptive parents may have to fight the urge to rename their children, there are some circumstances that warrant a change of first name. Although I know of one adoptive family with two boys named "Joe," if there already is a child in the home with the same first name, the new child probably should be renamed. Or if the name is likely to leave the child vulnerable to ridicule, it should be changed. If the first name is changed, the parents should try to find a name that sounds like the original name, and the original name should be incorporated into the legal name, perhaps as a middle name. It isn't unusual for an adopted child to have more than one middle name as a result of efforts to keep his original name part of his legal name.

Parents who intend to change their child's first name can inform the foster family or agency and ask that the child be prepared for it, so he doesn't have to make quite so many adjustments after placement.

Giving a Family Name

Adoption experts agree that the child's surname usually should be changed to the new family's name at the time of placement, rather than when the adoption is finalized. The surname is one way our culture defines who is a member of a particular family. One of the most important concepts to communicate to the adopted child, friends, teachers, and relatives is that by adoption we are creating or expanding our family. That process begins when the child arrives, not when he legally becomes a member of the family.

The child's teachers and school personnel should know what he is to be called. The child's name will not be legally changed until the adoption is finalized, and some school officials are reluctant to allow a child to use a name other than his legal name. The fact that the child's records from his previous school are in his original surname makes the problem even more difficult. Starting school or moving to a new school is hard enough without teachers, principals, and bus drivers calling a child by the "wrong" name.

Occasionally, and more often when a teenager is adopted, it is traumatic for the child to change his last name. The child may feel that changing his surname is being disloyal to his birth parents, or he may simply be too accustomed to the name he has had for thirteen, fourteen, or fifteen years to change it. The child's feelings should be discussed and ultimately respected. Though his refusal to take his adoptive family's name may seem to indicate an unwillingness to become integrated into the family, the child may resist becoming part of his adoptive family less if he knows it doesn't mean giving up important parts of his previous life. And with many blended families and women keeping their maiden names after marriage, it's not uncommon for a child to have a last name different from that of his parents or siblings.

2

Adjustment of the Family

๛ Adopted children are forced to break some ties with people or surroundings to which they have become attached. The length of time children have been in another place; the quality of the relationships with the people who cared for them; the number of times they have been moved from one home to another; and, to some degree, their developmental stage can all affect how children react to a move. It is not uncommon for a child, even an infant, to grieve when separated from someone she cares about or from a familiar environment—even if that person or environment was considered to be detrimental to the child's welfare. It may not make sense to us that the child is mourning, but she must be allowed to grieve and be comforted while she does.

The adoptee is not the only family member who must make adjustments. Siblings must adjust not only to the arrival of a new family member, but perhaps to additional scrutiny of the family by outsiders (see Chapter 12). Extended family members have to welcome the new family member, often without adequate preparation or a thorough understanding of adoptive relationships. There is likely to be some disharmony as family members learn how the addition of the new child affects them.

Perhaps the most difficult aspect of the adjustment period for those adopting for the first time is not knowing when—or if—it will end. The adjustment of our second child was not necessarily easier than the adjustment of our first, but our experience told us it was temporary. We were helped through our adjustment with our son by thinking back to incidents that happened with our daughter six months, one year, and two years after her arrival that were turning points in our development as a family. We should keep in mind that many of the most difficult times in the adjustment period are necessary for the development of attachment and a sense of belonging in a family, a subject discussed in Chapter 3.

Adjustment of Infants

Many people believe that babies adapt quickly to their new parents and home. However, some babies have noticeable reactions to what is a major change for infants who are so physically and emotionally vulnerable.

Before the age of six months, an infant doesn't distinguish between individuals; she doesn't even know what a person is. By six months, an infant not only is able to distinguish between individuals, but develops a preference for the one or two people whom she has learned to depend on to meet her needs. That feeling is called *attachment* (although it is sometimes erroneously referred to as *bonding*.) Like an adult, when an infant is separated from someone to whom she has an attachment, she doesn't like it. Because infants don't experience their world verbally, it's unlikely that they are conscious of "missing" a particular individual. What is likely is that their sense of trust has been disrupted. They are totally dependent, and the person they've learned to rely on to meet their needs is no longer there. Therefore, it's not surprising that they may be scared and anxious. Even before six months, when infants have not developed an attachment to a parent or other caregiver, they notice changes in diet, color, odors, routines, and other aspects of their environment, any one of which can be disruptive (see Chapter 3 for a more detailed discussion of attachment and disrupted attachments).

Infant Grief

An infant reacts to changes somatically, usually with sleeping or eating problems. She may refuse to eat, spit up her formula, have an upset stomach, or have chronic diarrhea. Or she may have difficulty sleeping regularly or for extended periods. The baby may be generally irritable or cry for prolonged periods for no apparent reason, fail to progress developmentally, lack vitality, have frequent illnesses and accidents, or lose weight or hair. She may also show her emotions through her facial expressions, tone of voice, and body language.

Lesley and Craig had never seen a baby show sadness other than by crying until their son arrived at seven months of age. His eyes and facial expression clearly showed that he was missing something or someone. Smiles were hard to evoke, and laughing was even rarer. He also had problems with eating and digestion and chronic illnesses. In the six months after his arrival, he had three ear infections, influenza, bronchitis, pneumonia, eczema, and chicken pox. Some of his problems were undoubtedly due to his exposure to viruses and infections, but it is also likely that his psychological state was either directly responsible for some of the problems, such as eczema, or lowered his resistance to disease.

Adoptive parents who discuss the adjustment reactions their infant is having often will have their diagnosis belittled by nonadoptive parents. "My baby had problems sleeping for three years," or "All babies have bouts of unexplainable diarrhea," they may say. The implication is that the adoptive parents don't know what they're talking about because they aren't biological parents, or that they are overemphasizing the effect that adoption has on a person's life.

An infant who is having ongoing sleeping or eating problems or is otherwise showing signs of distress should be checked by a physician to determine if there are any medical causes for the irritability or indigestion. But former social work educator Carol Williams suggests that in the absence of a medical explanation, a parent should assume that the baby is reacting physically to subtle changes she perceives in the world around her.

Babies and Toddlers Have Different Reactions

Psychiatrist Justin Call identified the reactions that parents can expect when infants are moved from one home to another at certain stages of development. Call believes that infants are most vulnerable to being distressed by a change in their environment between four and twelve weeks of age. Younger babies are concerned with having their bodily needs met and are not as aware of their surroundings. One to three month olds are alert enough to respond to stimuli, but not sophisticated enough to modify them when they receive too much. They are easily overloaded. Three- to six month olds are more adaptive to change. They are better able to use their bodies to modify stimulation, can handle more complex stimuli, and can adjust to changes in diet more easily. Six- to twelve month olds are again vulnerable to change because their attachment to their primary caretaker is intense at this time. Besides noticing a change in their environment, they will perceive the loss of an individual. A baby in this age group may go through the stages of grief that older children and adults experience, including denial, often expressed by the "searching" behavior that indicates that the child expects the previous caretaker to return; anger, expressed often by uncontrollable crying; depression, or withdrawal, and disinterest in food or play; and reorganization, or acceptance of the new situation. These stages may not be sequential and may repeat themselves. Two year olds show the same kind of reactions to change as do younger children, but more dramatically, Call reports. Their clinging is more intense and their withdrawal more striking. However, because they can express themselves better than can infants, they can actively participate in resolving anxiety, for example, by making their food or activity preferences known, or by using words to express emotions.

Easing the Transition

Although it is not often possible, an ideal way to ease the transition for an infant from one environment to another is for the adoptive parents to visit the infant before she is placed in their home. Doing so gives the parents an opportunity to observe the baby's routine and learn precisely how she is being cared for. Pediatrician Vera Fahlberg suggests having the foster parents, birth parents, or whoever is caring for the child begin each task, such as bathing the baby, and having the adoptive parents complete the activity. This practice does more than help the new parents learn the baby's routine. It gives the infant permission from her caregiver to accept nurturing from the adoptive parents. With an infant old enough to recognize familiar faces and objects, visits by the adoptive parents and perhaps even visits to the adoptive parents' house prior to placement can ease the "stranger anxiety" that is typical of six- to twelve month olds. Spontaneous smiling and an interest in interacting with inanimate objects in the new environment are signs that the baby is ready to make the move.

If visits with the infant before placement are not possible, adoptive parents can make the transition easier by learning and following the routine and method of care and interaction used by the previous caretaker. It is important to maintain the infant's schedule as much as possible and to replicate the way the infant is used to being fed, dressed, bathed, and even diapered. Some babies are used to being carried on someone's back, while others are familiar with a Snugli baby carrier. Some are massaged during baths. Some become more alert after feeding, while others are used to falling asleep with a bottle. Particular care should be paid to how the infant was soothed when distressed; even a baby who is well prepared for a move may show signs of grief. Even the same kinds of sounds can be important. New parents should try to make the same kinds of word sounds that the previous caretakers used with the child, such as those used in parent-child babbling games. Some social workers recommend wearing the same kind of perfume that the previous caregiver wore or using the same brand of laundry detergent to provide the child with odors that are familiar and that the child associates with being taken care of.

It often helps a child aged six months or older if familiar toys or other objects are transferred with her to the new home. One mother said that her eight-month-old son would grab his clothes with his right hand and put his right thumb in his mouth frequently after he arrived, causing her to wonder if he had been attached to a security blanket that wasn't transferred with him. She introduced one, and he immediately became attached to it. Another child in the family can make the transition easier for an older baby by providing diversion and entertainment.

Using a familiar object to bridge the move from one environment to the next is particularly effective with a toddler, Call says. The two year old has begun to claim some space in the home as her own. Her space in the new home should be made clear to her by the presence of toys or furniture. However, parents should take care not to introduce too many new aspects of the new environment at once. The child will take the lead in exploring the house. The backyard, siblings, pets, and other aspects of the new environment should be introduced one at a time, perhaps even on different days. In her book, *Toddler Adoption,* Mary Hopkins-Best gives more suggestions for easing the transition for a toddler, including the benefits at this time of a family pet.

Of course, it is not always possible to communicate directly with the foster parents or birth mother to learn the child's routine. Nor is it always feasible to have the baby and adoptive parents visit each other several times before the placement. And some agencies are not aware of the importance of replicating a baby's routine. Parents may have to insist on knowing how the child has been cared for or on being given a written description of her schedule.

Even when it is possible to take the time to ensure a smooth transition, adoptive parents are understandably anxious to have the baby in their home as soon as possible rather than wait several weeks while the baby gets used to them and the new environment. And some parents may resent having to care for "their" baby the way someone else did. They may want to put into practice their own style of child care. Yet it is important to remember that we are being asked to follow someone else's routine only temporarily, until the infant gets to know us. Then gradual changes can be introduced. Parents who strongly object to some way the baby was cared for—feeding on a set schedule, rather than feeding on demand, for example—have to weigh the advantage of demand feeding against the advantage of minimizing changes.

Transcultural Changes

A child from another country encounters even more dramatic changes in environment. Even though a baby is not talking or responding to verbal instructions, she is hearing new words and sound patterns. She may have moved from a humid, tropical climate to a cool, dry one. Because of differences in foods, the adoptive parents may have different body and breath odors than the child's previous caretakers. And the foods the baby is given may taste remarkably different from the ones she is used to.

Travel alone may require a major adjustment. The baby may have jet lag, or have her days and nights mixed up as a result of changing time zones. Although it is unusual, one couple discovered that their baby had been given a large dose of a tranquilizer to sedate him for the long plane trip. The first few days in his new home he was still "hungover" from the tranquilizer; then he experienced a mild withdrawal and refused to sleep for two more days.

Parents should find out as much as possible about the methods of care in the country their child is coming from. For example,

· What was the child fed and when?

We had a difficult time getting our Korean-born son to take his formula in the initial days of his placement. Finally, in desperation, I called the adoption agency to find out specifically what he had been fed. "Oh, just add a little Karo syrup to the formula," I was told. "The formula in Korea is sweeter." Babies in China seem to be accustomed to large holes in the nipples of baby bottles; they expect formula to come out easily and fast when they suck. Babies in Brazil are given coffee and sugar with their milk and are seldom given white milk or any cold foods. Parents may want to add smaller and smaller quantities of coffee and sugar, or even chocolate syrup, to the baby's formula until she gets used to the taste of plain formula.

Parents should continue to feed the baby with something close to the food she has been used to and make any changes slowly, perhaps mixing the baby's old formula with her new formula and gradually increasing the amount of the new formula in the mixture.

· What have been her sleeping arrangements?

Korean children generally sleep on a mattress on the floor and, like Latin American children, may sleep with many people in the same room. These children may have difficulty falling asleep in a crib or in their own quiet room.

· What methods of child care were used by the person who cared for her? How was she soothed when she was fussy?

Ann would place her infant on a blanket in the middle of the room, toys within easy reach, while she worked in another part of the house. She couldn't understand why her daughter wouldn't entertain herself for even a few minutes. Only later did she learn that Korean mothers carry their infants on their backs while they work.

Some babies from orphanages in China are not accustomed to the kinds of diapers typically used in Western countries and may feel some initial anxiety when their diapers are changed, although the Chinese diapers are not particularly comfortable so the adjustment is relatively easy. Some Chinese babies as young as eight months old have already been "toilet trained." Orphanage workers anticipate when the babies have to use the toilet and hold them over it, jiggling and cooing to encourage them to use it.

Some cultures dote on an infant, giving her freedom and attention that would be considered "spoiling" in the United States. Thus, adoptive parents who travel abroad to pick up their child should plan either to spend some time with the child's caretaker or learn how children in similar circumstances are cared for. The section at the back of this book includes sources of information on child care customs in other countries.

Variation in Adjustment Reactions

Some babies show adjustment reactions immediately after being moved into a new home. Others internalize their reactions to a move and develop sleeping and digestive problems months later.

Babies who have experienced more than one move may have either a minor reaction to the latest move or a severe one. If the baby was not attached to the last person who cared for her or the care was substandard, she may have few problems with the move. With other infants, a new move may recall all the previous moves, and they may show intense reactions to the new environment.

There is little that parents can do to help the infant who is grieving except give comfort and support. This may mean a lot of gentle rocking and walking the floors, even though it may not seem to be doing much to soothe the baby. Although it's difficult to try to comfort a baby who seems inconsolable, doing so not only lets the infant express her grief, but shows her that this is an adult she can count on in times of distress.

When the child is in good physical health, eats and sleeps well, progresses well developmentally, forms relationships, and otherwise lacks signs of distress, parents can assume the baby is making an adequate adjustment to her new environment.

While infants can have problems adapting to a new home, it is a mistake to characterize the adjustment period as an unpleasant time for the parents and baby. The joy of falling in love with the baby is there, just as every parent hopes it will be. And it doesn't take too many months before the baby stops thinking of her new home and caretakers as strange.

Prenatal Exposure to Alcohol, Tobacco, and Other Drugs

The adjustment of infants may be hampered by prenatal exposure to alcohol, tobacco, and other drugs, including cocaine. Infants exposed to such drugs may be restless, irritable, easily disturbed, and difficult to console. They may have a high-pitched cry and have difficulty feeding and sucking. Their bodies may be unusually stiff, and they may have a difficult time interacting with their caretakers. Their irritability may also show up as difficulty moving from one state of arousal, such as sleep, to another, such as wakefulness. Some infants have difficulty reaching a quiet state of alertness, which interferes with their ability to engage in their evironments, possibly impairing their cognitive development or their ability to form attachments. These symptoms should not be confused with "withdrawal" symptoms of an infant who was born addicted to narcotics, although they are similar. They are due to the effect of drugs on the developing brain. According to Dan Griffith, Ph.D., a developmental psychologist, cocaine disrupts a baby's ability to process and respond to environmental stimulation, so she is easily overloaded.

For example, singing to such a baby while rocking her could be more than she can handle. If it seems that the baby's behavior is making it difficult to have any meaningful interaction with her, that is exactly what the baby intends because "normal" infant-parent interaction is too much for her.

Although it can be difficult for parents who have waited so long to finally hold their baby in their arms, experts like Griffith say that they must learn how to stimulate the baby without overwhelming her and be alert for cues that the baby needs to rest. Swaddling a baby (wrapping her tightly in a blanket) and giving her a pacifier help reduce arousal so the baby can tolerate eye contact and voices. It may also be effective to hold the baby vertically, facing you, and gently rock her in an up-and-down motion, rather than back-and-forth in your arms. When the baby starts to sneeze, yawn, cough, stiffen, or thrash around, that's a sign that she is starting to become overloaded. Letting the baby rest then may stave off prolonged crying. Gradually, parents will be able to decrease the amount of time the baby needs to rest and increase the amount of time she can tolerate stimulation.

For infants whose drug-exposure has resulted in excessive muscle tone, or stiffness, exercises may be needed. Parents can consult a physical therapist for suggestions of ways to relax the baby's muscles. (The long-term effects of prenatal drug exposure are discussed in Chapter 6.)

Adjustment of Older Children

When preschoolers and school-age children move into a new family, it is often described as a "marriage" in which the various members of the family must learn about each other and adapt to the different personalities. Older children typically go through a period immediately after placement of near-perfect behavior, often called the "honeymoon." This period is followed by a testing period. The behavior of children during these two phases is tied to their grief over their separation from and loss of their foster parents or birth parents and to the process of forming attachments in their new family, which is discussed in Chapter 3. Many adoption advocates believe that parents who adopt older children should initiate family therapy before or immediately after the child's placement. Whether or not professional services are used at this time, it helps to understand the stages of grief that older children may be experiencing.

Grief in Preschool and School-age Children

Elisabeth Kübler-Ross, a psychiatrist and authority on death, identified five stages that people go through when dealing with death: denial, anger, bargaining, depression, and acceptance. Every time we experience a loss, we go through these predictable stages of grief, although if the loss is a minor one, we may go through the stages quickly. Psychiatrist John Bowlby reports that children as young as four mourn much like adults and that even two-and-a-half- and three year olds can experience the stages of grief that adults do. However, they can work through their grief, provided their questions are answered and their memories not discouraged.

Denial, Anger, and Bargaining

One of the first reactions to a loss is shock and numbness. Instead of collapsing or getting hysterical, people tend to function automatically, but report that the realization hasn't "hit them" yet. Children, too, may seem to react casually to news of a loss, but later cry uncontrollably or lash out angrily at those around them.

Realization of the loss is generally followed by denial and disbelief. Children often show "searching" behavior that indicates they expect the person to walk through the door at any minute. A child may even stare out the window, looking for the significant person to return. The adopted child may believe that the birth parent didn't mean to place her for adoption, that she was "stolen" or that it was all a misunderstanding and the birth parent will return for her. She may deny the loss by denying that the person lost was important to her, making statements such as "I really didn't like that place anyway." Strong emotions, such as anger, are common at this time, and the child may reveal them verbally or through other forms of behavior. It is crucial that the parents let the child know that they recognize how she feels, that those feelings are normal, and that she is allowed to express them. She may be saying shocking things or things that hurt, such as that she wants her "real" mom or that her real mom was bad and she wishes that her real mom was dead. Rather than stifle these feelings by criticism, such as "Don't you like living with us?" or "Oh, you don't really wish she were dead," parents should let the child express them so she can move to ultimate acceptance of her loss. Children need the support of their parents at this time, and holding or touching goes a long way toward reassuring them.

At some point children may try bargaining for a different outcome. They often believe they were to blame for what happened and that if they change, they will recover the foster parents or birth parents who were lost to them. The child may decide to behave perfectly or never to love her new parents so she can be rewarded by the return of the people lost to her.

The child in this stage of grief believes her loss can be reversed. Eventually she realizes that despite all her efforts, there is no hope of recovering her loss. That is when despair sets in.

Depression and Acceptance

One of the most difficult aspects of grief is the despair that accompanies it. The child has no hope of being reunited with the significant person that she lost, but still yearns for the person as much as ever. She may feel that life is hopeless and have difficulty functioning. She may contemplate suicide. A child may lose her appetite or look to food as a source of comfort. She is likely to withdraw and become apathetic. Screaming and crying is replaced by mournful wailing. Parents want to spare their children pain and will have difficulty accepting the fact that there is little they can do to mitigate their children's sorrow. But allowing the child to express her feelings is what is needed. If despair continues beyond a few weeks, though, the child may need professional help to move on to the next stage—an understanding and acceptance of the loss and the ability to move on with her life. As the child realizes that all the denial, searching, and bargains don't work to eliminate the loss, she will ultimately come to accept it.

Dealing with Grief

Bowlby points out that even though children mourn in much the same way that adults do, there are differences. Children have less control over their grief process—they may not be as able as adults to get the information they need to help them understand their loss, and it is not as easy for them to seek comfort from other people if those whom they depend on for support fail to provide it. Children are also more distractable and may seem to be having little reaction to their loss, when in reality their attention may have been diverted only temporarily. As a result, they may have sudden mood swings. Children need sustained comfort, an adult they can depend on, answers to their questions, and respect for their memories. Claudia Jewett Jarratt's book *Helping Children Cope with Separation and Loss* is an excellent discussion of how parents can help their grieving children.

One of the ways that a loss affects children is by demonstrating that relationships and situations they thought were permanent are not. Children then wonder what other seemingly permanent situation could be lost. Adoptees typically understand what it means to be placed for adoption years before they comprehend the legal system that makes adoption permanent. An awareness that they have lost their birth parents may be accompanied by a fear that their adoptive home is not permanent. This anxiety, according to Jarratt, may show up as a fear of going to school, insomnia, nightmares or night terrors (in which the child screams and may appear to be awake even though she is sleeping), nail biting, increased allergic responses, increased risk of infection, or other physical ailments. Jarratt, suggests surrounding the anxious child with softness—having her wear layers of clothes or sleep next to something soft like flannel sheets or a quilt. Adjustments in the child's sleeping routine also may be necessary, such as allowing her to fall asleep with the radio going or the light on. Parents may worry about establishing "precedents" like this—believing that a child who comes into a new home should understand "the way it's going to be." But some allowances do need to be made for the child who is experiencing grief. Adjustments in routine can be made when the child's needs change.

When the parents and child must be separated during this stage, the parents need to be particularly reliable about returning when they said they would or calling the child to let her know they have been delayed.

Even though children need to express their feelings, they may not be willing to do so, especially with "new" people like their adoptive parents. Parents may have to take the lead in initiating discussions of what the child may be feeling. Specific activities that the parents and child can engage in that can lead to discussions about feelings of separation and loss are discussed in Chapter 5.

Adjusting to a New School

At the same time that she is adjusting to her new family and grieving for those she is separated from, the older child is also expected to adjust to a new school and make new friends—formidable tasks for even an emotionally stable child. If possible, the older child should be placed in her adoptive home during the summer so she can start her new school in the fall, reducing her self-consciousness at being "new" at school. If school is already in session, the child should be enrolled as soon as possible. Even an unfamiliar school probably feels more comfortable to the child than staying home with parents she hardly knows. In addition, in many countries adopted children are not considered to have status equal to children born into a family. If an internationally adopted child is kept at home after her arrival while other children in the family go off to school, she may think she is not allowed to go to school because her status is not equal to that of the other children. Furthermore, the staff in some orphanages describe adoption as an opportunity to go to school and learn, as well as to have a family. The children therefore expect to go to school immediately.

A child who has been moved in and out of foster care or who has had enough turmoil in her life to be available for adoption may not be academically prepared for the same grade as other students the same age. This is particularly true for children adopted from other countries. Nonetheless, many parents and professionals recommend placing children in classes with their peers or with children who are no more than three years behind them. Although many children who are adopted at an older age are emotionally immature and may benefit socially by being with younger children, the stigma of being placed in a classroom with younger children may defeat the benefits—especially if the child reacts immaturely. Children with little or no English-speaking ability, do not benefit from being placed in a classroom with younger children; rather, they should be placed in English as a Second Language (ESL) or bilingual education programs. Authorities in the field say that it is no easier for an eleven year old to learn English in the third grade than in the sixth grade, since both classrooms will be filled with students who are proficient in English. Furthermore, some internationally adopted children have had so little education that they will struggle in the classroom no matter what grade they are in. Socially, it is better for an eleven year old to be in a sixth-grade classroom working at a third-grade level than to be in a third-grade classroom.

Educators counsel against subjecting a child who has just been placed in a new family to a battery of tests to determine the appropriate grade level. Testing is too stressful for children who are already making major adjustments in their lives. They may end up being labeled as learning disabled when they were simply having adjustment or language problems. Later, when the child is more adjusted, if a parent or teacher suspects a learning problem, testing may be appropriate.

Even with a carefully selected classroom, the adoptee may have difficulty with her schoolwork because she is using a great deal of energy to grieve and form new attachments. Jarett points out that the grieving child may have difficulty following directions or concentrating. She suggests giving children concrete suggestions to help them concentrate on their schoolwork, rather than the vague "buckle down." She also suggests giving them specific times, both at school and at home, when they can discuss their worries and concerns. They may then be able to push aside their feelings when they need to concentrate, knowing that there is a designated time when they will be able to think about their loss.

Parents should not place too much importance on the child's schoolwork, appearance, or other "learning" activities during the adjustment period, says psychologist Terrence Koller. It is more important for the child to concentrate on her new relationships. Of course, it will be difficult for parents to resist the pressure from teachers, relatives, and friends to focus on the child's developmental progress. If friends and relatives have expressed doubt that someone can have an influence on a child adopted at an older age, the parents are going to want to show them how quickly their child has advanced in school and improved her appearance. This is a time when support from other parents of children adopted at an older age can be valuable.

The parents should insist on a conference with the child's teacher before the child begins attending classes to explain her background. While emphasizing that they do not expect special treatment for the child, the parents should point out that the child may need extra attention, as well as empathy, for her intense feelings at this time. Psychologist Ann Jernberg points out in "The Special Student" that the newly placed child needs stability in her life, and teachers should be advised to provide her with as much predictability as possible. The child who has recently experienced a move may need more preparation than other students for changes in routine, such as a field trip or substitute teacher.

Teachers may also have little experience with children who do not readily form attachments and may need guidance in finding ways to get close to the child. (Attachment and the unattached child are discussed in Chapters 3 and 11.)

Most older children will want to reveal their adoptive status in their own way and in their own time. Parents should discuss this with the child and inform her teacher if she does not want her classmates to know she is adopted. Otherwise, the teacher may introduce her to the class with an explanation that she is new in school because she has just been adopted.

Because children are self-conscious about being new in school and about being adopted, parents should be aware that a newly placed child may have a greater need than other children to blend in with her peers and should be understanding if she seems to need to conform to the prevailing fashion or hairstyle.

When the new student is from another country, it may be advisable for a parent to visit the classroom and explain that a new student will be arriving who does not speak English. The parent can also explain that because of cultural differences, the child may behave differently or interpret the behavior of other students differently. For example, a boy from Asia may expect younger students in a classroom to defer to him. Parents should take care not to violate the child's privacy in explaining her situation. They can say that the child has not had the opportunity to attend school, but do not need to add that she had been living on the streets. It is a good idea for the new student to have a "buddy" assigned to her who is responsible for explaining things like the lunch procedure and serves as an intermediary with other students. The student should also have one person on the staff of the school who will trouble-shoot any problems that may arise, so that in addition to a new culture and a new language, the student does not also have to figure out the school bureaucracy.

Adjusting to a New Culture

Parents who adopt older children from other countries are often hindered in helping their children through the adjustment period by the language barrier. The first thing that parents should do to reassure the child is to let her know that the family taking her home is the right family. This can be done through an interpreter or by using any photographs or videos of the family that were sent to the child earlier.

Language is the most obvious, but not the only, cultural change the child must adjust to. The child may be experiencing both new foods and an abundance of food, different ways of expressing affection, alternative forms of discipline, and new values. Parents whose child is reluctant to be kissed or hugged sometimes think the child has never experienced parental love or is rejecting theirs. In fact, the child may just be unfamiliar with such a direct method of expressing affection. There may be other cultural differences. For example, some children will not be accustomed to having pets in the house, and others may not be familiar with bearded men. In the Philippines, forcing a child to make eye contact demeans her. In Korea, females are submissive to males, and a younger male child may expect his older sister to wait on him. Without an understanding of customs such as these, though, parents may find their child's avoidance of eye contact suspicious or think they have adopted a lazy child or bully who expects his siblings to do his bidding.

Children adopted in recent years from orphanages in Eastern Europe have been found to have problems resulting from detrimental conditions, particularly nutritional deprivation and the lack of staff. When orphanages are crowded and understaffed, children are not picked up or played with. Even stimulating toys may be lacking. The kinds of activities parents do to stimulate children, like playing pat-a-cake, are not done. As a result, some of these children do not respond to stimulation—sound, pain, touch, and movement—as other children do. Once they are in environments that are more interactive, some of these children show extreme reactions to sensory stimulation and have difficulty finding the middle ground. For example, some find slight movement overwhelming while others can't get enough bouncing and running. The touch of a parent soothing her hair may be overwhelming to the child, or she may gag on rough-textured food. Bumps in socks or labels in clothes may seem unbearable. Some find loud noises or sudden sounds alarming. Some find it fearful to have their head not in an erect position, as when their teeth are inspected by a dentist. It isn't clear how early sensory deprivation affects subsequent sensory processing. It may be that without adequate sensory input early in life, the central nervous system doesn't develop properly.

For the new adoptive parent, having a child who resists touch can be upsetting. Parents must remember that it is the sensation the child is rejecting—not them. Sharon Cermak, Ed.D., an occupational therapist and adoptive parent who has studied children from Romania, says that children who are hypersensitive to touch may not be able to endure prolonged touch, but may be receptive to quick touches. Parents sometimes find that pushing a child on a swing is one of the few ways the child can accept their touch. Children can also become desensitized to touch by playing games in which they rub themselves with a soft washcloth or having their gums massaged with a toothbrush.

Support groups and organizations such as the Parent Network for the Post-Institutionalized Child can help parents recognize and understand their children's behaviors and provide strategies for dealing with them, as well as provide referrals to professionals when evaluations are necessary.

Although many of us expect a child who has lived in an orphanage to be passive because of the lack of stimulation, some of these children often have effective "survival" instincts. Like street-wise children, they may be aggressive about taking food or hoard it when it is available. One parent found that instead of needing a security blanket when she went to sleep, her daughter needed to clutch a piece of bread. It may take many years for these children to learn that food is readily available. In the meantime, parents should leave food on the table day and night so the child learns it is always available. Parents may have to monitor their child's food intake by serving her, instead of allowing her to heap food on her plate, and by watching for the stashing of food in unexpected places.

Children from other countries are unlikely to have had the quantities of material goods that Americans are accustomed to. In her excellent discussion of East-West cultural differences, *Oriental Children in American Homes: How Do They Adjust?* Frances Koh notes that children brought up in a Confucian-dominated culture highly value material goods. These children may be strongly status conscious, flaunting their belongings and hoarding money. Of course, such behavior can also reflect a history of poverty in a child of any culture. Children who have not owned much in the way of toys or clothing may not be experienced with the concept of either "possession" or "sharing" and thus may not hesitate to take some-thing they want.

We can ease the transition for our internationally adopted chil-dren in several ways:

- Unless they are fluent in the child's native tongue, parents should have an interpreter available whom they can call on, even at odd hours, when sign language and a bilingual dictio-nary aren't enough to facilitate communication. Although many parents believe the child's adjustment will be much easier the sooner she learns to speak English, there is no need to rush her assimilation of the language; it will come quickly and easily as she is immersed in the new culture. In the meantime, they should tolerate her need to express herself in the way that is most comfortable for her. It is difficult enough for an adoptee to express her feelings, but more so if she is expected to do so in a new language (for more on the benefits of bilingualism, see Chapter 10). Parents should have the interpreter tell the child why the interpreter is there—a child is sometimes anxious when she meets someone from her country of origin because she fears this person is going to take her back to their country.

• Have some identification on the child, perhaps an identification bracelet. An older child sometimes runs away during the adjustment period and when found by the police, the newly adopted child may not be able to say her name or where she lives.

• Become acquainted with the customs of the country the child is coming from. If you must travel to the country to adopt the child, that is a good opportunity to learn the country's customs. Adoptive Families of America has a catalog of books for adoptive families, including several that describe cultural aspects of different countries. Pamphlets and information sheets on other countries are often available from the adoption agency placing the child, and travel guides available in any bookstore are other sources of information about different countries.

• Do not require the child to become Americanized overnight. She will abandon her original customs so quickly and so completely in an effort to fit in that her heritage will be virtually lost. There is no risk that allowing her to sleep on the floor, speak her own language, or eat familiar foods will hamper her adjustment (for a more detailed discussion, see Chapter 2). On the other hand, parents should know what the child has been accustomed to. One family took their five-year-old Korean son to a Chinese restaurant on the way home from the airport after his arrival. Each time he would pick up his fork to eat the rice they had ordered for him, they would indicate that it was quite all right for him to eat with chopsticks. Years later, the boy told them that in preparation for adoption in the United States, the staff at the orphanage she had been in encouraged the children to use knives, spoons, and forks; he did not know how to use chopsticks.

· Sometimes, in an effort to make the child more comfortable, parents arrange for someone from the child's country of origin to meet the child. In some cases, the child welcomes the sounds of her language or other familiarities. In other cases, however, such a situation can trigger memories of difficult times or even a fear of being returned to the homeland. Parents should be aware of such possibilities and act quickly to reassure and comfort the child if she seems distressed.

Adjustment of Siblings

How children react to an adopted sibling depends a lot on the age of the new member of the family, her age relative to the other children in the family, and the reactions of other people to the child.

The greatest adjustment will need to be made by the child who is most displaced by the arrival of the new sibling, for example, the child who had been the youngest and now is a middle child or the child who was the only girl in the family and now has a sister. The displaced child will probably have some behavioral problems as a reaction to the new child's arrival—regressing or becoming aggressive. Although the last thing parents think they need at this time is inappropriate behavior from a child they have come to expect good behavior from, it is really a healthy sign. Pediatrician Vera Fahlberg says that the displaced child will engage in "testing" kinds of behavior only if she feels secure in her family. If she does not show signs of jealousy or other behavioral problems, the parents may need to find out why she doesn't feel safe enough to let them know she is upset as a result of the new child's arrival.

Parents often expect exemplary behavior from the children who are already in the home when a new child arrives. They would like to be able to concentrate their energy on the new child and the changes they must make to accommodate her. They want the rest of their lives to be predictable, including the behavior of their other children. Adoptive parents are not sure they can control the new child's behavior, so they may try to increase control in an area where they know they have it—the behavior of the children who have been in the family.

The siblings will want to know how the family has been changed by the addition of the new child, particularly how their position in the family has been affected. So, they test the rules and their parents. Rather than see this testing behavior as normal, adoptive parents may find their self-confidence shaken. The problem is exacerbated if the new child is having a difficult time adjusting to the new home. Parents shouldn't neglect the children already in the home in their efforts to smooth the transition for the new child.

Reactions to Infants

When an infant is adopted, the reaction of siblings is much the same as it would be to a child being born into the family, but adoptive parents who try to prepare their young children for the arrival of a new baby may find that many of the books written for that purpose are unsuitable. Most of them discuss the mother's pregnancy, show pictures of a pregnant woman, or talk about the baby "coming home from the hospital." There are good books that discuss the feelings of jealousy and displacement that children feel when another child comes into the house. Tapestry Books, a mail-order catalog of resources for adoptive families, and Perspectives Press, a publisher specializing in infertility and adoption, offer several children's books to help siblings understand adoption and sort out their feelings.

There is a chance that an adopted baby can receive more attention than a child being born into a family. If the waiting period is so long that the parents become preoccupied with it, if the family has not adopted before and adoption is a novel thing for relatives and friends, or if the child is of a different race or ethnic background, she can receive more attention than she might otherwise. People may be especially interested in seeing a child from another country because they are curious about the child's skin color, hair texture, and features. They may fuss more about the child's appearance than they would about a baby who looks (to them) like every other wrinkled baby or spunky toddler. Or people may pay more attention to the child because they are looking for signs of mental or physical problems.

It is a good idea to bring a present for an older child when you bring a present to a family with a new baby or otherwise recognize that the older child is likely to feel jealous of the attention paid to a new baby. It may be even more vital to remember the older children if the baby is likely to receive undue attention.

Reacting to an Older Child

How children react to an older child depends on the child's age, and her age relative to the children already in the home and whether the child has emotional or behavioral problems. The children already in the home need some frank talk about what to expect when the new child arrives. They may be expecting a playmate and be surprised to find the new sibling stealing from them and competing for the parents' attention. Adoption activist Laurie Flynn says that agencies should prepare children for the arrival of an adopted sibling. Too often, though, the job is left to the adoptive parents who usually are not well suited for the task. Parents expecting the arrival of an older child may be anxious about how the adoption will affect their family and want everything to go well. Rather than wanting to discuss the ways the adoption may be unpleasant for the children they already have, they may look to these children to affirm their decision to adopt an older child. They may minimize potential problems because they hope the problems won't come up.

Some agencies and parent groups have preparation sessions for children whose families are adopting an older or special needs child. There also are support groups for children who have a physically or mentally disabled sibling, regardless of whether or not the sibling is adopted.

When the child being adopted has a history of serious behavioral problems, particularly inappropriate sexual behavior, the other children in the home need some additional preparation. But parents are sometimes justifiably reluctant to violate the new child's privacy by revealing her history to other members of the family. The best way to handle the situation is to discuss in general terms what kinds of problems any child might have who has been in similar circumstances. Instead of saying, "Jennifer was sexually abused by her father and made sexual advances toward the children in her last foster home," parents can say, "Sometimes children try to engage in sexual behavior with someone younger or smaller than they are. This is not OK, and if it should happen, you need to tell us immediately. You won't get into any trouble."

When the new child has serious behavioral problems, children already in the home may be embarrassed to be related to her. They don't always share their feelings with their parents. Children who previously have been welcome in all their friends' homes and who have been able to invite their friends to their house may find that their friends' parents are reluctant to let their children visit a house in which there is a child with a serious behavioral problem. And these children may be embarrassed if the new sibling lies, steals, or otherwise gets into trouble, particularly at school. Parents or school counselors can help these children understand that they are separate persons from other family members and not responsible for someone else's actions. It may be more difficult to help their friends' parents understand that.

During the adjustment period, children may observe that their parents seem to be tolerating behavior in the new child that they know would not be tolerated if they engaged in it. A child who has learned that her parents will not tolerate her shoplifting even a candy bar may see them apparently overlooking more serious stealing in the new child. Children may not understand that equal punishment for equal transgressions may be inappropriate when one child has serious behavioral problems. They may not understand that their parents may be pleased that the new child is doing less stealing than she was in her previous home, but only see that mom and dad would punish them severely if they were stealing at all. The lesson parents need to transmit to their children at these times is that life is not always fair. They can explain to their children that they have certain expectations of their behavior that may be different for each of them, just as they may expect one child to get straight As but be happy that another one gets all Cs, because each is performing to the best of his or her abilities. The problems that develop when each child is not treated the same are not limited to the adjustment period, but may be ongoing.

This is one of the most difficult dilemmas for families who adopt children with behavioral problems. The parents worry that if the new child is punished differently from the other children that the other children will think that standards have relaxed—that they can now "get away with" stealing or truancy. We must have some confidence that the values we are transmitting to our children will withstand some trial. Parents may see the normal testing behavior that children engage in when a new child arrives as an indication that the behavior of the new child is a poor influence on their other children. In addition, if the parents have been giving all their attention to the child whose behavior is so challenging, the other children in the family may try behaving the same way to get their parents' attention. Parents may need some professional assistance at this time if they are not already involved in therapy. A therapist or the family's social worker can help them decide whether the children who have been in the home are testing them to see how the family has been changed by the arrival of a new child or if their behavior represents a more serious problem. One of the reasons that placements of older children disrupt is that the parents perceive that the children are having an undesirable influence on other children in the home.

Adjustment of Relatives

The adjustment of an adopted child and the long-term adjustment of the family is affected by the level of acceptance and support given to the family by relatives and friends at the time of the adoption. Too often, though, adoptive parents expect their friends and relatives to give unconditional approval of the adoption without realizing that they, too, may need information about adoption. Not all couples share with their families the problems they are having conceiving a child or their reasons for considering the adoption of a child from overseas or with special needs. They forget that their relatives may have some of the same doubts, grief, and questions that they had before they decided that adoption was the right choice for them. As a result, instead of giving the parents a wholehearted endorsement of their plans, the extended family may be resistant.

Accepting Adoption

Though most relatives eventually accept adoption, their initial reaction is not always favorable, perhaps because they have had little, if any, experience with it. If they think that adoptees do not love and respect their adoptive parents the way they would their biological parents, the extended family may worry that the adoptive parents will be disappointed.

Sociologists William Feigelman and Arnold Silverman found that the more the child being adopted resembles a child the parents would have given birth to, the more accepting friends and family members initially are. Infertile couples who adopt infants of the same race receive the most support, while those who adopt older children, children of a different ethnic background, or special needs children receive less support—especially if they are able to have biological children. In their study, those who adopted Colombian babies received about the same amount of support as those who adopted Caucasian babies from the United States, those who adopted Asian children received somewhat less support, and those who adopted older African American children met the greatest resistance.

Resistance diminishes as family members and friends get to know the child and see that despite the racial or ethnic differences, the family attachments are "real." Nevertheless, the initial reaction is important to the short- and long-term adjustment of the family, and the more support adoptive parents receive, the smoother the adoption goes. David Brodzinsky and his colleagues at Rutgers University found that parents of transracially placed infants are often reluctant to leave their child in someone else's care, perhaps because they perceive a lack of support from friends or relatives. As a result, they may not take much time away from their child, though they may need rest from parenting as much as or more than other adoptive parents.

Although relatives usually accept the adoption eventually, the initial lack of support continues to affect the family. Having gone through the initial adjustment period without the help of family and friends, parents may get used to being self-reliant and not turn to their relatives or friends even after they have accepted the adoption.

Adoptive parents should remember that while adoption may be meeting our needs, it may not be meeting the needs of our extended family. We want to love and nurture a child and so adopt, but perhaps our aging grandparents want to know that their genetic line will be continued after their deaths. Perhaps our children are grown, and we want to extend our parenting roles by adopting special needs children; our parents feel their need for grandchildren to dote on has been met and don't understand why we want to take on more work at a time when we could be taking life easier. Maybe the extended family has not had much contact with disabled people or people of different races and isn't sure how to act around them. They may need time to get used to the idea of infertility, adoption, or transracial families. They may also need a neutral forum where they can ask questions, express their doubts, and obtain information without it interfering with their relationship with the adoptive family.

We can help our families accept adoption in the following ways:

- Introduce the idea gradually instead of springing it on the family as a decision that has been made and that they must accept unquestioningly.

- Give them an opportunity to get information they need. Many adoption agencies and adoptive parent groups recognize the need for relatives and friends of adoptive families to become educated about adoption and so provide information sessions or invitations to attend adoption meetings that are geared to prospective parents. Relatives can then ask questions of a social worker or other adoptive parent that they might be hesitant to ask a family member.

- Provide them with an opportunity to see other adoptive families. Once relatives see that adopted children treat their parents the same way that biological children do, many of their fears are assuaged.

- Provide them with an ongoing source of support and information. A subscription to *Adoptive Families* magazine, *Adopted Child* newsletter, or whatever publication parents have found to be particularly insightful could be sent to extended family members. *Supporting an Adoption* by Pat Holmes is an excellent booklet for relatives.

- Tell them what you need. If they haven't adopted, friends and relatives may not know how to provide support. Let them know, for example, that you appreciate their interest and you will let them know the minute you get word of your child's arrival, but in the meantime, their calls of inquiry are distressing.

- Include them in an entrustment ceremony or other rituals, such as naming, that demonstrate how the parents feel about the adoption and give participants a chance to express their feelings about the event.

- If, despite having an opportunity to become educated about adoption, relatives still seem resistant, parents should initiate a candid discussion about the subject. Parents could be misreading their relatives' intentions, or there could still be some reluctance to accept the adoption that needs to be discussed.

- Forgive relatives for any insensitive remarks they made while they got used to the idea of adoption. Adoptive parents forget that there was a time when they, too, may have had doubts about adoption, told racist jokes, or thought there was no choice but to conceive a child. Relatives who ultimately accept the idea of adoption and embrace the adoptee as a complete family member should not be held accountable forever for earlier remarks.

- Finally, encourage contact between relatives and the adoptees as early as possible. Just because the adoptive mother is not recovering physically from a pregnancy does not mean she doesn't need help with the care of a new baby. And while it is not a good idea to overwhelm an older child with visits or gifts from relatives immediately after her arrival, some marking of her arrival should be made—a special gift, photograph, or family keepsake could be given to her. A visit can follow as soon as the family regains its equilibrium.

If parents find they cannot count on their friends and relatives for the support they need, they should not hesitate to set up a new support system, perhaps turning to an adoptive parents group. (For information on the nearest parent support group, contact the North American Council on Adoptable Children.)

A Sense of "Clan"

In addition to giving the adoptive family needed support, extended family members have to remember that their relationship with the adoptee cannot be taken for granted. Although adoption gives them a legal tie, there is not the biological tie that usually bridges generations. The adoptee thinks of her adoptive parents as her parents because they raise her, but isn't always sure of her relationship to people who are referred to in terms such as "forebears," "kin," and "clan." As she grows up, particularly after her adoptive parents die, she may wonder whether she is an authentic member of the "clan."

Adoptees and their extended family members can and do develop deep, warm relationships, but these relationships must be based on meaningful human interaction, not on an assumption of kinship. Certainly, there are biological families in which grandchildren and grandparents are strangers because of geographic distance or other circumstances characteristic of today's families. But if the child does not know her grandparents well, at least she knows there is a connection—she's been told that she gets her determination from her "pioneer stock" or feels an obligation to show her Irish heritage by wearing green on St. Patrick's Day. The adoptee who doesn't know her extended adoptive family well has only a legal document—to which both the adoptee and the relatives were passive participants—to bind her to them.

It is important, then, for extended family members to make an effort to develop strong relationships with the adoptee. Parents and relatives should make sure the adoptee knows who makes up her extended adoptive family. One adoptee's family made her a book with a page for each extended family member containing a photograph of the person and a drawing of him or her doing a typical activity. The words on the page indicate the relationship between the adoptee and the person shown and tell something about him or her. Especially nice is the theme running through the whole book: *This is your family, and all these people love you.*

Extended family members should also be encouraged to write, send E-mail, create videos, make telephone calls if affordable, and send small gifts to the adoptee, especially if they don't see each other often. Children are easy to please. An interesting picture from a newspaper, wildlife or other stamps that are sent to every mailbox, or an inexpensive sticker or balloon are treasures to a child. Older children could be sent magazine or newspaper clippings on a topic that interests them. An inexpensive tape recorder can record stories about grandparents and great-grandparents, or best of all, stories about the adoptee's parents when they were young. Relatives can also read a children's book from the library into a cassette for a personalized present. These all show the child that her relatives care enough about her to do something special for her.

Although the adoptee and her extended family members do not share a heritage, they can build their own traditions. Relatives can try to develop particular activities to share; for example, Uncle Ralph can become the uncle who always takes the child swimming, and Grandpa can be remembered for sharing his record collection.

3

Bonding and Attachment

◐ My friend Julie was clearly exhausted from four consecutive nights with little sleep. Her newly arrived Filipino daughter had her days and nights mixed up, and Julie and her husband had been taking turns walking the floors with her.

"This can't go on much longer," she said to me.

I nodded. "It's even more difficult when you don't love her yet, isn't it?" I asked.

Julie looked at me in amazement. "I'm glad you said that," she said quietly, "I was beginning to think there was something wrong with me."

Julie and her husband lost many hours of sleep while their daughter adjusted to her new surroundings, but in the process their daughter learned to depend on them, and they received satisfaction from meeting her needs. This grew into what is now a strong attachment between them.

Adoptive Families Do Form Attachments

People do not adopt unless they believe they can love a child who was not born to them. Although love for a biological child is the same as love for an adopted child, the attachment between a child and his adoptive parent develops under different circumstances than the attachment between a child and his biological parent. But some theories of how bonding and attachment develop between a child and a biological parent have raised doubts about whether adoptive parents and their children can form relationships that are as deep and secure.

Some child care manuals emphasize that activities during pregnancy and birth contribute to the "bonding" of the mother and baby. This philosophy grew out of research published in the 1970s indicating that early contact between a parent and a baby was essential to the formation of a bond between them.

Obstetrical practices were altered to give fathers an active role in the babies' deliveries. Hospital environments changed to allow babies to stay with their mothers and breastfeed immediately. Parents began to think that natural childbirth, rooming-in, and breastfeeding were essential for bonding. They believed that if these practices were used, then bonding would be virtually accomplished before mothers went home from the hospital.

All this has not been lost on adoptive parents. Intellectually we know that natural childbirth, rooming-in, and breastfeeding are helpful but not necessary for attachment. Still, we're anxious to form an attachment with our children as soon as possible so we can dismiss our doubts and those of our parents, in-laws, and friends.

Fortunately, there is now evidence of what adoptive families have known all along, namely, that adoptive parents and their children bond, or form attachments, as successfully as do biological families. Researchers Leslie Singer, David Brodzinsky, Douglas Ramsey, Mary Steir, and Everett Waters found no difference between the development of attachments between mothers and infants when nonadoptive families were compared to adoptive families in which parents and children were of the same race. Nor was there any difference between adoptive families of the same race and interracial adoptive families. Interracially adopted infants were more anxious than nonadopted infants, but the researchers suggested that parents who adopt a child of a different race may need more time to feel comfortable with a child who looks remarkably different. These researchers concluded that adoptive families—even those adopting interracially—can be optimistic about the development of warm, secure parent-child attachments. Rather than immediate contact after birth to make this attachment, parents need confidence in their ability to take care of the child and a warm, consistent atmosphere of caretaking that is based on the infant's needs.

Unlike animals, which become independent adults quickly, humans are dependent for so long that they need to develop the kind of close relationship with a caregiver that will ensure that they will be cared for. From an evolutionary standpoint, infants need to be able to form this attachment with *any* caregiver—not just a biological parent, and they need to be able to form attachments with a few people, not just one.

Though there is much controversy in the attachment field, this point—that infants can just as easily form attachments with foster parents and adoptive parents—is virtually undisputed. Furthermore, because *learned trust* is the basis for attachment, attachment experts say that giving birth to a child does not predispose the child to attach to the biological parent or give the biological parent any kind of "head start" in developing attachment.

Early contact between a parent and child can get attachment off to a good start, but experts on infant care discourage parents from thinking of attachment as something that happens instantaneously. The fact is, it often takes time before biological or adoptive parents feel their child is an irreplaceable part of their lives; it takes time for the child to think of his parents as special people who are not interchangeable with any others.

Bonding and Attachment

Although we often talk about the development of love between parents and children as "bonding," those who have studied the phenomenon differentiate between "bonding" and "attachment."

Bonding, as Frank G. Bolton, Jr. explains in *When Bonding Fails*, is a unidirectional process that begins in the biological parent—primarily the mother—during pregnancy and continues through birth and the first few days of life. It is the parent's instinctive desire to protect the infant.

Attachment takes more time and more interaction between a parent and child. It is a reciprocal process between a parent and child that develops during the first year they are together and is solidified throughout the relationship. It is the development of a mutual feeling that the other is irreplaceable.

Given these definitions, what most of us are talking about when we refer to "bonding" is actually "attachment." In fact, some people question whether the attachment behavior that humans engage in can be compared to the instinctive "bonding" activities of animals.

There may be some development of emotional ties taking place in the adoptive family prior to the arrival of the child. Many parents report feeling a closeness based on the photograph they have of their child and mourn if that child can't be placed with them for some reason. But in both the adoptive and biological family, the feeling of attachment between the parents and child develops after the child arrives.

Attachment to an Infant

Attachment between the parents and the child develops as the child learns that he can count on his parents to meet his physical and emotional needs. We as parents learn to take pleasure in subordinating ourselves to the needs of our child. This process is the same whether the child has been born to us or was adopted.

A newborn's initial needs are for food and physical comfort. He can't begin to relate to people until he has the security that these needs will be met. A baby comes well equipped to make people take care of him. With his large head, big eyes, soft skin, puffy cheeks, and short limbs, he looks helpless. Parents, especially adoptive parents who have waited a long time for a baby, respond because they want to be needed.

Reciprocal Relationship

At about three months of age, the baby begins to relate to people and starts to develop a reciprocal relationship with his primary caretaker, usually his mother. He learns that if he smiles, his mother smiles back. If he makes silly gurgling sounds, his father does, too. If he cries, a parent comes running. It is important for parents to be playful. The "coochie-coochie-coos" that embarrass some adults are an important way of interacting with a baby.

The adoptive parent should be cautious about overstimulating the infant. We are often so anxious to be "good parents" that we overreact to the baby's signals and create anxiety, rather than security, in the infant. This is especially likely to happen when the baby has been abused or neglected and the parent is trying to compensate for the child's unpleasant experience.

Babies may respond to such intensity by withdrawing. The adoptive parent who misinterprets the baby's need for rest as rejection may try even harder to communicate with the baby, prompting even more withdrawal. Babies are made to tell us what they need; all we need to do is be open to the cues they are giving us.

Gradually the baby learns it is not a coincidence that when he smiles, mom does, too. He discovers he can make the grown-up do something for him. His actions begin to be intentional.

In addition, around six months of age, a baby begins to conceptualize the idea of a *person*. Before then, he may have recognized his mother's face, but he did not understand that the face belongs to an individual. Once this happens, he begins to differentiate between the people who respond to him and comes to prefer the one or two people who are most dependable in providing him with care. He directs his signals to them and prefers that they alone respond to him. In his book *Becoming Attached*, Robert Karen eloquently describes how attachment forms: "As mother comes into view as an individual, their mutual history of dovetailed responses coalesces into the single phenomenon of love."

Separation anxiety is determined by the attachment process, not the child's age. Most child care manuals say that an infant will fuss when he is left at about six months of age. That will be true for an adopted infant if he was placed at birth. Our children arrived at about seven months of age. They did not begin to show separation anxiety when I left them until they were perhaps a year old and the attachment process had progressed to the point where I mattered to them more than someone else. I remember a friend reaching for my eight-month-old daughter and then drawing back to ask, "Does she go to strangers?"

"Of course," I answered. "She's living with strangers."

Exploring the World

Gradually (in the second six months of life for an infant who has been with his caretaker since birth), the baby feels more confident of his ability to make his parent do things and begins to test other people. When he finds he can influence other people as well, he begins to feel powerful, and his dependence on his parent tapers off. The baby continues to test the degree to which he can make others do what he wants until he is about three years old. At times of stress, however, he will still turn to the person with whom he first felt safe.

The infant who formed an attachment to his biological or foster parents before he was placed may look for that person in times of stress. This doesn't mean that he is rejecting his adoptive parents. In time, he will come to recognize them as his primary caretakers. Searching can be a good sign; the child who has been able to form attachments in the past will form new attachments more easily than the child who has never felt an attachment, because he has already learned to trust.

We must allow our children the opportunity to make attachments to other people, including those outside the family. These attachments do not diminish their attachment to us, but demonstrate that they feel secure enough to try to test the rest of their world. A parent who thinks he or she is the only person capable of properly caring for a child or playing with him is fostering dependence, not attachment.

Open Adoptions

Adoptive parents who have open adoptions—direct contact with their child's birth parents—may wonder if their child will develop an attachment to the birth mother if they have contact while the child is young. Understandably, they are concerned about whether such an attachment will leave the child confused about who his parents are or will lead to divided loyalties later on. Adoptive parents need not be concerned. Because a child is not born with what we call "attachment" to his birth mother, but grows attached to whomever becomes his primarily caretakers, the birth mother's occasional presence will not inhibit attachment in the adoptive family. A bigger issue may be whether the birth mother's presence inhibits the adoptive parents' own sense of entitlement (see Chapter 1). Both these issues—*Do I have the right to be this child's parent?* and *Will we love each other the way biological parents and children love each other?* are fundamental questions for adoptive parents. One advantage of open adoptions is that they bring these issues to the foreground, but developing a family life in which the answer to both questions is *yes* is fully within the control of the adoptive parents.

If the child has been with the birth parents or foster parents long enough to develop an attachment to them, he will feel disrupted, confused, and grief stricken if he is suddenly moved to the adoptive family. Subsequent contact with the birth parents or foster parents could be difficult for the child and may slow attachment to the adoptive parents. Adoptive parents may want to react to this by cutting off contact with the birth parents, but it must be remembered how important these people have obviously been to the child. We all probably can recall the vivid images of two-year-old "Baby Jessica's" abrupt move from the couple she had been with since birth to her birth parents and the birth parents' wish to keep the child apart from the people she thought of as her parents so she could build a new attachment to her birth parents, who would now be raising her. Many people questioned whether the abrupt move and the complete lack of contact with her "parents" was really the best way for Jessica to be moved.

A gradual move, as discussed in Chapter 1, with the child getting to know the people who will become his parents, is more likely to help the child during what will be a difficult transition even under ideal circumstances. The child learns that he does not have to be dependent on the people who have been taking care of him but can begin to depend on these new parents. The foster parents or birth parents likewise learn to "let go" and are reassured as they see the child adjusting well to his new parents. An entrustment ceremony, also described in Chapter 1, can be the culmination of this process. When the transition is smoothed in this way, contact with the birth parents or foster parents after the placement can then serve its intended purpose—to keep the child in touch with people who are significant to him—without such contact being disruptive.

Ways of Interacting

Feeding, smiling, eye contact, and body contact are all ways that infants and their parents interact. Through these reciprocal activities, a child learns that he can affect other people, even though they may be bigger and stronger than he is.

Eye contact is a good way to communicate with a baby who cannot yet send verbal messages. Eye contact stimulates other interaction between the parent and child. Few parents can look into their baby's eyes for long without stroking the baby's cheek or picking up the baby. And when the parent moves away, chances are the baby will follow her with his eyes. It is a simple action, but it tells the parent she is important enough that the baby will want to see where she's going.

Eye contact between a parent and the baby often leads to an exchange of smiles. The smile is another small but powerful means of communication. A smile from the baby in the morning erases a lot of the resentment that parents may feel because the baby kept them walking the floors all night.

Cuddling, stroking, kissing, and other means of bodily contact are also ways of enhancing the attachment process. Positive messages are transmitted back and forth. Of course, not all children or all parents are cuddlers. Alex came from a foster home where there were several children. When his adoptive mother held him, he did not put his arms around her or put his head on her shoulder. His arms flailed about him. He has never been able to sit on his mother's lap for long periods or snuggle in bed. However, they hug, hold hands, and sit close while reading books.

When a parent or child finds touching of any kind objectionable, a powerful message of rejection is sent. Professional help is needed to deal with this situation if it arises (see Chapter 2 for more about sensory deprivation among children who have been institutionalized). In most cases, however, parents and child find physical contact pleasurable.

When a parent feeds a baby, he is doing more than letting him know that when he's hungry he'll get what he wants. He is usually touching and having eye contact with the child as well. Parents who feed the baby according to their schedule, rather than the child's needs, or who remove the bottle before a baby is finished nursing are communicating that the child can't depend on them.

Although it contradicts the long-held child care belief that infants who are picked up when they cry will have that behavior reinforced and cry more, attachment theorists currently believe that infants cry because they are distressed and need to be comforted. Infants who learn they will be comforted when distressed become secure; after a while, when they are distressed, they cry less because they know they will be comforted.

Length of Time for Attachment

It is not possible to predict how long it will take to feel that a child is irreplaceable. It may take weeks, months, or a year or longer. The mother and father probably won't form an attachment with the child at the same rate or in the same way. A child may take less or more time than the parents to feel they are essential. A parent should not feel a need to rush the attachment process or feel like a failure if it takes more time than expected. The important thing is that the parents and child do develop an attachment, not how long it takes to do so.

A child's responsiveness to a parent and the parent's confidence in recognizing the child's needs are a good measure of successful attachment. Another sign of a secure attachment is the child's willingness to move away from the parent, returning to the parent during times of stress to regain the confidence he needs to be on his own again. Similarly, a parent's willingness to let go—to be enthusiastic about a child forming close relationships to others within or outside the family—is a sign that the parent feels the relationship is strong. Attachment is a never-ending process—the parent and child will continue reinforcing the attachment that began in infancy throughout their lives.

The Window of Attachment

It would seem to make sense that a child who had been starved for love would gobble it up when it became available. However, researchers believe that when the mother (or primary caretaker) does not respond to an infant's signals—perhaps because the mother is depressed, absent, abusive, or unable to decipher the baby's needs—the child's later behavior will reflect the lack of trust he has in his ability to get his needs met by giving out signals. In the most extreme situations, in which the infant has never received consistent care, the child grows up not expecting closeness. If affection is offered, he is suspicious of it and may reject it. Author Robert Karen says that the child avoids activating his attachment needs so he can stay near people without being rejected for wanting something from them. Some of these children show *indiscriminate friendliness*—a behavior sometimes seen in children who spent many years in understaffed orphanages. The children seem to be affectionate, but are as likely to be as affectionate with a stranger as they are with a family member; the behavior has no emotional basis because the child did not learn that he should expect any more from someone close to him than from a stranger.

When caregiving has been inconsistent, the child learns he will sometimes get his needs met, but he isn't sure when or how. He may be anxious about being needy or suspicious about offers of affection.

Attachment researchers are fairly certain that infants who do not receive regular, trustworthy care from a few recognizable individuals during the first six months of life are at risk of future attachments and the behavioral problems that can result when a child hasn't learned to trust or care. However, with effort and professional assistance, many of these children can also learn to trust. A much better outlook is envisioned for those who have formed secure attachments during the first six months of life but have those attachments disrupted. These infants will grieve for the loss of the most important people in their lives (see Chapter 2), but it won't be long before they learn that just as they once depended on their birth mothers or foster mothers to meet their needs, they can now depend on their adoptive parents. Because they learned early that they could trust that their needs would be met, they can transfer this trust from one person to another.

Breastfeeding the Adopted Baby

Breastfeeding is one way to use feeding time to become close to a baby. Because the baby's sucking at the breast is the primary stimulation for lactation, or the secretion of milk, breast milk can be produced without a pregnancy.

While it is possible to breastfeed an adopted infant, breastfeeding is not the right decision for every mother and baby. Before making a commitment to breastfeed an infant, a mother should consider the advantages and disadvantages and her motives for wanting to do so.

Adoptive mothers generally want to breastfeed to minimize the emotional and health disadvantages of their babies' separation from their birth mothers. Today's child care manuals emphasize the nutritional, cognitive and immunological benefits of breast milk. They also say that nursing is the best way to form an attachment to a baby (some incorrectly imply that it's the only way).

More recently, the American Academy of Pediatrics has issued new guidelines encouraging mothers to breastfeed for at least one full year. Given this advice, some adoptive mothers may feel they are second-rate mothers if they feed their babies the "second-best" choice of food—formula—and may be anxious to speed up the attachment process to reassure themselves.

Adoptive mothers should not feel guilty if they do not want to breastfeed their babies. It is possible, but it's complicated. At the same time, those who do want to breastfeed should be encouraged in their choice. If the adoptive mother is going to attend the birth or be at the hospital at the time of the birth, she may want to discuss with the birth mother who will feed the baby. The birth mother may have plans to breastfeed as a way of being close to the baby for the short time she plans to be with him. Because breastfeeding promotes attachment, either the birth mother or the adoptive mother can feel threatened if the other is breastfeeding. However, there may be situations in which the birth mother would welcome the adoptive mother's plan to breastfeed as an indication of how loved the baby will be. As always in an open adoption, communication on points of potential conflict is essential.

Nutritional Benefits

Adoptive mothers who breastfeed usually provide 25 to 75 percent of their infants' nutritional needs. The average is about 50 percent. In one study, Kathleen Auerbach and Jimmie Lynne Avery found that most adoptive mothers had to use supplements for the entire time the infants nursed, and more than a third needed to feed at least two bottles of formula a day.

The milk of women who have stimulated milk production without a pregnancy lacks colostrum—a protein and antibody-rich substance found in the first milk of biological mothers. The first milk of adoptive mothers is comparable to the milk produced by biological mothers after about ten days; it has a lower level of protein and a higher concentration of water than colostrum.

Babies will compensate for the lower concentration of protein by drinking more milk. However, some infants, especially premature babies, will not be able to tolerate the additional quantities of milk they have to drink to obtain enough protein. They may spit up or vomit after feeding. Feeding the baby formula may be preferable in such cases.

Emotional Benefits

The foster mother of Pam's two-month-old baby neglected to tell her that she had been breastfeeding the infant. Pam struggled with the distraught baby who guzzled bottles of formula but remained dissatisfied. The baby was well nourished, but clearly missed the emotional benefits of nursing. It took nearly a year for the baby to adjust to that emotional loss and develop a strong attachment with her new mother.

Most adoptive mothers who want to breastfeed are trying to enhance the mother-child relationship. I remember holding my daughter one day and thinking that if I were breastfeeding her, I would be able to hold her even closer.

The closeness that develops during breastfeeding is realized regardless of the amount of milk produced. Of course, if the infant is getting so little milk that she is frustrated or if mother feels she is a failure because she isn't producing vast quantities of milk, breastfeeding is unlikely to be a positive experience.

Adoptive mothers should breastfeed if they want to, but not because they think they will be depriving their child of first-class care if they don't. Formula still provides infants with a highly nutritious diet. And breastfeeding is only one of many ways to form an attachment with a child. What is more important to the development of a close relationship with a baby is not whether the infant is breastfed or bottle fed, but whether the mother is comfortable with her choice. The mother-child relationship is unlikely to be enhanced if the baby is being breastfed out of a sense of duty rather than desire.

How to Breastfeed an Adopted Infant

A mother who decides to breastfeed her adopted infant will not need injections of hormones or other drugs. She will need to prepare for the demands of a breastfeeding infant through proper diet, exercise, and rest. Pregnant women are constantly reminded to eat right and get enough exercise, and people understand when they say they need a nap. It may be difficult for the expecting adoptive mother to treat her body as though she was pregnant or get the support she needs to do so. But this is necessary to meet the physical demands of nursing.

Milk is produced in a woman by the baby's sucking at the breast. Lactation is not immediate; it takes time for the stimulated breasts to produce milk. A baby is unlikely to keep sucking at a breast when hungry if he is not receiving any milk. An adoptive mother can either manually stimulate her breasts prior to the arrival of the baby, so milk already is being produced when the baby begins to suckle, or she can use a nursing trainer that provides the baby with milk from an external source while he sucks at the breast.

Breasts can be manually stimulated either by expressing milk from them by hand or by using a breast pump a few times each day. Two to six weeks of frequent stimulation is necessary to produce milk. This method is impractical in most adoptive situations, though. Adoptive mothers do not always know exactly when their infants are due to arrive, and because delays in even an expected arrival are not uncommon, this method is not recommended. A woman may be willing to rearrange her life to accommodate the nursing schedule of a demanding infant once the baby is in her arms, but she will probably find that sitting down with a breast pump several times a day in anticipation of the baby's arrival only increases the anxiety that adoptive parents feel during the waiting period.

The Lact-Aid Nursing Trainer System and the Supplemental Nutritional System are devices developed for women who want to breast feed adopted infants. A presterilized bag that can contain up to four ounces of milk is attached to a nine-inch flexible tube about the width of a strand of spaghetti. The mother attaches the bag to her bra or hangs it around her neck and positions the tube next to her nipple. As the baby suckles at the breast, he receives milk from the bag, so he keeps suckling, which eventually causes the mother to produce milk. The disadvantage of a nursing trainer is that it makes the uncomplicated act of breastfeeding decidedly more difficult.

Elizabeth Hormann, an authority on breastfeeding adopted infants, says that adoptive mothers should use nursing first to pacify infants, rather than to feed them. Assuming the baby is on a four-hour feeding schedule, Hormann says to give him formula first, then the breast. Two hours later, just offer him the breast. In another two hours, use formula again followed by the breast. It is a good idea to nurse the baby to sleep because he will be less resistant when he is tired.

Adoptive mothers should not feel personally rejected if their babies refuse the breast at first or even after several valiant attempts. Biological mothers often have difficulty getting their babies to suck properly. Infants are conservative creatures who resist change, and those who have been bottle-fed may not want to work as hard as they have to for breast milk. The younger the baby is, the easier it will be for him to make the transition. An infant older than eight weeks is as likely to reject as accept the breast. La Leche League members can provide emotional support and technical advice to adoptive mothers who want to breastfeed.

It is important for an infertile woman who wanted a pregnancy but was unable to achieve it not to attach too much importance to her success at nursing. She shouldn't feel like a failure as a mother if her baby refuses the breast or she does not produce large quantities of milk. The goal is a healthy, well-nourished infant, secure in the love of his new parents, not milk production.

Attachment to An Older Child

The older the child being adopted, the more intensified are the parents' concerns about forming an attachment with him. As children grow, their personalities, habits, likes, and dislikes become more established. Parents understandably worry about whether they will even like the child, much less love him. One mother said, "What worried me more than anything else about adoption was that I might get a child and just not like him. So I felt I had to get a kind of 'bonding' feeling with a picture of a waiting child. I needed some kind of immediate attraction to the child that would make me stop turning the pages of the adoption exchange book and think, 'Oh, I've got to check on that child.'"

An additional concern about the adoption of a child who was not placed at birth is the child's possible history of abuse or neglect that could make him wary of physical contact and new attachments.

The process of attachment between a parent and an older child is similar to infant attachment, but with a few twists. The infant first learns to depend on a particular adult to meet his physical needs. Then he learns that he can make this adult smile or stop what she's doing to play with him. At that point, the attachment becomes reciprocal. A baby toddles over to his mom, who is reading a newspaper, holds out his arms, and says, "Up, up, up." Mom somewhat reluctantly puts down the newspaper, lifts the baby up, and is rewarded with a hug or a smile, making the interruption worthwhile.

This is significant because parents often expect an older child to be at a later stage in the attachment process when he arrives. They don't expect that they will have to prove to him that there will always be a meal on the table at the appropriate time. They expect him to have more patience in his demands than a two year old who stands next to mom screaming, "Up, up, up," until she finally puts the newspaper down. They expect that the same kinds of activities that would reinforce the attachment between a parent and a biological seven year old can be used to develop an attachment with the seven year old adoptee, who is joining the family.

Initially, that seems to be the case. Older children typically go through a "honeymoon" period immediately after placement. Their behavior is appropriate, they seem to be accepting of their adoptive parents and siblings, and they may be responsive and responsible.

When attachment begins to develop, the honeymoon period is replaced by what is sometimes called the "testing" period. During this time, the child begins to behave in ways that threaten the developing relationship.

Attachment Ambivalence

The older child at the testing stage of attachment has some ambivalence about the close feelings he is experiencing. All his past relationships with adults have ended in separation; he may be worried that this one will, too, and try to end it before he gets too close. At the same time, he is drawn to the parents. Sometimes this period is explained as a time when the child tests the parents to see if he's accepted as a family member only if he behaves well, or if he can be "bad," too. He wants to be a family member, but wants to find out how far he can go in his behavior.

The child may try to put distance between himself and the parents by, for example, using abusive language, lying, fighting, refusing to make eye contact, or acting too grown-up for his age. The same child also may cling, whine, have difficulty eating and sleeping, and regress in toilet habits. For the parents, this behavior is as frustrating as lying and fighting. But while lying and abusive language are ways to push the parents away, clinging and whining are designed to draw them closer.

For example, a mother may think she has a serious problem if she discovers her child taking small items that the child couldn't even use, such as an earring, to school. The child isn't stealing; he is trying to take a part of his mother with him to school. His actions are not much different from the toddler who has to take her favorite blanket with her to the day care center.

Psychologist Terrence Koller says that the older child often acts like a young child in the early stages of attachment. Whining, clinging, and baby-like behavior are acceptable ways for an infant to draw the mother closer. They have the opposite effect for a seven year old, especially when combined with "disengaging" behavior like refusal to make eye contact.

We need to remember that a school-age adoptee can regress physically, emotionally, and morally. We don't expect a toddler to keep his pants dry, go to bed without a fuss, or know that it is wrong to take objects from his mother's dresser drawer. We expect a seven year old to know these things. But the recently placed seven year old may behave like the toddler because that's where he is in relation to the family—he's not an infant in age, but he is an infant in the family.

It helps to learn to distinguish between behavior that is clearly designed to push parents away and behavior that attempts to bring them closer and to respond as though the child was much younger, by allowing the seven year old to suck his thumb or ask for a drink of water three times a night, for example.

The difference between "come close" and "go away" behavior is not always easy to see, especially when the child is doing both at once. A parent needs to look hard for the signals that the child wants to be close and may have to find creative ways to meet the child's needs, especially for physical contact. The twelve year old who seems to be defiantly resisting instructions to go to bed may want to be rocked to sleep as an infant would. He may allow his parent to do so. However, he also may resist being treated "like a baby." Another way of giving him the comfort and physical contact he needs at that time may have to be found.

Attachment Following Arousal

In her book, *A Child's Journey through Placement*, pediatrician Vera Fahlberg suggests that children are most open to attachment after a period of high arousal. She believes children go through cycles of high arousal that are brought on by some physical or psychological need. Once that need is satisfied, a period of relaxation follows. During that time, the child is open to attachment. The calm period following a child's temper tantrum is one time when the child may be open to attachment, but parents may be inclined to want to leave him alone while they rid themselves of their own anger. Ironically, that may be a good time for a hug.

Seeing a child through an illness or injury also can enhance closeness. The child's defenses are down, and he learns he can count on someone in times of stress.

Fahlberg points out that the move to an adoptive family is itself a time of stress. Helping the child express his feelings about the move and about his birth family and foster family can lead to a period of relaxation in which the child is open to attachment.

Indeed, if the child does not adequately grieve for the relationships he has lost, he will have difficulty forming new attachments.

Fahlberg says that another way to enhance attachment with a child who is older at the time of placement is to share positive interactions—just as sharing smiles and playing pat-a-cake enhance attachment with an infant. Sometimes the older child will also want to play baby games. He may be regressing because he intuitively knows that these kinds of games are how parents and babies build interactions that lead to attachments. Even though infantile behavior in an older child can be unpleasant, it may be a hopeful sign that the child is willing to allow attachment to grow.

Finally, Fahlberg points out that claiming behaviors can be important signals to a child. By "practicing" what it is like to be a family, we actually help create those relationships. Having the child take the parents' last name, putting the child's picture with family photos, and having an entrustment ceremony are ways parents can communicate to the child that they are welcoming him into the family. Sharing family stories, informing the child of family rituals and including him in them, and helping him understand family rules are ways of communicating that he belongs.

This testing stage is difficult. However, it may help to realize that much of the behavior that is making life chaotic is a sign that there is a future together as a family.

Attachment Disorders

The attachment of the parents and child does more than give the family a warm and fuzzy feeling; it creates order. Children who don't have a reciprocal, caring relationship with family members are unlikely to modify their behavior to please their parents and may not be motivated to keep from hurting them. Obviously, this can make life with these children chaotic and even dangerous.

Although children who were not securely attached to their parents were once described as unattached, it is now thought that attachment is a continuum, with securely attached children at one end, completely unattached children at the other, and the vast majority somewhere in between.

In a healthy, well-balanced relationship, says Fahlberg, a child seeks the caregiver to whom he is attached when he is in need, but feels secure enough to move away from the caregiver to explore his environment. A child who has not learned to trust that someone will always be there to meet his needs may respond by being anxious about moving away from the parent into the environment for fear the parent won't be there when he needs her again. Another child may respond just the opposite—not looking to the parent at all to meet his needs, but roaming the environment looking for other ways to get his needs met.

The child's early history of relationships is only one factor in his ability to develop attachments. Fahlberg points out that because attachment is dependent on the child's and the parent's capacity to receive, interpret, and send messages, factors such as temperament, prenatal drug exposure, and brain damage can be barriers to positive interactions between parents and children, inhibiting attachment. Even "mismatches" in temperament between parent and child can contribute to difficulty with attachment.

Parenting techniques that are based on making a child feel appropriately guilty for breaking rules or temporary withdrawal of parental love do not work with the child who doesn't care. Consequently, it is important for parents who suspect their child has an attachment disorder to get a thorough assessment. Parents should have their child evaluated by a professional who is knowledgeable about attachment disorders, but well grounded in neurological function, family and individual therapy, grief and loss issues, and psychodynamics. Although an increasing number of professionals identify themselves as specialists in attachment disorders or attachment therapy, parents should not jump to this diagnosis. Nor should parents expect a quick fix, although those who are completely frustrated by their child's unmanageable behavior may be vulnerable to anything that appears to be a simple, speedy "cure."

Although a child who has not formed a secure attachment in the first six months, or even the first three years of life, is at risk of attachment disorders, experts in the field caution that the situation is not hopeless. A number of treatments have been successfully used to facilitate attachment in children with attachment disorders. Parents should select a therapist who uses a variety of treatments, beginning with the least intrusive, and who actively involves the parents in the therapy. Even when treatments fail, parents may still be so committed to the child that they want to raise him regardless of his behavior. After all, just because the child may have difficulty forming attachments doesn't mean the parents don't care about him. Friends and relatives may not understand why parents are so committed to the child and may even recommend that the parents "disrupt" the adoption, or return the child to the agency. Parents and their caseworker should discuss this option before taking any action. For parents who remain committed, there are parenting techniques that can be successful with a child with attachment disorders. A group for parents who have adopted older children can provide emotional support from those who have had similar experiences, as well as referrals to professionals and even respite care when times are particularly difficult.

The Lifelong Process of Becoming a Family

We don't need to be in a hurry to form an attachment; we should enjoy the process, have fun with the child, and build up a reservoir of pleasant experiences to draw on when there is friction in the family. We must try to identify and meet the child's needs without hovering over him. Especially with an older child who demonstrates his growing closeness in seemingly negative ways, parents have to learn to recognize signs of attachment and gather strength from them.

Part II

At Home
with Adoption

4

Talking About Adoption

At one time, parents hid the fact of their child's adoption from not only the child, but from friends and family as well. There are even reports of prospective adoptive mothers wearing padded maternity clothes before their adoptive babies arrived. Today, however, adoptive parents seldom question whether they will tell their children they were adopted. We are living in an age of greater candor, and while this has led to extremes, such as people revealing remarkably personal information on afternoon talk shows, it has also provided a supportive atmosphere not only for telling a child she was adopted, but for providing her with details about her origins. Rather than wonder *if* they should tell their child she was adopted, most adoptive parents have questions about *when* to start talking about the subject and *how* to provide information to their children about their origins.

Adoptive parents are also more forthcoming with information about their families to other people. Indeed, being open about adoption with other people is said to be a sign that the adoptive parents have a healthy attitude. Sometimes, though, parents feel uncomfortable talking to people outside their immediate family about their child, the circumstances of her adoption, or her birth parents. The questions that people ask may feel intrusive, yet parents worry that if they are evasive, it may seem to be implying that there is something about the child that they want to hide—especially to the child who may be overhearing the conversation.

Revealing Adoption Information to Others

Although our families are formed in a way that sometimes seems public, with coworkers knowing details about our infertility, potential birth parents perusing our files, and social workers and judges evaluating our worthiness to be parents, we do not have to feel as if we're on display, even when our children are so physically dissimilar from us as to evoke questions. Indeed, we owe it to our children to draw a line between healthy openness and legitimate privacy. When we do, we are not only protecting them from unwarranted intrusions into their personal lives, but teaching them how to make decisions about when and to whom they can reveal personal information.

There is a difference between legitimate privacy and the kinds of secrets that have been so harmful in adoption. Secrets keep information concealed from people who have a relevant need to know it. They create power differences, with those "in the know" having important information and people who need that information shut out. They isolate people and inhibit communication about important events. Furthermore, they lead to feelings of shame. Secrets are held when someone believes that the possibility of the wrong people learning the information is so harmful that even people who ought to have the information can't be trusted with it.

With privacy, we make case-by-case decisions about whether information should be shared. If the information is relevant to a particular person, it is shared; if it is not relevant, it isn't. If the information is potentially harmful, we assess whether the possible harm of the person not knowing the information outweighs the harm that may come from revealing it. We are also influenced in revealing personal information by the level of intimacy we have with the other person; if we know we can trust someone with information that may leave us vulnerable, we are more likely to share it with him or her.

Most of us feel comfortable telling other people that our child was adopted. However, when we're asked *which* of our children was adopted or whether our children are *really* brother and sister, we may bristle. Suddenly, we are aware that this information may make a difference to the person asking the question. Some people do have odd notions about adoption; they expect adoptees to be less intelligent, more troublesome, or otherwise less "satisfactory." Nearly every adoptive parent has had someone express condolences that they "had to" adopt or otherwise indicate the view that adoption is really second-best. We therefore become a bit wary of even revealing the most basic information about our families. At the same time, we worry that our desire to maintain privacy may be misinterpreted as confirmation that we really are not completely comfortable with adoption.

Not everyone needs to know that our children were adopted, but it is important that professionals, such as physicians, psychologists, and even teachers, are informed so that they can provide our children with necessary services. And close friends and family members deserve to have us trust them enough to reveal this information. Seldom, however, do strangers or casual acquaintances need to know why a parent and child look dissimilar, why the family appears to have two children less than nine months apart, or *which* child was adopted. A polite, but evasive answer can be given—as long as it is not going to be confusing to the child. For example, if someone asks a Caucasian woman with an African American child, "Is her father black?" she should reply that he is not, *if the father that the child thinks of as her father is not black*. But to the person who asks where your daughter got her red hair, it is sufficient to reply, "Isn't it beautiful."

Naturally, there may be times when we choose to reveal that our child was adopted, but we should do so knowing that the news may not be greeted with complete support or respect. More intrusive questions may follow, and unsolicited opinions or advice may be given. Although we may think we have opened the door by being candid, *we can close the door at any time.* "Well, you'll have to ask her that when she's older," or simply excusing yourself politely can be acceptable ways to communicate that the conversation has moved into an area that is none of the person's business. Some people find it useful to inquire politely, "Why do you ask?" That way, if the person does have a relevant interest, you have not closed the door. If the person does not, you have politely asked him to look at his own motives.

There are some details of our child's life, including the circumstances surrounding her conception or relinquishment and details about the birth parents, that are so personal that they should not be revealed to anyone but the adoptee. For example, if the birth mother became pregnant as a result of rape, if the child was sexually abused, or if the birth father was a criminal, these facts should be considered the child's private information, not to be shared without her permission. Information like this should not be given even to extended family members. Once information is shared with one person, it may be shared with others, and some relative may inadvertently reveal it to the child before the parents thought her ready to know it. Furthermore, there may be a serious breach of trust if the child learns her parents were sharing such private information with others. Rather than provide the child's history, parents can tell people, "We have as much information as we need, but we want to share it first with Michelle when she's old enough and let her decide whom she wants to tell." Even when the child has ongoing problems related to past treatment, the parents can simply say, "Michelle doesn't like to be touched," without explaining the conditions in the orphanage that led to her sensory deprivation.

Talking to Professionals

When details of the child's history need to be shared with a professional, parents must be clear that they intend that information to be held in confidence. They should also tell the professional whether the child knows the information or is aware that the parent is providing it to the physician, psychologist, or teacher.

There is some controversy among adoptive families about whether teachers should be given any details about the child's background, including the fact that she was adopted. Parents are concerned that if the teacher and school administrators know a child was adopted, they will expect less of the child academically. They also fear that any behavioral problems will be blamed on adoption. They don't want their child treated differently because she has been labeled "adopted." Yet they expect the teacher to be sensitive enough to adoption issues that she will not assign a "family tree" project or ask the students to trace the origins of the color of their eyes.

I felt the same way when we enrolled our two-year-old son in a day care center and a question on the application asked if he was adopted. After the initial shock, however, I realized that a child's adoptive status is part of his social history and that schools need to know the social histories of their students. At the same time, parents should not expect that teachers or administrators are informed enough about adoption to know when it may be an issue for a child. So, at the same time that we inform the teacher of our child's adoptive status, we should also take a few moments to ask if the teacher has any classroom assignments coming up that deal with families or genetics. We should discuss with the teacher how he plans to handle those assignments in such a way that our child is able to complete them without being singled out as an "exception." In many cases, when children are given enough flexibility, they can come up with their own creative and insightful ways of completing an assignment so they satisfy the teacher while maintaining a sense of privacy and control.

Talking to Other Children

Just as parents use the pregnancy of a friend or relative to explain conception and birth to children, they often use a friend or relative's adoption plans as a way to instruct their children. Curious children in the extended family or neighborhood may ask adoptive parents questions, including some that seem intrusive. Some people have an even harder time evading a child's question about adoption than they do an adult's. They want to inform. They want to help the child develop a positive attitude toward adoption. However, the same rules of privacy should prevail. Children, like adults, can be told that the information they are asking for is "Heather's story" and that they'll have to ask Heather to tell them when she is old enough.

Sometimes children ask questions about adoption because they are trying to figure it out. However, sometimes they ask questions because they get a lot of attention when they do. If a child's questions are becoming a nuisance, check whether she is gaining something besides knowledge by asking them.

One prudent couple wrote a letter to their relatives and neighbors prior to the arrival of their child in which they gave information that they felt comfortable sharing and a polite explanation for why they would not be sharing more. They gave some specific suggestions for communicating information about adoption to other children, such as using "birth mother" and "birth father" instead of "real mother" or "natural father" and not expecting a child who could not yet understand reproduction to be able to understand adoption. As a result, they had few complaints about how their friends and relatives dealt with their adoption.

Dealing with Insensitive Comments

When we are confronted with a rude or insensitive remark, most of us ignore the insult, but spend days thinking up responses we *could have* used. Generally, these responses would have hurt the other person as much as we were hurt by the original remark or question, and our intent in fantasizing about how we might have responded is a way of dreaming about "revenge." In most cases, other people do not intend to hurt us. When they do, we can let them know that we were hurt by saying something like, "I'm sure you didn't mean to imply that had we known I'd get pregnant, we never would have adopted. We love little Peggy so much; we just wouldn't trade her for anything."

Even when we choose to ignore the remark, we only extend the hurt by repeating the insult in our minds as we try to come up with an "appropriate" response or by repeating the offensive comment to people who will share our outrage. It can be more helpful to remember the times when we too may have inadvertently offended people with a thoughtless remark. Psychologists say that by reminding ourselves of our own imperfections, we can accept others' imperfections more readily, and by forgiving them, we can heal.

Talking with Adopted Children

Years ago, adoptees were often kept in the dark about their adoption indefinitely or were not told until they had discovered the fact themselves. Later, parents were told to tell their children sooner that they were adopted, but not to tell them much beyond what they asked. The child who asked no questions about her adoption was thought to be well adjusted, while the inquiring child was thought to have problems. Today we know that many adoptees are reluctant to initiate a discussion of adoption with their adoptive parents. Many keep their questions to themselves, which can lead to fantasizing and even magical thinking—a belief that thinking about something can make it happen. We know now that discussions of adoption should be open and ongoing and should even be initiated by parents in some circumstances.

Parents sometimes wonder when they should tell their child she is adopted. That sounds as though talking about adoption is a one-time event with the parent doing the talking and the child doing the listening. It is more appropriate to question when to "start talking with" a child about her adoption—when to begin a dialogue about being adopted that will continue throughout the adoptee's life.

Adoptee Betty Jean Lifton writes in *Lost and Found* about adoptive parents who try to find the "right" age to tell a child about her adoption, as though picking the proper moment will eliminate the doubts, fears, questions, and fantasies adoptees grow up with. Instead of worrying about the proper time to start talking about adoption, parents should be concerned about setting the right tone. Then when the doubts, fears, questions, and fantasies arise, the child will feel free to discuss them with her parents. No one can say when the timing will be right with one particular child; no one can give parents the correct words to say. But we need to feel at ease with adoption so we will be prepared not only to answer questions, but to anticipate them and communicate our willingness to discuss our children's concerns. Before talking with our children about adoption, we should make sure we're ready to talk about such issues as infertility and why birth parents place children for adoption. To prepare ourselves, we can read about the experiences of adoptees and talk to our spouses and other adoptive parents. Unless we feel comfortable talking about adoption, our adopted children may be reluctant to talk with us again about adoption issues or, worse, may conclude that the reason there is tension during such discussions is because adoption is something bad.

Starting to Talk about Adoption

Each of Kristy and Dan's children has a book that was made for them before they arrived. The book tells the story of why the child was wanted, why the child needed a family, the process Dan and Kristy went through to adopt the child, and their first meeting. The pictures are simple but recognizable as their house, their family, and their dog. The text is brief enough for a preschooler; the pages—

plastic-covered cardboard designed for holding photographs—are durable enough for toddlers. Kristy and Dan began reading the stories of how their family was formed long before their children were able to understand what the stories meant. At first, the children just enjoyed seeing pictures of people and things they knew. Gradually, the stories took on meaning and led to more detailed discussions of their adoptions.

Kristy and Dan realized that the importance of sharing that story when their children were young was not to teach them about the adoption process, but to establish an atmosphere in the family in which adoption was discussed openly, honestly, and naturally.

An additional reason to start discussing adoption with a child early is that there is then no risk that the child will hear about her adoption first from someone other than her parents or in anything but a loving atmosphere. Furthermore, delaying the revelation of adoption for five to seven years almost inevitably will involve some deception that could work against the parent-child relationship.

This "early telling" theory is the prevailing philosophy on revealing adoption, but not everyone agrees with it. Some experts believe that the child should not learn she is adopted until she can understand what it means, usually at the age of five, six, or seven. A child can't fully understand adoption until she understands about conception and birth. She can't understand that she was the biological offspring of another man and woman until she understands how babies are conceived.

Advocates of "telling later" fear that to label children "adopted" before that time may cause them to think there is something wrong with them. Psychiatrist Herbert Wieder is among those who believe that early telling is disruptive to psychological development. He points up the need for clinical studies to determine whether early or late telling is less traumatic for the child.

Parents of internationally adopted children or children who are racially different from them have little choice but to tell their children as soon as possible that they are adopted. Although young children don't comprehend enough about genetics to realize that children usually resemble their parents, other people will comment on the physical difference and ask if the child is adopted in the child's presence.

Even if my children were not Asian, I would subscribe to the early-telling theory. I think it is risky for parents to pretend that their child is not adopted. We can't acknowledge and build on the unique aspects of our families while we are pretending that there is no difference between our family and a biological family. Furthermore, it is essential for adoptive parents to develop an attitude of openness with their children on the subject of adoption. If children are sent out of the room so their mother can talk to the physician privately or hear their grandmother being hushed when she starts to mention something about them, they can imagine something terrible is wrong with them. Most important, if children feel they were deceived about being adopted, it can affect the level of trust they have with their adoptive parents on that subject.

When I've met people who delayed telling their children they were adopted, they usually tell me that the longer they waited, the more difficult it became to reveal the truth. Adoptive parents who are reluctant to tell their child that she was adopted should spend some time exploring what is behind their reluctance. Are they worried that the child won't love them if she knows she has other parents? Are they aware of disturbing information in the child's background and do not want to begin a process that will lead to revealing it? One mother, who had delayed talking about adoption with her daughter for five years, realized that she was afraid she would start to cry when she told her the story. When she was told that it was OK to cry—that doing so showed the daughter that adoption involved a lot of feelings—she felt like a burden had been lifted.

The fact remains, however, that these are just theories without clinical data to back them up. Experts can suggest what they think is the best time to start talking about adoption, but ultimately the choice rests with the parents. The best that parents can do is be informed about the advantages and disadvantages of each approach and consider them along with the personality and reactions of each child.

Adoption Concepts

Regardless of when parents start to talk with their children about adoption, there are certain concepts that need to be communicated. Naturally, the younger the child, the more simply these attitudes and ideas will need to be conveyed. More details can be provided as the child matures. It is helpful, of course, if the child asks questions indicating what she wants to know. But adoptees sometimes are reluctant to bring up the subject of adoption because to do so may feel disloyal or because they have somewhere received a message that the subject is off-limits. Parents can initiate discussions or seize opportunities to comment on something related to adoption. At the same time, they can go too far in talking about adoption. Excessive discussion of adoption can indicate that the parents have not resolved their infertility or are not yet comfortable with the topic. It tells the child: "We're constantly aware of your being adopted." It tells her she's different. For example, a man whose home I was visiting introduced his five children by their first names. With the last he said, "And this is David. He's adopted." There is a fine line between talking about adoption enough that the child knows this is an acceptable topic for conversation and talking about it so much that the child starts to think there's something wrong with being adopted. The key is to talk about adoption when it seems natural and relevant to do so.

When talking with their children about being adopted, adoptive parents should start at the beginning—the child's beginning. That means talking about the child's birth and places that she lived before being adopted. The child's life did not start with her adoption, although she may have no conscious memory of her life before her adoption, and her parents may have little information. The birth parents should be referred to as real people—by first names if that information is known—who exist somewhere, though they may not be part of the child's current life.

Parents should discuss the decision to place a child with empathy for the birth parents: they were people caught up in their circumstances, who engaged in behavior perhaps without forethought about the consequences. When faced with the reality of the pregnancy, they made a difficult decision that they thought was best for the baby. Adoptive parents used to be told to convey the selflessness of the decision by telling their children: "Your birth mother gave you up for adoption because she loved you so much." Therapist Claudia Jewett Jarratt points out that this is a confusing idea for a child who is told that her adoptive parents love her a lot, too. The child may worry that her adoptive parents will also love her "enough" to place her with another set of parents. As the child grows older, she may also have difficulty reconciling loving someone with placing someone for adoption. When she falls in love, she will want to be with that person, and she may have difficulty believing that anyone would willingly separate from someone they love. It is important to tell the adopted child that her birth parents probably loved her and that it was probably difficult for them to place her for adoption, but that they thought that was what would be best for her. Jarratt suggests that parents should add that the birth parents probably think about her often.

A child should be reassured that her birth parents placed her for adoption because they weren't able to act as parents of any baby, not because there was anything wrong with her. As the child approaches adolescence, parents can talk about what is involved in raising children, what makes it difficult, and what kinds of skills parents should have. Then they can discuss the realities or probabilities of why her birth parents could not cope with a child.

It is important that a child know that there are thousands of children who are adopted or who do not live with both biological parents. Children should know that they are not freaks because they were adopted or because their birth parents did not choose to raise them. They need to know there are many other children in similar circumstances.

The child should understand that even though she has birth parents, her adoptive parents are responsible for raising her and that this is a permanent arrangement. Parents shouldn't assume that the child knows her adoption is permanent—after all, she already has lost her birth parents. We need to tell our children in concrete terms that our plan is to be their mother or father even though we sometimes get mad or go away on a trip.

I am a naturally curious person, so I have no trouble understanding that adoptees are curious about their origins. But not every adoptive parent thinks such curiosity should be encouraged—and some people think there is something abnormal about an adoptee who wonders about her birth parents or circumstances of her life before she was adopted. Although researchers have not come up with a clear-cut answer to the question of why some adoptees are interested enough to search for their birth parents and others are not, most experts agree that being curious about one's origins is normal. Adoptive parents need to let their children know that it is OK for them to have questions about their past and to come to their parents with those questions.

When information is not known, parents should be honest about that, too. But they can suggest what they think is the case: "We don't know how old your birth mother was, but most women who place children for adoption are in their twenties. It's likely that your birth mother was very young."

Not every mention of adoption requires a formal setting in which the parent pulls the child onto her lap and talks in serious, low tones. Sometimes it is better to handle the subject casually, with what may appear to be an offhand remark. It is similar to the way parents help their children understand other important concepts, such as the danger of crossing the street without first looking for cars. Sometimes they have serious, formal discussions on the subject. But those talks are reinforced whenever an opportunity presents itself. When driving down the street, a mother may point out some children who are not playing safely and then resume the conversation she was carrying on in the car. If every mention of adoption turns into an intense analysis of feelings, children may avoid the subject.

What Children Understand About Adoption

Researchers at Rutgers University, including psychologist David Brodzinsky, found that children have similar levels of understanding about adoption at roughly the same age, whether or not they are in adoptive families. Children seem to develop a general understanding of what adoption is and how it works from their social environment, rather than by accumulating facts and pieces of information from their parents. Adopted children learn what it means to be adopted whether or not their adoptive parents tell them about it. The job of the adoptive parents, therefore, is not to explain the social concept of adoption so much as to provide information about the child's particular situation. Parents should also provide emotional support and reassurance for the child and create an environment in which the child's questions can be discussed.

The Rutgers researchers found that children's knowledge and understanding of adoption change in predictable ways with their development. As a child's understanding of family, reproduction and birth, social relationships, values, and legal and social institutions increases, so her understanding of adoption and adoption matters grows and changes. Children, then, need to have the adoption story repeated because they will focus on certain aspects of it at different developmental stages. At one age a child is concerned with how old her birth parents were; at another age she is more concerned with the legal process of adoption. Fortunately, we now have some understanding of what children especially need to know at certain stages of development.

The following sections give a brief idea of what children should know and can understand at different ages. For a more complete discussion, see *Making Sense of Adoption* by Lois Ruskai Melina and *Being Adopted* by David Brodzinsky, Marshall Schechter, and Robin Marantz Henig.

Preschoolers—A Little Information Goes a Long Way

Dawn was delighted that her four-year-old son Kevin could recite the story of his adoption. She was pleased that he seemed to accept his adoptive status and was proud of it. Then one day she heard him saying, ". . . and Jeremy's adopted, and Ben's adopted, and Adam's adopted, . . . " naming all his friends who were born into their families. Kevin accepted his adoptive status so well because he had no concept of it being unusual. Sure, he grew inside another woman before coming to live with mommy and daddy. That's how it's done.

While I do advocate the "early telling" theory, one problem of talking to preschoolers about adoption is that they often appear to understand more than they really do. The researchers at Rutgers found that preschoolers usually cannot differentiate between being adopted and being born into a family. The two concepts are fused in their minds. Preschoolers simply do not understand the concept of a "blood tie." To children that age, anyone who lives with them is part of the family. The reason they seem so willing to accept their adoptive status is because they don't understand it. When preschoolers tell the story of how they joined the family, they are usually just parroting what they've been told, not showing a real understanding of the circumstances of their lives.

Parents who talk with preschoolers about being adopted should think of their discussions as a foundation for later elaboration. The goal with a young child is to establish a comfortable atmosphere in which family stories are shared honestly and compassionately.

Talking to children about their adoption is considered stressful by many parents, and the preschool years offer an opportunity to practice. Three year olds are not going to ask any tough questions. And because children are not really gathering information during these years, parents can make mistakes that can be easily corrected later. When Kristy and Dan made their first "welcome home" book, one page read: "Then Kristy and Dan heard about a baby who didn't have a mother or a father." They read this to their daughter for a couple of years before they realized they were ignoring the existence of the birth parents and avoiding the issue of why she was placed for adoption. They changed the page to read: "Then Kristy and Dan heard about a baby whose mother and father couldn't take care of a baby." Their daughter didn't seem to notice the change in the story line, but in a few years she would have.

If parents are uncomfortable with any part of the story, this is a good time to examine why and to try to become more at ease with it. Perhaps there is some underlying grief that has not been resolved or a sense of competition with the birth parents. Parents should understand that if there are parts of the story that they are uneasy with, they are likely to convey their discomfort to the child, no matter what words they use. Consequently, it will not only help the parent, but also the child, for the parent to become more comfortable.

No matter how many times parents have gone over the adoption story with their preschooler or how well their preschool child can recite the story, the child probably does not have a real understanding of being adopted. The job of talking about adoption has not ended, nor are parents "safe" from uncomfortable questions about adoption just because discussions with preschoolers have seemingly gone so well. They cannot respond to the five year old who asks: "Did I grow inside you, mommy?" with a curt, "You know you didn't. Remember, you were adopted." The five year old who asks that question may be thinking about it for the first time, even though she seemed to understand the circumstances of her birth at the age of three or four.

Since preschoolers are not going to be picking up much actual knowledge, it is hard and perhaps unnecessary to suggest what they should be told. It is probably adequate to say: "Mommy and daddy wanted a baby very much, but couldn't make one that would grow inside mommy. Your birth mother and birth father couldn't take care of *any* baby born to them at that time in their lives, so they asked us to be your parents (or "so you came to live with us"). They were probably very sad that they couldn't raise a baby at that time, and mommy and daddy were sad that you couldn't grow inside mommy. You might be sad, too, sometimes. But your birth parents were also happy to know you would be taken care of, and we are happy to be your parents."

Ages Five to Seven—Awareness of Life and Death

Children in this age group are interested in life and death issues, such as "Where do puppies come from?" and "Where is heaven?" Around the age of six, the Rutgers researchers found, most children can differentiate between birth and adoption because they understand conception. Even parents who have talked about adoption before may have to start from the beginning of the story with children in this age group who are just beginning to realize what it means to be adopted.

Former social work educator Carol Williams says that children in this age group need to know that they were born just like every other person. So often adoptive parents talk about adoption by saying something like: "You know your friend Ben grew inside his mommy. But you didn't grow inside me. Mommy and daddy couldn't make a baby, so we called an adoption agency and they found a baby for us, and that was you." This story, while accurate, skips an important step—the birth of the child. It is not unusual for the adopted child to conclude that "adopted" means being hatched or born through some other nonnormal process. Karen, a thirty-eight-year-old adoptee, said that because her adoptive mother never talked about her birth, she never thought of herself "of woman born." As a result, she never thought of being naked ("as a newborn babe") as her natural state. She thinks this is why she was excessively modest and sexually reserved. Now that she's met her birth mother, she has a healthier attitude about her body.

When information about the child's birth is available, it should be shared with her. Knowing the actual circumstances of her birth can help a child understand that her birth was normal and had nothing to do with becoming available for adoption. Adoptees sometimes believe they were placed for adoption because they were "bad from birth."

There are other reasons for starting to talk with a child about adoption by talking about how she was born. Talking about the child's birth leads naturally into talking about why she was placed for adoption. And talking about the child's birth acknowledges that the child has a history that began before she joined the family and communicates that it is OK to think and talk about that time.

The birth father shouldn't be ignored in discussions about adoption. The mother of five-year-old Kelly explained to her daughter that being adopted meant that she had grown in the uterus of another mother. When Kelly asked her how babies were made, she responded accurately and matter-of-factly. It didn't occur to her to discuss those two topics simultaneously, but Kelly put them together. Eventually it became clear that Kelly thought her adoptive father had impregnated her biological mother. That was the only explanation Kelly could come up with, given the information she had. Like many adoptive parents, Kelly's mother and father had never mentioned her birth father.

Although the birth father is as essential to a child's existence as the birth mother, he is often left out of the story. It is impossible to talk about how a child came to be adopted without mentioning the birth mother—the birth mother got pregnant, the birth mother couldn't take care of a baby, the birth mother made a plan for the baby. However, we often ignore the birth father because we look at his role as merely sexual. In our uneasiness with that subject, we leave him out of the explanations. The result is that many adoptees fantasize, like Kelly, that their adoptive father is really their birth father.

A scenario for talking with a five- to seven year old might be: "A man puts his penis into a woman's vagina. Sperm from the penis joins with an egg from the woman and out of that a baby grows. It was sperm from your birth father and an egg from your birth mother that made you. You grew inside your birth mother. When it was time for you to be born, you came out through her vagina." Parents can add that this is usually a loving thing that happens between a man and a woman.

If the adoptive parents know the identity of the birth parents, have a photograph, or have a letter from the birth parents written at the time of the placement, these can be included as part of the adoption story. For example, the parents can add, "And that woman's name was Andrea" (or "The woman you grew inside and who gave birth to you is your Aunt Cassie" or "We have a photograph of you with your birth mother when you were born. Would you like to see it?"). Of course, because children are concrete thinkers, the adoptee who is told her birth mother's name is Andrea may think the Andrea who works at the video store or who attends the same church is her birth mother. Adoptive parents may have to clarify the issue with every Andrea the child meets.

If the circumstances of the child's birth are not known, the likely circumstances can be discussed ("You probably were born in a hospital . . . "), along with what probably or actually happened after birth and up until the time she was placed for adoption. Parents should not say anything to imply that the child was responsible for being placed for adoption, but that "for some reason," the birth parents couldn't take care of any baby. Parents might want to ask the child why she thinks parents might not be able to take care of a baby.

The Rutgers study found that four- to seven year olds who had an idea of why parents place children for adoption thought children were placed for three main reasons: because of some negative characteristic of the child, because of the parents' financial problems, or because of the lack of time to care for the baby. This is a good time to correct any misconceptions a child may have about why she was placed for adoption. The child who says she became available for adoption because her parents died could be told, "No, your birth parents are still living, but they were still in high school and didn't know how to be parents yet," or if the information is not known, the parents can say "We don't know if your birth parents are alive, but they probably are. They probably were very young and didn't know how to take care of a baby." The goal with children this age is for them to understand the process of adoption—how children join a family. Later, they will begin to question *why* it happened, whether it is permanent, and what it means to them and to other people.

Ages Eight to Eleven—Feelings of Separation and Loss

Children eight to nine years old are beginning to have a notion of "blood relations" and how they differ from other kinds of relationships. These children can now have a fuller understanding of birth and adoption. However, the Rutgers team found that most children cannot understand the legal system that makes their adoptive status permanent until about age eleven. This greater awareness of blood relations and adoption but lack of understanding about the legal system may cause the eight or nine year old to feel unsure of her place in the adoptive family. It isn't uncommon for children this age to think the biological parents could possibly reclaim them.

A common fear of all children at this age is that they may lose their parents. Adopted children have already experienced this loss. They want to know *why* it happened, in part so they can try to keep it from happening again. When providing information or explanations, parents should take care to speak in concrete terms. Something as simple as telling a child this age that if she continues to misbehave at the dinner table, she will have to leave, could be misinterpreted by the child as having to leave the *family*, rather than the *table*. However, parents should realize that children this age long to solve problems on their own, and are developing the skill to do so. We should give them opportunities to work out their questions about adoption on their own, while remaining sufficiently in contact with them that we can guide them should they go off track.

While children are trying to figure out why they were adopted when nearly every other child they know is living with at least one birth relative, they may feel their place in the family is insecure. Although it may be unusual for a child this age to be reluctant to spend the night at a friend's house or adamantly resist having mom go on a business trip, such insecurity is normal for a child who was adopted.

Because the realization that someone made a decision to relinquish them for adoption hits children at age eight or nine, they may have a normal grief response at this time. Their reaction may be mild or severe, although it probably won't be comparable to the way they would react to a death. Still, parents may not expect their child to grieve for her biological parents eight or nine years after she was separated from them and may not recognize that the child's sad feelings are a reaction to her growing awareness of adoption. The child is rapidly increasing her knowledge and understanding, but is unable to keep up emotionally with the new information and awareness. Parents should encourage their child to express her feelings and let her know that it is not only OK to feel sad, but perfectly normal. They should also let their child know they understand what she is feeling sad about and that it is OK to talk about her birth parents if she wants to. It also is important to tell the child that the feelings eventually will go away, and that's normal, too.

By age ten or eleven, children understand that somehow the legal system ensures the permanence of their adoption, although it still isn't as clear as it will be in a few years.

Children eight to eleven years old usually are concerned about how they measure up to their peers. They compare material possessions, rules, and activities. Carol Williams says a child at this age wants to know if being adopted makes her different from her friends. She needs to know she is not the only adopted person in the world and that even though she's adopted, she's like other children. Because of their increasing understanding of various relationships, eight to eleven year olds may want to know about the relationship between the birth parents, particularly whether or not they were married. They may want to know if being conceived out-of-wedlock makes them different from other children. If they don't already know, children at this age will be curious about where they were born.

In addition, the child's awareness of relationships will stimulate her to think about her relationship to her siblings—both those in her adoptive family and biological siblings who may have remained with the birth parents. Parents who know that a child has siblings that the birth mother or birth father is raising often wonder when they should share this information with their child. They are concerned that if the child knows the birth mother kept other children, she will feel doubly rejected. It's hard to predict how any individual child will react to this information. Parents should be aware, however, that at this age a child is sufficiently knowledgeable about relationships to arrive on her own at the possibility that she has siblings who are being raised by the birth mother. By bringing up the actual situation, parents at least open the door to letting the child explore what this means and how she feels about it. When discussing children the birth parents are raising, parents should emphasize the birth parents' situation *at the time each child was born or was relinquished for adoption.* Parents can help children think about times in their lives when they took on more responsibility than they could handle and how it affected them when they were faced with even *more* responsibility.

During the middle childhood years, children also try to understand what being adopted says about them. Does it mean they aren't loved as much? Does it mean the siblings born into the family are cherished more? Are they really part of their extended family? Do people think less of them because they were adopted? Just as adoptive parents encounter the attitudes of those outside the family that call into question their own experience as a family, so do adoptees. Rather than shield children from these attitudes, which can be found not only in unwelcome comments from acquaintances but in movies and magazine articles, parents can use other people's opinions about adoption as opportunities for the family to explore what really is a complex sociological issue: how relationships formed through the legal means of adoption compare to those formed through biology. Because the issues raised by adoption are complex and often paradoxical, we serve our children better when we help them explore the complexities, sometimes concluding that there is no easy answer or one that fits every circumstance, and that that's OK. It may be tempting to try to provide children with simple, reassuring answers, but they will be no more satisfied with them than we were when we were first coming to grips with the issues of adopting and experienced adoptive parents offered us platitudes. By acknowledging that adoption is a difficult subject to understand, by raising questions, and by pointing out inconsistencies ourselves, we help our children arrive at their own answers, which will be far more satisfying to them in the long run, even though it may be a frustrating process at times. For example, I remember some interesting, and often humorous, discussions we had at our dinner table about whether adoptive siblings could marry when they grew up. During one of these discussions when my children were young, my son concluded a marriage between siblings would result in too much discord, while my daughter was worried that any children of such a union would not have any aunts or uncles. While they were off the mark because of their ages, they were starting the difficult but important process of examining adoptive relationsips.

It is important to be honest when talking with children of all ages about their adoption. Children aged eight to eleven may ask difficult questions that parents may be tempted to avoid or answer evasively. Let the child take the lead. If she is asking a question, she probably is prepared to deal with the answer. In fact, she may be more able to deal with the answer than the parent.

Children Who Are Reluctant to Discuss Adoption

Sometimes it seems that children do not want to discuss adoption. Different children have various degrees of curiosity about their adoption or their birth families, but there may be explanations other than a lack of interest for why some children do not seem to want to talk about adoption.

Some children talk more than others about adoption because they are more verbal. Parents who are unsure whether their children are fully expressing their interest in their origins may want to look at how their children gather information or express themselves on other topics. Is this a child who talks through a problematic situation, or is she more likely to work through issues alone or express herself through art, music, or movement? A child who tends to be more intense about expressing her feelings may express more intensity about adoption than a child who is more easygoing.

Although all children have some interest in adoption, they may not be interested in adoption at all times. Parents whose children do not seem interested in discussing adoption may want to consider whether they have been approaching their children at times when their children do not want to talk about it. Children are more likely to express their thoughts on adoption if discussions take place at a time when they have questions or concerns or when the subject comes up naturally, perhaps as the result of a casual comment from a stranger, a television show featuring adoption, or something happening in the family. Thus parents need to be alert for natural, appropriate times to talk about adoption. While parents may be more comfortable talking about adoption in the privacy of their own home, sometimes the natural, appropriate place to discuss adoption is while walking through the shopping mall or driving in the car.

Parents can also overdo discussions of adoption, going into more detail than children need or can handle at that time. When they do, children may change the subject or walk away. It is one way a child says she is overwhelmed by the information and needs time to process it.

Parents sometimes report that their daughters are more interested in adoption than their sons. Although there is little empirical evidence on this question, search groups often say that female adoptees are more commonly involved in searching for birth relatives than are male adoptees. Although some may argue that women are simply more curious than men, the more likely explanation is that it is more acceptable for women to express their feelings and vulnerabilities. Both male and female adoptees may feel they were rejected by their birth mothers when they were placed for adoption, but the idea of being rejected by a woman has a different connotation for a male than for a female. As a result, boys may have a more difficult time admitting that they care about their birth mothers or expressing an interest in them.

The more parents can do to communicate to their sons that it is all right for them to express their feelings, to need nurturing, and to be powerless, the more able they may be to express their thoughts about adoption. However, it is important to realize that children receive powerful messages from sources other than their parents about how boys and girls "should" be.

Another reason that some children may not be talking about adoption is that they haven't put their thoughts into words. If asked, "Do you have any questions about adoption?" they are likely to answer that they don't—not because they don't, but because they haven't verbalized the questions even to themselves. Concrete questions, such as, "Have you ever wondered if your birth mother has any other children?" help children put their thoughts into words. Children may not immediately respond to such questions. They may need to think a while about the issues their parents have raised. In the meantime, they have learned that it's OK to have those thoughts and discuss them with their parents.

Sometimes children act as if they are uninterested in adoption or their birth parents to hide the hurt they feel. Just as a child might try to act like she doesn't care that she wasn't invited to a friend's party, a child who is feeling abandoned or rejected by her birth parents may try to act as though she doesn't care about them at all. Similarly, when information about the birth parents or contact with them is impossible, rather than express longing for what they can never have, some children may try to act as though the information or contact isn't important to them.

Some children may be reluctant to discuss adoption with their parents because they perceive the topic makes their parents uncomfortable. Some parents may have difficulty discussing adoption because they have unresolved issues that make it difficult to acknowledge they aren't their children's biological parents. When this is the case, parents may want to work through those issues by discussing them with each other, an adoptive parents' support group, or a therapist.

Parents may also be anxious because they are not sure how to talk about some aspects of adoption without children feeling hurt. We need to remember that children are sometimes going to feel sad, angry, and hurt about being adopted. Trying to discuss adoption in ways that leave children feeling only happy and positive about the experience is unrealistic and denies children the right to have and express their emotions. It's unlikely that children will want to discuss adoption with their parents if the message they receive is that they're always supposed to be happy and grateful they were adopted. They will be more likely to enter into conversations with their parents if they know they will be allowed to have and express whatever feelings they have about adoption.

Parents will probably find that their children's interest in adoption ebbs and peaks. During the early part of a new developmental stage, as changes in their mental ability allow children to view adoption differently than they have in the past, they may be more curious about their origins or more confused by their new awareness. As they become more comfortable with the answers they receive to their questions and their ability to understand new aspects of their adoption improves, their need to work through adoption issues may decline until they reach the next stage of development or they encounter another situation that causes them to reevaluate what they've learned about being adopted.

Explaining Parents' Motives for Adopting

Amy grew up with the "chosen-baby" story that was told to so many adoptees. In this story, the adoptive parents walked up and down the aisles of a hospital nursery or orphanage until they found the perfect baby for them. In Amy's case, her mother compared it to looking for the "perfect tomato" in the grocery store's vegetable case. Adopted children were told that other parents were "stuck with" the children they got, but that adoptive parents chose their children.

Adoptive parents are no longer encouraged to use the chosen baby story to explain their motives for adopting. In the first place, the story is no longer valid—if it ever was. Parents who adopted after the "boom" of available babies began to decline in the 1970s did not have bassinets full of babies to choose from. Many parents have waited years, perhaps circumventing the adoption system, to get their babies. Instead of choosing the "perfect" baby, prospective parents tell agencies that the sex of the child won't matter, perhaps that the race or ethnic background of the baby isn't an issue, and what disabilities they would accept.

In addition, that chosen baby explanation of how the child came into the family places an enormous burden on the adoptee. If she was chosen because she stood out from all the other babies, she has an impossible image to live up to. She was chosen because she was perfect. She could be unchosen if she reveals herself to be imperfect.

In his book *Shared Fate,* sociologist H. David Kirk encourages adoptive parents to become closer to their children by acknowledging that they were all in a painful situation: The parents wanted a child and couldn't conceive or carry one, the child could not be raised by her birth parents, and adoption was the best solution for all. In this view of the adoptive family, parents are not the rescuers of their children who have to feel eternally grateful.

Parents should, therefore, be honest about telling a child why they decided to adopt. When they think the child is ready, they can tell her that mommy and daddy couldn't make a baby (or that mommy and daddy's babies died before they were born), but that they wanted a child to love and take care of.

Like their understanding of adoption in general, children's concepts of why people adopt change with age. Four- to seven year olds who were studied by Rutgers researchers saw adoption in terms of the parents' needs: the needs to love a child, to choose a specific type of child, and to increase their families. Older children, aged eight to thirteen, were more likely to see infertility, concern for the child's welfare, and the joy of watching a child grow as reasons for adopting.

Adolescents—Exploring Who They Are

By the age of twelve or thirteen children understand that adoption involves the legal transfer of parental rights and responsibilities from the birth parents to the adoptive parents. They also have a better understanding of the reasons children are placed for adoption. New issues come to light, however, because of adolescents' newly acquired ability to think in abstract terms and their own developmental issues of identity and independence.

Every adolescent struggles to define herself as a unique individual and experiments with ways to assert independence while maintaining her ties to the family. For adoptees, the struggle to develop a sense of identity is complicated by their history of having been separated from their biological families and placed with families who were chosen, it may seem, arbitrarily for them. An individual's sense of who she is begins early. By adolescence, however, the development of abstract thinking enables individuals to consider not only what *is* but what *might have been*. Furthermore, as they begin to separate from their families and move out into the world without the protection and identity of their families, their sense of identity coalesces in important ways.

Teenagers develop a sense of identity by looking at the people with whom they are most similar—their parents and siblings—and evaluating how they are alike and different from them. An adopted adolescent has to complete this task twice: once in relation to her adoptive family (the environmental influences that have shaped her) and once in terms of her biological family (the genetic influences that have shaped her). Of course, this process is not necessarily conscious or even accomplished at a verbal level. Teenagers can make these comparisons without putting them into words. They may explore identity issues out of a sense of being uncomfortable with themselves. They may experience the need for more information about their own biological origins as a vague yearning or emptiness.

If the task of the preschooler is to understand *how* adoption happens and the task of the child in middle childhood is to explore *why* it happened and what it says about her that she was adopted, the task of the adolescent is to determine how adoption has shaped her in specific ways. What does it mean that she has had *these* adoptive parents? This upbringing? And in particular, what does it mean that she had *these* birth parents? The more information the teenager can have, even though it may be disturbing, the better able she will be to answer these questions.

For teenagers who were adopted transracially or internationally, the questions are the same but involve more layers. What does it mean to have been raised in this culture? What is their relationship to other people of the same racial or ethnic background? What beliefs, customs, or attitudes do they have that may be different from those of other people of their racial background? What experiences have they had that are influenced by their racial or ethnic heritage and not understood by their adoptive families?

Many of the other issues of adolescence, such as privacy and control, are also influenced in subtle ways by the teenagers' experiences as adoptees. Because this developmental stage can be so confusing and chaotic, it is natural for teenagers—and their parents—to long for a simple explanation or a "quick fix" that will illuminate or resolve the challenges. For some, *adoption* seems like the cause of all their problems, and some aspect of adoption, such as a reunion with birth parents, seems like the solution. For others, adoption may not even be an issue compared with other issues in their lives. The solution to the agonies of adolescence is seldom that simple. What teenagers need is to develop their critical thinking sufficiently to be able to work through whatever complexities they are facing, including the development of identity. We cannot give them the answers; it is time for them to find their own solutions. What is a family? Why do they have to listen to us when we didn't give birth to them? What is their relationship to their birth families? They must arrive at the answers to these questions on their own, just as we did when we chose to adopt. We can explore these and other questions with them if they will risk letting us know what they are thinking and if they believe their opinions are respected. In doing so, we can hope that the questions will seem more manageable and the answers less elusive. Sometimes teenagers do not want us to know what they are thinking, especially on topics so personal. When that seems to be the case, we can focus the discussion on other people. One adoptive mother tried talking to her son about an upcoming meeting with his birth parents, saying, "You might feel a little uncomfortable because. . . ." Her son cut her off. "Don't try to tell me how I'll feel," he said. "If you want to talk about the way other adoptees feel, that's fine, but don't think you know what I'm feeling." Grateful for this direction, the mother rephrased her thoughts, saying, "Some adoptees who meet their birth parents for the first time during adolescence feel uncomfortable because. . . ." This subtle difference made it possible for her son to be able to listen to what she had to say.

As the adolescent develops a sense of her unique identity, she gets the strength to move away from the family. Like the toddler exploring her boundaries, a strong sense of attachment will enable the teenager to become more independent while knowing there is a secure base to return to in times of crisis. Part of the dilemma that parents of adolescents struggle with is the facility with which teenagers jump from wanting to be independent to wanting to feel that security. What is different for adoptive families is that the teenagers' rapid progression to adulthood and the independence that accompanies it can raise old adoption issues for the teenagers and their parents. If I assert my independence, will my parents still be there when I need them? Is her independent streak a rejection of me as her mother? And most important, if we aren't connected biologically and became a family because this child needed parents, what will keep us a family when she no longer needs our daily nurturing? Adoptive parents who haven't considered these questions sometimes respond to the adoptee's quest for independence with resistance. That, of course, only makes the need to break free more critical and can lead to parent-teenager conflict. Adoptive parents can take reassurance from knowing that what has made them a family all along—the quality of the relationships they have built—will withstand separation. If the infant becomes attached to the parent because she learns she can depend on that adult to meet her needs, the adolescent or young adult remains attached—though perhaps far away physically—because her parents have continued to meet her needs, in this case, the need to move out into the world on her own.

Books and Other Resources

Many parents find that children's books help them discuss adoption issues. There are also several books specifically for adopted children that explain the adoption process and explore adoptees' feelings. Some that are directed at transracial and older child adoptions are described in *Selected References and Resources* at the back of this book. While books are often helpful, parents should use them as a point of departure for discussions, not as substitutes for talking with their child about her particular situation.

There are also several books that will help parents understand what adoptees want to know and what they can grasp about adoption at different developmental stages. These, too, are listed in *Selected References and Resources*.

Group sessions offered by some adoption agencies and therapists help children understand that their feelings about being adopted are natural and shared by other adoptees. Similar sessions for adults are effective in helping parents realize the questions and concerns their children may be having. Adoptive parent groups provide support for parents, but also provide an informal social setting in which adopted children can meet other adoptees.

Talking About the Unpleasant Past

Adoptive parents are encouraged to be honest, open, and complete when talking to their children about their pasts. It is often difficult to be so, and even more so when a child's mother was an alcoholic, the child was physically or sexually abused, or the child was moved from family to family while an attempt was made to find parents who were willing to adopt her. The past cannot be changed. As much as adoptive parents would like to have prevented those events from occurring, they cannot do so by pretending they didn't happen. Eventually, the full story of her past will need to be shared with the child if for no other reason than because it is that person's story and we each have a right to know our own story.

Naturally, children shouldn't be told unpleasant information until they are able to understand it without being confused and without feeling responsible. Sharing too much too soon can give the child a negative image of her birth parents and a negative self-image. For example, a child may wonder how a mother could neglect her child unless the child was somehow unworthy of being cared for. There is no magic age at which parents should share unpleasant information about the child's past; it depends on the child and the nature of the information. During the child's early years, parents should speak positively about the birth parents and their decision to place the child for adoption. But they should not say anything that may later be contradicted when the full story is revealed. Whatever information is shared with a child should be shared with the idea of building on that information later.

Children are perceptive, and at some point it will become clear to them that there are gaps in the information they have been given. When this happens, they often imagine something far worse than the actual circumstances. Therapist Claudia Jewett Jarratt says that the information parents are reluctant to share with their child is often the piece that makes the whole situation make sense to her. For example, she says that an adoptee who has been told that her birth mother placed her for adoption because she "couldn't take care of her" eventually will want to know why. She may assume it's because she was a difficult baby to take care of. Because of the stigma attached to mental illness, adoptive parents may be reluctant to tell the child that her birth mother was committed to a mental institution. Rather than being embarrassed by this information, the adoptee may be relieved. It makes sense to her that her birth mother couldn't take care of her if she was mentally ill.

Even though it can be difficult, parents are the best people to share unpleasant information with the child because they can be there to provide comfort and reassurance. Being honest doesn't mean being harsh. Even painful information can be softened. Parents can reassure the child that the events in her past didn't happen because she was bad and that she is not bad now because something bad happened to her.

As responsible adults, parents may be furious at the behavior of the child's birth parent or foster parent. But the adopted child is connected biologically, historically, psychologically, and spiritually to the people in her past. By attacking them, parents attack the child and jeopardize their relationship with her. Former social work educator Carol Williams and therapist Claudia Jewett Jarratt encourage adoptive parents to discuss the birth parents and foster parents empathically and to help children comprehend the adults' responsibility for their separation from their birth parents by incorporating the children's own experiences into their explanations. For example, a child can better understand how overwhelmed her birth mother felt by the responsibility of caring for a baby if she can remember a time when she was asked to do something that was too hard for her. This helps the child understand the situation without feeling responsible for it. Much of the material in the following sections is derived from Jarratt's book *Helping Children Cope with Separation and Loss.*

Abandonment

Like many children who were adopted from other countries, eleven-year-old Tiffany has little information about her background. Her adoptive parents were told that she was "abandoned" as an infant and that her biological mother and father were "unknown." Her adoptive parents have told Tiffany that they don't know who her birth parents are, but are unsure of what to tell her when she asks more specific questions that will lead to the information that she was found at a market and taken to an orphanage. They want to talk about the birth parents in a positive light and think that telling Tiffany that she was abandoned will sound like her birth parents deserted her with little concern for what would happen to her.

We have difficulty understanding abandonment because we misunderstand customary adoption practices in other countries. Some countries do not have established procedures for formal adoption. And not all societies have the tolerance for unmarried motherhood that has evolved in our country. Until 1976, when it became legally possible for Koreans to adopt nonrelatives, "abandonment" was the only way a child could be placed for adoption with a nonrelative. Even in Korea today, and in other countries, a child is sometimes abandoned so that an unmarried birth mother does not have to answer embarrassing questions. But this doesn't mean that she left the child without concern for her welfare. For example, one orphanage in the Philippines had a "revolving cradle" on which a child could be placed from the outside, then swung around to the inside of the orphanage where she would be taken care of without anyone questioning who the child was or why she was being taken to the orphanage. Sometimes a friend or relative of the birth mother takes the child to an orphanage or police station so that she can be placed for adoption, but to avoid questions, says she found the child abandoned. Some children have been placed in care supposedly temporarily, but the parents had no intention of returning. In some cases "abandonment" is a legal technicality—the child does not have any legal documents saying who her parents are; therefore, she cannot be placed for adoption any way other than by being declared "abandoned."

In recent years, an increasing number of international adoptions have been from China, and many of these children are girls who were abandoned. There is a common misunderstanding that the reason so many girls have been abandoned in China is because females are not highly valued. Faced with a government policy that only allows them to have one child per family, the Chinese abandon girls born to them in deference to the boy they might have later. Therefore, it is not surprising that parents who adopt these girls are concerned not only about how to put the birth parents' abandonment in a positive light, but how to keep these girls from viewing themselves as having been "discarded" because of their gender. Those who are familiar with Chinese politics and culture say the circumstances surrounding the abandonment of children are more complex.

Girls are highly valued in China, says Kay Johnson, an Asian studies scholar who adopted a girl from China. Traditionally, however, sons are permanent members of their families while daughters belong to their husbands' families after marriage. Sons are therefore needed to fulfill family obligations, such as caring for elderly parents in a country where there is no social security system. Families who can only have one child feel a necessity for that child to be a healthy son.

Furthermore, the one-child policy has been ignored and circumvented, particularly in rural areas. Some families openly have more than one child, while others "hide" the daughters through a system of family or informal adoption. Families could say they hadn't added to the population problem in China because they had adopted. In the late 1980s, this practice of "hiding" girls through "adoption" was recognized as a way to undermine family planning regulations. In response, the government loosened its one-child policy in one way, but enforced it more strictly in another. Families were allowed "one son or two children." In addition, the government made it more difficult for families to adopt.

Adoption has long been practiced in China, although girls were often adopted as a way for a family to obtain a servant or daughter-in-law cheaply. The Communist government opposed the adoption of girls for these reasons, so it encouraged adoptions only when the adopting parents were childless. In this way, they could ensure the adopted child would be treated as an equal member of the family. In the 1980s, when the government determined that informal adoptions were undermining family planning policies, it began requiring that couples be childless before adopting.

As a result of these policy changes, families who exceeded their allotted number of children faced severe penalties. Nor could these families take their child to an orphanage because doing so would be admitting that they had violated the government policy. People in China are even reluctant to take a child whom they find to authorities for fear they will be suspected of fabricating the story to cover up their own culpability.

Abandonment is a potent issue for all adoptees. Everyone wants to feel that she or he was irresistible, and even adoptees whose birth parents made deliberate adoption plans can feel abandoned. It isn't until they can think in abstract terms, and therefore see the situation from their birth parents' point of view, that adoptees will be able to understand what happened as something other than a personal rejection. Parents should probably wait to explain the circumstances of a child's abandonment until the child has some abstract thinking ability. Before that, they can construct a story that is consistent with the truth, but not necessarily complete. Parents can present the idea that sometimes people feel overwhelmed by responsibilities and difficult tasks. They can suggest that it was probably difficult for the birth parents to be separated from the child, but that they did so in a way that ensured she would be taken care of (later filling in the fact that the child was abandoned in a crowded place where she was sure to be found). They can discuss how scared birth parents might have been when they realized they had "broken the rules," whether those rules were getting pregnant as a teenager or violating China's one-child policy. At the same time, they can be aware of the need to build the child's self-esteem, so that when all the facts are known, she can draw on her self-esteem and see that she was a person worthy of being cared for. One mother learned that her daughter had been "abandoned" in a particular park near a statue. When she visited the park, she found the statue—of a family. She felt certain her daughter's birth parents wanted her to know that she was valued, even though they could not raise her. Another couple learned that their daughter's birth date had been sewn into the clothes she was wearing when she was found. They, too, hoped their daughter would see that as a sign that her birth parents intended her to be found and loved.

Death

There are more adoptees who have been told they became available for adoption because their parents died than there are actual orphans. Adult adoptees placed years ago have told me how amused they are when they get together and discover the rash of airplane and car accidents in which their birth parents supposedly died. Although it is not as common a practice today as it was in the past, adoptive parents have told their children they were orphaned because they wanted to spare the children the stigma of being born to unmarried parents and spare themselves questions about the birth parents. Too often, however, the story of "adoptee-as-survivor" leaves the adoptee feeling guilty over being alive when the rest of her family is dead.

Children sometimes do become available for adoption after the death of their birth mothers or both birth parents. When the child is told about it, she may feel guilty that she survived or even feel responsible for the death, especially if her birth mother's death was due to a complication in childbirth. Carol Williams suggests separating a discussion of the child's birth from a discussion of the parent's medical problems, so that the child doesn't feel responsible.

In recent years, an increasing number of children have become available for adoption because their birth mothers were dying of AIDS. Parents can explain that a child became available for adoption because her birth mother was too sick to take care of a child. Because children who are concrete thinkers may associate illness in a parent with being relinquished for adoption, parents should keep this in mind whenever they are sick. They can say in concrete terms, "Mommy is sick and has to stay in bed until her tummy feels better. This is not the way your birth mother was sick. Mommy will feel better soon and will be able to take care of you then. Until then, Daddy (or whoever will be caring for the child) will take care of you." If the birth mother contracted AIDS through irresponsible behavior, that will eventually have to be explained in a way that does not excuse the behavior, but is empathic to the individual.

Physical Abuse

A child is hit not because she is bad, but because the adult is out of control. If there is anything children have experience with, it is being out of control when they are angry. Parents can try to explain why someone would abuse a child by relating it to the child's own experience with anger: "When you are really frustrated and really angry, do you sometimes hit somebody or something, even though you know you shouldn't?" Most children have. Parents can explain that grown-ups are supposed to be able to control themselves when they are angry, but that some people haven't learned what to do with their feelings. They hit. And because they are bigger than the children, it hurts. They probably knew that they shouldn't hurt a child, but they lost control. This doesn't excuse the behavior, but can explain it in a way that places responsibility for the abuse on the adult, not on the child. An abused child often thinks that if only she had been better, she wouldn't have been hit and would still be with her birth parents. The child should be helped to understand that she was abused not because she was bad, but because the adult did not have the experience or skills to handle a child.

Sexual Abuse

Children who have been sexually abused also need to be assured that it was not their fault. A child usually can understand that adults need to be close to someone and don't like to be rejected. The parents may ask the child to talk about her own experiences of wanting to be close to someone and not wanting to be rejected. She can be told that the adult who touched her just wanted to feel close to her, but that while it is OK for two adults to get close by touching each other that way, it is not all right for a grown-up to touch a child that way. It's important to distinguish between the inappropriate sexual exploitation of children and the appropriate expression of sexual feelings between adults so that the child doesn't grow up thinking that sex is always bad. The child can be told that the grown-up knew what he was doing was wrong and probably gave some clues that showed he was aware of it, for example, having the child promise not to tell anyone and never touching her that way when anyone else was around.

The child whose sexual abuse is discovered because she told about it may have a particularly difficult time believing that she did the right thing by revealing it. While telling stopped the abuse, it also probably resulted in either her or the abusive parent's removal from the home—something she may view as a "punishment" for telling. The other parent may have reacted angrily and acted as though she didn't believe the child. These children need to know that the other grown-ups probably were angry because they couldn't make the abuse stop and that telling was the right thing because it helped the grown-ups deal with the problem.

No child enjoys being abused, but some receive secondary gains from it. A child may become the favored child or be rewarded with treats or special privileges for keeping silent and submitting. It can be particularly difficult for the child to sort out her feelings about the abuse when part of it frightened her and part of it seemed to be advantageous. The abused child needs therapy to sort out these ambivalent feelings and to deal with other results of being molested. But adoptive parents don't need to consult a therapist to answer an abused child's questions about why she couldn't continue to live where she had been living. They can answer these questions honestly, empathically, and without infusing a child with guilt.

Substance Abuse

Most children will not have experienced anything comparable to intoxication or addiction, so they cannot draw on their own experiences to understand a parent who was an alcoholic or drug addict. If they are old enough, though, they may remember what it was like to live with that parent. If they were removed from the home when they were young, they can be told what other people observed. They may remember that meals weren't always prepared or that they were sometimes late for school because their mother or father couldn't wake up in the morning. Or they can be told that other people noticed their parents were only taking care of their own needs and not their children's. The reason for this was that the parent was taking drugs or drinking too much and wasn't able to make the appropriate decisions or function as a responsible parent. A child may think, "If they loved me, they would have stopped what they were doing and taken care of me." Adoptive parents can say they don't know why the birth parents didn't stop what they were doing—even doctors don't know why—but that it had nothing to do with how much they loved the child. Even though alcoholism and addiction are considered diseases, children younger than adolescents cannot distinguish between diseases of the mind and those of the body. To tell them their birth parent was "sick" can encourage them to think that anytime somebody gets sick, the children need to go somewhere else to live.

Mental Illness

Just as they probably have not had feelings that parallel addiction, children usually have not had any experiences similar to being mentally ill. Again, they are best able to understand mentally ill parents if they are asked to remember behavior in the parents that they observed or that someone else saw. If the parent is schizophrenic, the child may be able to understand how people can be frightened of something that other people tell them is not fearful, such as the dark. She may have had the experience of not knowing if she was dreaming or awake or of thinking she heard someone talking when no one was around.

A child can be helped to understand that it was not easy for the parent to control herself. If it is true, the child should be told that the parent had these problems before the child was born. Children may hear their parents saying, "You're driving me crazy." They need to know that this is not what happened to their birth parents.

Difficult Behavior

Although parents try to explain why a child was moved from one family to another without placing the blame on her, sometimes children are moved because of their behavior. Some children set fires, run away, abuse members of the family, break the rules, and otherwise create chaos in a household. There's no way to ignore the fact that a child's behavior had consequences—a move to another home. But she can also be helped to understand that her behavior was the result of choices that she made and that she can make other choices in her new family. It can also be pointed out that her behavior made the adults she was living with scared and angry. As a result, she needed to be moved to a family where the adults were not as frightened of that kind of behavior. This tells the child that her behavior carries consequences and that she has a choice as to what kind of behavior she demonstrates. If she doesn't want to move again, she can avoid the behavior that precipitates it. But it also takes some of the blame off her by pointing out that some adults have an easier time than others living with children who behave as she did.

Mental or Physical Disability

Children should not be made to feel unlovable because they are in a wheelchair or have some other disability. Parents can engage them in a discussion of what is involved in taking care of someone with their condition and explain that their birth parents did not feel capable of doing it. The birth parent is not condemned for her lack of ability, nor is the child responsible for the birth parent's inadequacy. Parents can say: "Maybe your birth mother didn't have friends at church who would be willing to build ramps in the house" or "Perhaps your birth mother didn't know how she could take care of a blind child because she lives alone."

Incest, Rape, or Prostitution

When a child was conceived as a result of rape or incest, parents are frequently concerned about how to explain this fact to her. They are understandably concerned about how the child will feel about herself when she realizes her birth father's behavior was violent and criminal toward her birth mother. Furthermore, they are concerned that the child will feel that her placement was not so much due to the birth mother's inability to care for a child, but was an actual rejection of her because she reminded her of the violent act. Because these are such difficult issues, parents will want to wait until the child is old enough to deal with them emotionally as well as intellectually. At the same time, we should keep in mind that what is disturbing to us as parents may be a helpful insight to adoptees. Until the parents determine that the child is ready for the full story, they can give her information that is accurate, though incomplete.

The first issue the child will deal with is why she was relinquished for adoption. Parents can explain that at the time she was born, her birth mother was dealing with some traumatic events in her life. They can explain that she did not have any energy to deal with a child because she was using all her energy to take care of herself.

By adolescence, the child's need to have all the facts about herself will probably require that she be told the full truth. Then she will need to deal with the question of what it means to have had a birth father who was capable of such an act. While it does not make the acts any less objectionable, we know from talking to men convicted of rape or incest that they do not always see their acts as offensive. The man who commits incest may have had a misguided way of expressing affection for his child or sibling. The rapist—particularly one who perpetrated a "date rape"—may have invested in the all-too-pervasive cultural belief that women mean yes when they say no. Seldom, experts say, is the rapist a psychopath choosing unknown victims at random, although such acts certainly do occur. The birth fathers are really men who made the wrong choice, having grown up in a society that has tolerated violence toward women for too long.

However, before telling the child that her birth father raped her birth mother, the parents should check out the accuracy of that information. Most women, when faced with a crisis pregnancy, remain in their communities. They face some stigma in having become pregnant, and even more stigma if they plan to place the child for adoption. "They should have been more careful," people say, or "They should take responsibility for what they did." Some pregnant women find that by saying they were raped, they do not encounter this criticism. Furthermore, some birth mothers may think that by saying they were raped they can avoid involving the birth fathers in the adoption plans. Some adoption facilitators may accept this description of the birth father with little question because they, too, want to avoid involving a birth father who may object to the adoption. (When this happens, it is not only unfair to the birth father and the adoptee, it is unethical on the part of the adoption facilitator and can jeopardize the security of the adoption.)

Forgiveness

No matter how well adoptive parents explain the circumstances that led to their child's relinquishment and no matter how well the child understands the circumstances, she is bound at times to feel hurt—to feel rejected or abandoned. Adoptee Marcy Axness explained at an open adoption conference in Traverse City, Michigan, that intellectually she recognized that her birth parents made the right choice in relinquishing her. In her heart, however, she wanted to be so valued by them that they would have made any sacrifice. There is a healing that must take place in adoption that is both emotional and spiritual. Intellectual understanding of the circumstances is helpful, but ultimately the adoptee must forgive the birth parents in her heart for not being able to be there for her in the way she needed at the time. Some adoptees must forgive the birth parents for even more—for rape, abuse, or drug use that interfered with parenting. Adoptive parents, too, may have to forgive the birth parents, for nothing makes a parent more angry than someone who has hurt their child.

Although some people believe that forgiveness follows healing, experts in the field say the opposite is true. Forgiveness promotes healing. Forgiveness involves understanding that everyone is imperfect. It requires that we remind ourselves of the ways we have failed other people. Maybe we haven't abandoned a child in a Beijing marketplace, but we haven't been available when someone needed us. Maybe we haven't beaten a child, but we have let our anger at someone we love get out of control. By being empathic, we can accept the failings of the person who hurt us.

Life Books

One way to initiate discussions about the child's past is for her to make or read a life book—a chronological outline of where the child has lived, who the people were that she lived with, and why she moved on. While life books are most helpful to older children who have lived in many places and may be confused about the various people and houses in their pasts, they are also useful with children who were adopted as infants.

The life book reconstructs each important episode in the child's life, starting with her birth. The text is written by the child, with assistance from an adult to ensure accuracy. Photographs, when available, or pictures drawn by the child illustrate the story. The life book can also be a record of the child's life, not just her adoption, and include such items as when the child first walked, what her first word was, and other milestones. Mementos, such as a hospital identification bracelet or an airplane ticket, can also be included.

By working on a life book with their child, parents can discover the child's own theory of why she was adopted or moved from one family to another. It is an obvious time to provide information to the child that she doesn't already have or help the child separate her fantasies about an experience from the facts. The parent can say, "I know that's how you would have liked that experience to be, but this is what really happened." When information about the child's past is missing, parents can discuss the likely possibilities: "We don't know why your mother couldn't keep you, but most mothers who make adoption plans for their children are young and don't know enough about how to raise a child."

It isn't difficult to initiate the construction of a life book. Parents can start by saying, "Let's talk about everything that happened to you before you came here." Once the child gets involved in the cutting, drawing, writing, and pasting, she will enjoy the activity. A four year old is mature enough to become involved in creating a life book.

Parents can be creative about the media used in making a life book. It isn't necessary for the life book to be a storyline illustrated with drawings and photographs; diagrams, letters to people the child knew before, and tapes of discussions may be more appropriate with some children.

Parents shouldn't try to make a life book in one day—to reconstruct the child's life one episode at a time is sufficient. Parents should also remember to let the child do the work. This is her story;

let her tell it. We are there to guide her and make sure that the final product is an accurate record, not a work of art.

Reconstructing one's past can be so emotional that the child may be able to tolerate the activity only for fifteen to thirty minutes and may need to run off steam afterward. Reliving painful memories may also cause some children to regress in their behavior. But parents shouldn't assume that because working on a life book makes their child feel sad or angry that the activity should be discontinued. Even though it may sometimes be painful, understanding the past is important for the adoptee.

Parents who are looking for guidance in making a life book can consult the references listed in the back of this book.

The Adoptee's Role

As parents, we will not be able to anticipate all our children's questions. We may be too busy to talk to our child one day and only later realize that the topic was important. We may discover that we have been using outdated language or sending double-messages when we talk about adoption. Every time I make a mistake as a parent, I am sure I have done irreparable psychological damage to my children. I have learned, however, that we usually get a second chance. The topic comes up again, or we can bring it up again, saying something like, "I think I may have confused you when I told you your birth mother placed you for adoption because she loved you. What I meant was that even though she loved you a lot, she realized that you needed things from a parent that she couldn't provide at that time in her life."

I also believe that our attitude as parents is often more important than the language that we use or our ability to engineer discussions with our children. If we are sincere in trying to know what their issues are and make an effort to meet their needs and if we are open, empathic, and honest, I believe they will excuse our shortcomings.

It's also important to remember that we will not be able always to answer our children's questions or provide answers that are immediately satisfying. Our children are on their own adoption journey. In the process, they will have to determine for themselves why they belong in our families, what their identity is, and why they are valuable human beings worthy of being loved. We can give them information, validation, perspective, support, comfort, and other tools to help them on this journey, but we cannot give them short-cuts.

5

How Adoption Affects the Family

რ Once the family and the adoptee have adjusted to one another and the first discussion of what it means to be adopted has been successfully handled, is being an adoptive family any different from being a biological family? Some people think not; they suggest that the only time adoption is an issue is when discussing how the child joined the family or whether the adoptee should have contact with the birth parents. "Once he's in your home, forget he's adopted," they tell adoptive parents.

Adoptive parents do forget their child is adopted, in the sense that they do not think daily about the way their child joined the family. Yet infertility, the adoption process, the way people outside the family respond to the child's being adopted, and the knowledge that there is another set of parents responsible for the existence of the child all affect adoptive parents and their children. These internal and external factors shape both parents and adoptees. The dynamics of the adoptive family are different from those of the biological family because the family was formed differently.

Adoptive Parents: Intensely Concerned

When asked to characterize adoptive parents, most professionals—as well as most friends and relatives—describe them as intensely concerned, deeply committed parents, who believe strongly that they can make a difference in their children's lives. Some may argue that only people with that attitude toward raising children are likely to adopt or be approved for adoption. That may be true, but I think there's also strong evidence that infertility, as well as the adoption process and the reaction of people outside the family to the idea of adopting, contribute to parental attitudes. Adoptive parents bring their attitudes to every aspect of their role. For example, we may not recognize a parent's eagerness to help a child with his homework night after night as an adoption issue. We may be inclined to describe that parent as a caring mother or father. But it is entirely possible that the parent's extra effort is the result of the great weight he places on the role of environment in academic achievement—a philosophy that may be directly influenced by the parent's experience with adoption.

Caring and Commitment

Adoptive parents make the decision over and over again to become parents. Even when parents adopt one of the many older or disabled children "waiting" for families, adoption is a lengthy, complicated procedure. The pregnant woman and her husband who have doubts about parenthood, discover that an expected promotion didn't come through, or develop marital problems find that it isn't easy to rescind their decision to become parents. Prospective adoptive parents know that a simple phone call can halt the entire process. People who proceed with adoption repeatedly commit themselves to becoming parents. Those who have decided on adoption because of infertility have spent years trying to have children, deciding each month that they want to be parents. Certainly, many biological parents make conscious decisions to have children and are committed to their roles. Most, however, have not had their decisions and commitment tested to the extent that adoptive parents have.

Some adoptive parents do manage to adopt without this level of commitment; the husband goes along with the adoption to please his wife, or both the husband and wife think a child is the solution to their problems, and they are able to fool not only them selves but their social worker. But most professionals characterize adoptive parents as highly committed to the decision they have made to adopt and to carry out their responsibilities. Committed parents are naturally caring and concerned. They want to do a good job. One strength of the adoptive family is the adoptive parents' concern for their children. Sometimes, though, parents can become overly concerned and too intense in their commitment. When they do, caring becomes hovering; concern becomes control; and, as a result, the parents don't give their child enough room to explore or make mistakes.

Impact of Infertility

One reason adoptive parents are sometimes thought to be over-protective is that infertility leaves us a legacy of loss. Each month we lost our expectation of a child. Some of us actually experienced pregnancy loss or the death of a child. Although we may know intellectually that our adoption has been finalized, in our hearts we may be preparing ourselves for the past to repeat itself.

Playing into this fear is another irrational belief—that perhaps infertility was a "sign" we weren't meant to be parents. Those who were brought up in a Judeo-Christian religion may be aware that in the Old Testament, infertility was a punishment, while fertility was a reward for righteous behavior. We may wonder if we are "worthy" enough to be parents. We may feel that by adopting, we escaped our "fate" (childlessness) and that, as in a Greek tragedy, we will eventually lose what we most sought to gain.

Author Ellen Glazer says that even infertile couples who ultimately conceive and bear a child carry this legacy with them. For the parents who adopt, however, there is the additional risk that we will lose our child to the birth parents—either physically or emotionally. The highly publicized adoption custody cases of Baby Jessica and Baby Richard were every adoptive parent's worst nightmare— that the child they loved and had come to think of as a member of their family would have to return to the birth family. Those cases are rare. Yet all adoptive parents deal with the fear, at some level, that they will lose their children emotionally—that someday they will discover that the love they share is not as deep or as lasting as they thought it would be and has been overcome by the children's ties to the birth parents.

We need to recognize that the losses we experienced with infertility have shaped us and our outlook on the world. Yet we do not have to be crippled by these experiences. Indeed, we can build on these losses once we have acknowledged them and expressed our feelings about them. From these experiences we can learn to cherish each day that we have with our children and to not take love for granted—even the love between a parent and a child—but to work daily to nourish and strengthen our relationships—not out of fear, but out of a healthy respect for the individual and the relationship.

We must learn to temper our concern so that we are not overprotective. Nobody wants his or her child to get hurt, but the child who gets no bumps or scrapes probably isn't exploring his surroundings. It's hard not to intervene to settle an argument between children, but sometimes children need to be left alone to work out their own solutions. We resist letting a child go to school without a coat when the weather is chilly, but sometimes we have to let him learn to make decisions and take the consequences. It is a delicate balance—caring without going overboard. Just recognizing the tendency to err on the side of overprotectiveness can help adoptive parents achieve that balance.

Liza adopted her daughter as an infant after six years of waiting for a child. She felt that because someone entrusted her with a child, she had to rear her perfectly. Mother and daughter were constantly together; for two and a half years, Liza refused to leave her daughter with another caretaker. "I went overboard," Liza said. "If we talked about leaves, I'd show her twenty, not two." She gradually recognized that her intensity was not beneficial.

High Expectations

Many people go into parenthood with idealized visions of what they will be like as parents and what their children will be like as a result. For adoptive parents, though, infertility and the adoption process, as well as the attitudes of those outside the family, can combine to raise their expectations of themselves and their children.

Because infertility puts parenthood out of reach for a couple who desires that role, the goal becomes all the more valuable. Couples often fantasize after years of attempted pregnancy about what their lives will be like with children. Often they become obsessed with getting pregnant. If they decide to adopt a baby—most infertile couples who decide on adoption prefer an infant—because of the high demand for healthy babies and the small supply, their goal is once again put out of reach. They may become preoccupied again with becoming parents. It's hard to think about the realities of raising children at this time. I remember a nurse at my physician's office who said, "You want to adopt? I've got a fifteen-year-old you can have." But I wasn't in a frame of mind to hear about how difficult it was to be a parent.

All expectant parents idealize to some degree what it will be like to be parents, but some infertile couples who are waiting for a placement are in such distress they begin to think that all their problems will be solved by the presence of a child. Couples who expect such a high degree of satisfaction from parenthood are likely to be disappointed.

In addition to expecting parenthood to bring them a high degree of happiness, adoptive parents often believe that they are expected to be "superparents" and that they have the ability to live up to those expectations. Those who are "competing" for the few healthy babies who are available believe they have to present themselves—to the social worker, birth parents, physician, or other intermediary—as the best possible choice of parents. The home study that "approves" them, plus the letters of recommendation from their friends that are required by many agencies, reinforce the idea that they are above-average parent material. When we were adopting a second time, I read a letter of recommendation to the agency from a friend and neighbor. The glowing terms in which my husband and I were described made me feel that this friend had a saintly image of me that I had to maintain. Fortunately, I became more realistic. Sometimes couples believe that since the birth mother decided she wasn't able to raise her baby and chose instead to have her placed with people who could, the adoptive parents are not allowed any mistakes. Parents in open adoptions, who have ongoing contact with their child's birth parents, may feel particular pressure to be faultless. Not only did the birth parents choose them on the basis of exemplary qualities that they saw in them, but the birth parents are able to see them "in action" with the child. Adoptive parents want to live up to the birth parents' trust and expectations, especially if the birth parents are around to observe them.

People who are properly prepared for the adoption of a child with special needs are less likely to have idealistic visions of what it will be like to raise that child. Yet some may have unrealistic expectations of what raising such a child will take or of their own limits.

As a result of their experiences, adoptive parents often jump into their roles with eagerness. There is nothing wrong with an enthusiastic parent; indeed, another strength of the adoptive family is that parents take their roles seriously. But there is a danger that adoptive parents can expect too much of themselves and of being parents. Couples may expect that after all they went through to adopt, they will not have any doubts about the decision once the child is taken home. They may think they should be capable of dealing with any situation. Adoptive parents may expect that because they chose to adopt, had plenty of time to reflect on it, and made the decision over and over again, they should be able to meet all the challenges of parenthood willingly and happily.

Being aware of the pitfalls in adoption that can lead to unrealistic expectations can help us avoid them. Adoptive parents shouldn't expect to be more patient than biological parents would be when raising children becomes overwhelming. Just because they wanted the child very much and waited a long time for him doesn't mean they are resistant to the rigors of parenting. All parents sometimes long for the freedom and more carefree days of childlessness. But adoptive parents, especially those who are infertile, may have a difficult time acknowledging those feelings.

One way to keep expectations realistic is to select sources of child care information carefully. Joseph Procaccini and Mark W. Kiefaber, in their book *Parent Burn-out,* are critical of the child care manuals that focus only on the needs of the child and imply that deviating from the "correct" methods of child rearing will have disastrous consequences. Parents should also avoid those manuals professing that a certain goal, such as toilet training or reading, can be attained only if the parents follow the guidelines exactly. Parents should choose child care guides that are realistic, humorous, and talk about the needs of parents as well as children. My favorites have been the Gesell Institute of Child Development series of books written by Louise Bates Ames and Frances L. Ilg. With titles like *Your Three Year Old: Friend or Enemy,* and *Your Four Year Old: Wild and Wonderful,* these books let parents know that some obnoxious behavior is both normal and transient. David Elkind's books *The Hurried Child* and *All Grown Up and No Place to Go* discuss the disadvantages of pushing children to mature too fast.

Observing other children the same age as one's own is another way to ascertain what behavior is appropriate to a certain stage of development. Unfortunately, because they are typically older when they become parents for the first time, adoptive parents often find that friends their own ages have children much older than their own. Therefore, they may want to look for other opportunities to associate with families who have children the same ages as their own.

Emphasis on Environment

Another reason adoptive parents may expect too much of themselves is because they may place too much faith in the capacity of a child's environment to influence his development. To commit themselves to raising a child born to other parents, adoptive parents must have a strong belief that the environment they have to offer the child will make a difference in his life. Claudia Jewett (now Claudia Jewett Jarratt), writing in *Adopting the Older Child,* says that parents who choose to adopt may see themselves as having a more active role in manipulating the child's fate than biological parents do. Consequently, they may expect to be able to solve all the child's problems.

Those who adopt infants usually want to adopt a baby so they can have as much opportunity to influence the child as possible. And even those who adopt older children, whose personalities are already formed, place a high degree of confidence in environment. With another teacher, the right therapist, and enough love, they think, they can overcome any negative factors in the child's past.

All this effort and concern is important, but adoptive parents cannot and should not forget that their child comes with a genetic code that influences more than the color of his eyes and the texture of his hair. Researchers are finding that genetics plays an influential role in the development of intelligence, personality, and even vocational interests. By accepting the role of heredity in child development, parents are not relinquishing the responsibility they have to provide a good environment for their children. There is a complex interplay between nature and nurture. A child may inherit his intellectual capability from his birth parents, but will never realize his potential unless he is challenged and motivated by his adoptive parents and teachers. A naturally sensitive child who is belittled for not being tough enough will develop a personality quite different from the child whose parents find his sensitivity to be charming.

Recognizing the limitations of environmental influences can help parents be more unconditionally accepting of their children. It also can go a long way toward relieving parents from the burden of thinking that any problem the child has is the result of inadequate parenting. Adoptive parents are not responsible for the ultimate outcome of a child—nor is any parent. We need to allow our children to be who they are and accept them as unique individuals, rather than try to mold them to fit some preconceived ideal. One of the joys of parenting is the discovery that continues as our children grow. One of the joys of adoptive parenting is the differences we are able to experience by raising children with different genetic backgrounds.

Outsiders' Reactions

Even when adoptive parents recognize that they do not have a perfect family and are sometimes dissatisfied with their roles, they may feel a need to project an image of a family devoid of problems. If their friends and relatives expressed doubt about their decision to adopt, adoptive parents may feel pressure to show these people that all is well. For instance, adoptive parents may respond to others' doubts that adoptive parents and their children love each other as fully as do biological parents and their children by trying to project that they always have a warm, loving relationship with their child. Even though they may recognize that parents who love their children sometimes lose their tempers or resent the responsibilities of parenthood, they may feel they have to hide these feelings. The first time I had this feeling was at a Friday evening gathering after a difficult week with two young children. When someone at the gathering asked me about my family, I told her exactly what my week had been like. She looked at me with surprise and a little disappointment. "You sound just like a real mother," she said. At the time I felt as though I'd betrayed my children and the institution of adoption. Today, I think I would realize that the problem is the other person's unrealistic idea about adoptive families.

When adoptive parents are honest about the difficulties they are having, friends and relatives are not always supportive. In particular, those who adopt children with emotional problems find that others are not always sympathetic to their situation. The single career woman who chooses to have a child on her own is in a similar situation. Because she chooses a situation with predictable difficulties, she is not allowed to complain about them afterward. She is expected to be a "superwoman." "You asked for this," some people say to adoptive parents, in reference to the fact that adopting requires repeated, conscious choice.

On the other side are those who believe that adoptive parents are angels. "You are wonderful to take in a child without a home," they tell us. Who can tell a person who makes that kind of statement that the child has been intolerable all week? If we are labeled "wonderful," we must live up to the expectation. Either way, adoptive parents come to realize that we are not always seen as a "normal" family. Because we lack a biological connection, some people see us as a family with fragile bonds, and we sometimes feel we are scrutinized for signs that those bonds are cracking. Others mistake the love that we share for charity and gratitude. Both views hurt because neither recognizes and accepts us as we are.

Some people are able to put these attitudes into proper perspective. They complain about the day-to-day hardships of parenthood without worrying that their complaints make them appear to be dissatisfied with their children. Others are more sensitive to outside opinions. But everyone needs someone with whom he can be honest about the problems of daily life. At the very least, a husband and wife should not hide their doubts and dissatisfaction from each other. They may also need close friends who can listen to them without passing judgment. Some adoptive parents turn to adoptive parent support groups to have this need met. There they can talk about what it's like to be parents without feeling defensive about having doubts or problems after they deliberately chose to become parents. They also get feedback and understanding from couples in similar situations. Reading Jana Wolff's book, *Secret Thoughts of an Adoptive Mother,* will also help adoptive parents know that they are not the first parents to have concerns that they may be reluctant to share with others.

Reconciling Expectations with Reality

The picture that emerges is of adoptive parents who care deeply about the responsibilities that they willingly and knowingly undertook. These people believe they have the skills, talents, or intuitive abilities to be good parents. They have waited a long time and gone through a difficult process to become parents, and they are anxious to begin their roles as mothers and fathers. They are full of enthusiasm. Another strength of adoptive parents is their belief in themselves and in their ability to overcome problems. But, at the same time, if they fail to adjust their view of themselves as "superparents" to the realities of raising children, they may put too much pressure on themselves and on their children.

Procaccini and Kiefaber say that parents who have high expectations about how they would perform as parents and the amount of satisfaction and happiness that would result from parenthood are at risk of "burning out." When the realities of family life set in, these parents begin to feel fatigue, disenchantment, and self-doubt—that parenthood isn't quite as ideal as they thought it would be. Some parents respond by adjusting their expectations to the realities. Others try twice as hard to make their family life perfect. Unless they eventually change their expectations, parents are likely to retreat from their jobs as parents, withdraw from their families and friends, and feel angry and resentful.

Parent burnout is estimated to affect about half the parents in the United States in some way and perhaps as many as 20 percent severely. It can affect any parent, but adoptive parents may be at risk because of the many factors that influence them to expect more of themselves.

Ironically, the adoptive parents who are the least likely to burn out are the ones most people think have the toughest jobs—those who have adopted many special needs children. They tend to have more realistic expectations and are aware of the children's limits. And the more children in the family, the more the parents' intensity is diluted. With disabled children, the more severe the handicap, the less likely that the parent will burn out. Apparently, parents realize that the probability of substantial change in the child's condition is slim, and they adjust their expectations accordingly.

Procaccini and Kiefaber suggest that one way for parents to avoid becoming disillusioned with raising children is to take care of themselves. Parents need to take some time for themselves, perhaps just a half hour, to exercise, meditate, work on a hobby, or enjoy some other favorite activity. Parents who put everyone else's needs before their own are setting themselves up to feel angry and resentful. Parents also need to take time for each other, nurturing their relationship as well as the relationship with their children. Because children are so impatient and their needs so pressing, it is often easy to insist that the spouse wait to have his needs met until the children are taken care of. Husbands and wives must let each other know that they still consider the other a priority.

Adoptees: Seeking Perfection

Adoptive parents sometimes falsely assume that if their children are not talking about having been adopted, they aren't thinking about it. How much an adoptee thinks about being adopted depends on his personality, how much factual information he has, and the attitude in his home toward his past. But we do know that a person who has been adopted will sometimes feel insecure about his adoptive home, will fantasize about what his life would have been like had he not been adopted, and grieve for the people he has been separated from or never knew. Unless the adoptive parents establish an atmosphere in which the adoptee feels that he can express his feelings, they may not realize that their child's "moodiness" is related to his adoptive status.

Pressure to Be Perfect

One way that adoptive parents with high expectations of themselves gauge how well they are meeting their expectations is by evaluating their children's behavior. Although there are a number of influences on children besides their parents, we tend to believe that children's behavior is a good indication of the quality of parenting. Parents who have unrealistic expectations of themselves are likely to have unrealistic expectations of their children. Strong believers in the influence of environment, adoptive parents may put undue pressure on their children to achieve more than they are capable of or push them into activities or situations that the children are not interested in.

In addition, adoptees sometimes think they must be model children to stay in their adoptive homes. The results of a study by psychologists at Rutgers University confirm what adoptees have been telling us for a long time: Adoptees sometimes believe they were placed for adoption because they were "bad" or in some way defective. They believe that if they had only been better, their birth parents would have kept them. The logical outgrowth of this mistaken belief is that they must behave very well to stay in their adoptive home.

Although the practice has fallen out of favor, some adoptees have been told that biological parents have to keep the children they have, while adoptive parents wanted their children and picked them out because they were special. This explanation puts pressure on the children to live up to whatever extraordinary qualities they had that led their parents to select them instead of other children.

While adoptive parents seldom want to be thanked by the children for adopting them, society implies that gratitude is required. And children express gratitude to their parents by being the kind of children their parents want. Not only is this an impossible expectation to fulfill, it is an unfulfilling expectation. As Betty Jean Lifton points out in *Lost and Found,* how can the adoptee possibly be perfect enough to repay his parents for rescuing him from being an orphan?

The pressure that adoptees put on themselves and that society puts on them can be eased by ongoing discussions of adoption. Adoptive parents, knowing that younger children tend to think they were placed for adoption because they were imperfect, should ask their child, perhaps in the course of making a life book, why he thinks he was placed for adoption. Misconceptions that he was placed for adoption because he cried too much, was messy, or was otherwise defective can be discussed. Frank discussions of why the parents chose to adopt can also communicate to the child that the adoptee was not the only one in need; the parents had needs that were met by adoption.

Family Romance Fantasies

Most of us can remember a time as children when we were angry at our parents and decided they were being mean to us because they were not our "real" parents. The only explanation for what we saw as horrendous parental behavior was that we had been adopted. Our "real" parents would have been more understanding because they would have really loved us. We may even have fantasized about who these other parents were—a Juliet who fell in love with a Romeo but couldn't marry him because the families were opposed to the marriage.

These family romance fantasies are neither unusual nor abnormal. Psychiatrists, beginning with Sigmund Freud, have suggested that they serve several purposes: to express disappointment with the parents, to reduce guilt associated with incestuous feelings, or to meet other defensive needs.

The adoptee also has fantasies about his birth parents. Thinking, as all children do at some time, that his adoptive parents aren't letting him have his own way because they don't love him, he may imagine a set of birth parents who are every child's ideal. They are everything his adoptive parents aren't—young, attractive, understanding, and rich. Psychiatrist Herbert Wieder suggests that some adoptees have difficulty reconciling this ideal image with people who would "give away" a child. If she was so rich, she wouldn't have had to relinquish her child for adoption, for example. At the other end of the spectrum, the adoptee may fantasize that to place a child for adoption, the birth parents had to be horrendous, and the adoptive parents were the saviors. Of course, this explanation is also flawed because he knows his adoptive parents are not ideal. Or he may decide that the birth parents didn't intend to place him, that he was stolen from them or that the placement was somehow beyond their control. Once his birth parents find out where he is, he thinks, they will rescue him.

Whatever the fantasy, it is more difficult for the adoptee to solve his temporary disappointment with his adoptive parents by fantasizing that he was adopted. The fantasy is mixed up with reality. While the biological child can let go of the fantasy as soon as his anger or resentment at his adoptive parents subsides, the adoptee's thoughts about his birth parents do not go away so easily. And there is a danger that he may start thinking of one set of parents as "bad" and the other set as "good."

How it Feels to Be Adopted, by Jill Krementz, *Being Adopted,* by David Brodzinsky, Marshall Schechter, and Robin Marantz Henig; *The Adoption Triangle,* by Arthur D. Sorosky, Annette Baran, and Reuben Pannor; and books written by adoptees, such as Betty Jean

Lifton's *Twice Born* and *Lost and Found*, can help adoptive parents understand that many adoptees think about their birth parents and what it means to be adopted far more often than most of us would imagine. Once we understand the kinds of thoughts that adoptees may have, we have a basis for discussion with them. We can tell them about the family romance fantasies we had as children and ask if they ever think their birth mothers were princesses, using that idea as a way to initiate a discussion of their feelings and correct any misconceptions. Parents could say, for example, "It is nice to think that your mother is very wealthy and will someday buy the toys for you that we can't afford. Probably she would want to buy nice things for you, just as we want to. But she probably isn't rich." Adoptive parents can also help their child understand that his ambivalent feelings toward them are quite natural and do not threaten their relationship. He can be angry at them, be disappointed in them, and think they are doing something wrong, just as they sometimes are angry at him and think he's making an incorrect decision. Those feelings don't diminish the fact that the parents and child love each other and are a family.

Knowing that ambivalent feelings and fantasies about the birth parents are normal doesn't always eliminate the sting that adoptive parents sometimes feel when their children compare them to their birth parents and find the adoptive parents wanting. We must remember: This doesn't mean we've failed to communicate how much we love them or that they don't love us. It is normal for children to think some other mother and father would be better to live with. Most important, however, adoptive parents can't let their children know that a comparison between them and the birth parents is a vulnerable point or the children may use it to manipulate the adoptive parents.

Unresolved or Renewed Grief

Adoptive parents often expect their children to need some time to adjust to a new family and to grieve for their birth parents or foster parents. But they may be surprised to find the children grieving for these losses years after the move.

The adoptee may never have seen his birth father and may have been separated from his birth mother immediately after birth, but our society values biological connections. He may not have formed attachments to his birth parents, but our society tells him he has lost people whose relationship to him is a valued one. When he realizes that, he is likely to grieve. Psychologist David Brodzinsky and his colleagues at Rutgers University found that children don't understand this loss until about the age of eight. At that time, they may show signs of mild or even severe grief.

The signs of grief that children experience when they realize they have had a loss are similar to those any of us experience with a loss (see Chapter 2). However, as Brodzinsky and his colleagues point out in *Being Adopted,* children who were adopted as infants usually "do not express the shock, deep depression, uncontrollable crying, or intense rage that are commonly part of acute or traumatic loss." Instead, they may be withdrawn, distracted, confused, "clingy," or have occasional bouts of sadness or anger. Although it isn't common, some adoptees around the age of six, seven, or eight suddenly begin to have severe behavioral problems or angry outbursts without any apparent cause. The explanation may be that they are grieving.

It may not make sense to the parents that the child is grieving for a loss he had years ago. The child himself may not realize that's what's going on. Some children this age describe feeling "empty" or having a "black spot" on their hearts. They may feel angry for no apparent reason—especially at their adoptive mothers. They may be anxious when they are away from their parents. Because they may not be able to put words to their feelings, their parents have to be ready to help them.

Parents may have difficulty recognizing symptoms of grief that aren't severe. Is John fighting more with his classmates because he's grieving or for some other reason? It can be hard to tell. And parents may not want to believe that the cause is adoption-related. They may want to believe that since they have formed an attachment with their child and told him he's adopted, adoption issues are behind them. Or they may think it's too simple to blame every problem on adoption. Perhaps they prefer to look for explanations of problems that they can have more control over so they will have a better chance of solving them.

Adoption issues are never completely put to rest. Although it is unfair to blame every problem on adoption, it is unrealistic to think that adoption will never be a factor in a situation. In *Being Adopted*, Brodzinsky and his colleagues suggest that the loss of parents that a child experiences with adoption is more complicated than the loss of a parent through either divorce or death. The child may have no history or relationship with the birth parents—no memories to sustain him. Furthermore, because in most cases the birth parents are still alive, the child may harbor fantasies of reversing the loss. That, too, presents a dilemma to the adoptee: To reverse the loss for which he is grieving would require that he lose his adoptive parents, whom he knows and loves. He is truly in a no-win situation. It's no wonder that this experience can be confusing and painful for a child. One of the ways parents can help is by letting children know that it is normal and all right to have conflicting emotions in a situation—that they can grieve for the loss of their birth parents and wish it had never happened without meaning that they wish they didn't have their adoptive parents. One wouldn't have happened without the other, but they can have separate feelings about each event. We will be better able to communicate this idea if we think about our own similar experience. Adoptive parents who are infertile grieved for failed attempts at pregnancy or actual pregnancy loss. We may still have times when we are reminded of those losses and feel sad that we were unable to conceive or give birth to a biological child.

We know that if we had given birth to a biological child, we probably would not have adopted the child we love beyond words. By feeling the sadness of infertility or pregnancy loss, we are not wishing we hadn't adopted; we are having an appropriate emotional reaction to a separate event.

Although neither the adoptee nor the adoptive parents can change the fact of the child's loss, they are not powerless to deal with the emotional aftermath. Parents can help their children name their feelings and identify the reasons for them. They can say, for example, "I notice that you get scared when I go on a business trip. I think you may be worried that I won't come back. Maybe you are thinking that you lost your birth parents and you don't want to lose me too." Parents can then explain that the birth parents didn't disappear, but made a plan for the child's well-being, and that while the future is uncertain—accidents can happen—the adoptive parent's plan is to come back and continue to be that child's parent.

By maintaining an open atmosphere in which the child feels comfortable discussing his feelings, by validating those feelings, and by providing unconditional support, parents can help him through his period of mourning toward acceptance and understanding.

Triggering Memories of Past Losses

Children often grieve for past losses because they were not allowed or able to mourn at the time of the loss. But sometimes children who have resolved a loss find themselves repeating some of the stages of grief when they experience a new loss, on an anniversary of the loss, or on holidays. Their reaction is not likely to be as severe as it would be if the loss was recent, but it is equally real. Sam had an early history of foster and adoptive families. He was placed again for adoption when he was seven years old. His foster mother, unwilling to deal with Sam's reaction to another move, told him he was going to stay with the new adoptive family only for Christmas, she would pick him up after the holiday. Sam had a lot of behavioral problems in his new adoptive family, but never more so than at Christmas time each year. His mother believes he was deliberately trying to destroy Christmas for the family. One year he damaged all the Christmas presents. Another year he shot out the windows of the neighbors' houses. Yet another Christmas he stole a checkbook and wrote a series of bad checks. The money it took for his parents to cover the bad checks almost eliminated the possibility of their buying any Christmas gifts. The double stress of the anniversary of his placement in the home, for which he had been poorly prepared, and the holiday season combined to trigger extreme behavioral problems.

Sometimes the exact day of an anniversary does not trigger remembrances of the loss as much as the time of year, Jarratt says. Children may associate the loss with the feel of the air in a particular season or the lengthening or shortening of days. Lorraine Dusky, a birth mother who wrote about her experience in *Birthmark,* associated the loss of her daughter, born in April, with the blooming of forsythia.

In most adoptive families, adoption anniversaries are marked in some way. It just feels right to celebrate such a significant occasion. However, adoptive parents should recognize that the day the child was placed in his family was also the day the child had to be separated from his birth family or foster family. It is a day of mixed feelings. Many adoptees who grew up with their adoption anniversaries celebrated say they appreciated the acknowledgment and wanted it continued even after they grew up and left home. Some were hurt, however, if the anniversary was the only time their adoption was mentioned or if the celebration dwarfed the celebration of the day they were born. Some adult adoptees who never had their adoption day celebrated have invented their own ways of marking that important occasion.

Families can fall back on familiar routines in celebrating "Adoption Day." However, they can also invent their own ritual. For example, they can gather around the dining room table on which items of significance have been placed, such as the clothes the child was wearing when he arrived, or the referral photo of the child. Family members can read a meaningful poem or story, such as the biblical story of the adoption of Moses; sing a song; or play meaningful music (see *Designing Rituals of Adoption* for some suggestions). Then the child's adoption story can be told. Families can have two vases filled with different flowers on the table and move a flower from the vase representing the birth family to that representing the adoptive family as they tell the story of the child's placement. If the birth mother wrote a letter of good-bye to the child at the time of the placement, it can be read. After the story is told, the family can honor the birth parents by offering a prayer or good wish, acknowledge the sadness that had to happen for their family to come together, and have family members make a statement or participate in an action that symbolizes their feeling of unity as a family. Another poem or song, such as John McCutcheon's song *Happy Adoption Day*, can conclude the ritual.

Because the adoptee may have similar ambivalent feelings when celebrating other events that emphasize family, such as a birthday, wedding day, holidays, or family reunion, it is important for adoptive parents to be aware that memories of past losses may be haunting their child at these times.

People are usually sensitive to the way a widow feels on Thanksgiving or how a mother may feel on Mother's Day after her child has died. But we often don't expect the adoptee to think of his birth parents or foster parents on "family" holidays, probably because they don't belong to our past—but they do belong to the child's.

Because Christmas is generally the biggest holiday of the year, it is often particularly stressful for the adoptee. The emphasis on being together as a family and on the birth of Jesus combine to remind adoptees that they are separated from some significant people. Adoptees may wonder if they would have been placed for adoption had they been as perfect a baby as Jesus and may engage in other fantasies of what might have been. In Jill Krementz's book *How It Feels to Be Adopted,* an adopted boy talks about his feelings at Christmas. If he had been bad, he would think Santa wasn't going to bring him presents and would put coal in his stocking, and his mother would take him back to the adoption agency. Unusually good behavior or unusually problematic behavior can be warnings that a child is having a holiday grief reaction. Unusual tension in the child is another sign.

The key to helping a child work through grief is to allow the child to express his feelings, but that may be more difficult at Christmas when the emphasis is on being happy, Jarratt says. She points out that even the Christmas song "Santa Claus Is Coming to Town" tells children they'd better not cry or pout. For the parents who recognize that their child needs to discuss his feelings at this time, Christmas does provide opportunities. Christmas stories about Rudolph the Red-nosed Reindeer or Charlie Brown's scrawny Christmas tree are good starting places for talking about feelings of being rejected because one is imperfect. And the story of Mary and Jesus can be used as a starting point for discussions of mother-child relationships.

In Jewish homes, the High Holy Days of Rosh Hashanah and Yom Kippur emphasize family connections and the linkage of the family unit to Jews elsewhere and to history. The solemn evaluation and personal scrutiny that are part of these holy days may result in some thoughts by the adoptee about how he fits in with the family and with the history of his family. He may even wonder if he is "really" Jewish.

New Losses

Subsequent losses, even minor ones, can trigger memories of past losses, especially if the person has not fully grieved for the previous loss. Psychologists believe that anyone who experiences a significant loss is likely to feel new losses more acutely. The death of a pet, a broken toy, or a friend who moves away can provoke grief in a child that may seem out of proportion to the actual loss, Jarratt says. This intense grief may indicate that the child is mourning for more than just the broken toy or absent friend. Psychiatrist John Bowlby suggests that when a person loses someone or something to which he is attached, he turns for comfort to an earlier attachment figure. If that person is not available, the loss is felt again. (For a discussion of how adopted children react to divorce or the death of a parent, see Chapter 12.)

Whatever the loss, a child's response may seem more severe than the loss would warrant, perhaps because he is grieving for more than the immediate loss. Allowing the child to grieve, rather than implying that he shouldn't be feeling the loss so intensely, is essential.

Permission to Love Again

Parents can choose some concrete activities to help children resolve their feelings of separation and loss, either at the time of placement or later when they are experiencing renewed grief. Life books, discussed in Chapter 4, are designed to help a child understand where he has been and why he had to leave those places. Feelings the child has as a result of having to move can be discussed quite naturally at this time.

Jarratt believes it is important for a child to have a chance to say "good-bye" to the people he has lived with and receive a blessing from them—permission from someone he cares about to be happy in the new family, to be loved, and to love. Even children who never knew their birth parents learn from society that there's a certain loyalty children should have toward their biological parents. At some point, they may need to know that it is OK for them to love their adoptive parents. The letters that some birth mothers write to their children at the time of placement can explain to a child why he was placed for adoption and can give him the permission he needs to love his adoptive parents. In the absence of such a letter, Jarratt suggests that the adoptive parents help their child write a letter or place a phone call to the people he needs to say good-bye to or receive a blessing from. If direct contact isn't possible or desirable, "make-believe" can be used. The child can be encouraged to make a phone call on a toy telephone or use puppets or dolls to act out the event, with the adoptive parent playing the role of the birth mother or foster mother. The adoptive parent can direct the activity by saying, "What do you think you would say to your birth mother if you called her?" "How do you think she would respond?" "I think she would say, 'You sound like a fine, strong boy. This family must be the right place for you.'" The adopted child then has had an opportunity to say good-bye and move on with his life.

Adoption is Different

More than thirty years ago, sociologist H. David Kirk suggested that adoptive parents who have not given birth experience what he termed a *role handicap* arising out of the discrepancies between the expectations of how their families would be formed—based on a cultural expectation of fertility—and the reality of how their substitute parenthood came into being and developed. In other words, because adoption is not the way we tend to think of families being formed, but is seen as an *exception* to what is "normal," it raises questions about whether we can have the same expectations of the experience. *Can I discipline this child the way I would have a biological child? Will our family life be as satisfactory? Will my child love me as much? Will I love him as much?* Kirk suggested that if adoptive parents do not recognize the ways in which adoption alters expectations and raises questions, their ability to perform their parenting role competently could be compromised. What is necessary, he said, is to substitute a "script" that is normal for adoptive families for the cultural script written for biological families. We have to recognize the discrepancies and see that although they make us different from the majority of families in society, they are common among adoptive families and therefore "normal." It is normal for adoptive families to have experienced losses for which they must grieve. It is normal for us to have children who are physically dissimilar from us. It is normal for adoptive parents to be unprepared for the arrival of their child or for the child's arrival to be precipitous. It is normal for us to be anxious or overprotective because of our experience with loss and the unpredictability of adoption. It is normal for other people to scrutinize us because our method of forming a family is different from the cultural model. It is normal for us to respond to that scrutiny by feeling defensive, by withdrawing, or by projecting an overly positive image. It is normal for us to believe strongly in environmental influences in raising children. It is normal for our children to experience grief that may distract them, lead to feelings of insecurity, or be expressed as anger. It is normal for us and for our children to be somewhat more vulnerable to other losses or memories of earlier losses. For parents who adopt children with a history of abuse or neglect, it is normal for there to be ongoing behavioral problems and regular family therapy. For those with open adoptions, it is normal for them to have an "extended family" of relatives composed of the biological relatives of the adoptees, as well as their own. For those who were adopted transracially, it is normal to have a sense of racial identity that is different from the majority of people of the same racial group.

Kirk suggested that parents who could acknowledge these differences and make the necessary adaptations would feel more competent and less alienated. Presumably, they would therefore be more successful parents. Kirk also suggested that parents who could tap into their own feelings about these losses and discrepancies would be more empathic to their children's feelings about their losses and the challenges adoption poses for them.

Kirk was looking at adoptive families as a sociologist—studying the "system," that is, the adoptive family, the ways it adapts, and the potential consequences when it does not adapt. Other researchers have focused on adoptive families from a psychological perspective, looking for the ways in which the differences evident in adoptive families may cause psychological distress. This subject is discussed in Chapter 6.

6

Are Adoptees at Risk?

☙ News accounts of crimes often mention whether the arsonist or murderer was adopted, as though this fact somehow explains the events. It reflects a belief held by some people—including many professionals—that adoptees are more vulnerable to psychological disturbances than are nonadopted persons. While there is some evidence that adoptees may be at a greater risk of emotional and behavioral problems, the risk is not as great or as inevitable as we are sometimes led to believe.

Perhaps we are not surprised when children who were adopted at an older age have behavioral or psychological problems. Neglect, abuse, failure to set appropriate limits, frequent moves, and failure to form attachments affect a child and are likely to continue to affect her to some degree after she is placed in an adoptive family. In these cases, it isn't adoption that causes the problems, but factors experienced before the child was placed for adoption. Nevertheless, one of the most important and controversial questions in adoption is whether adoption itself is so traumatic as to cause lasting psychological damage—even in those who were adopted as infants. Research on this issue has yielded conflicting results and a variety of interpretations of the results. Discontinuous mothering, unresolved grief at the loss of the birth parents, failure to make an attachment to the adoptive parents, confusion about the meaning of adoption, and feelings of rejection and abandonment may put an adoptee at risk of emotional problems. But not all adoptees develop problems, and enlightened attitudes on adoption and an awareness of its effects may prevent or mitigate problems. It is too simple for parents, relatives, or professionals to explain away any behavioral or emotional problems an adoptee has as being related to her adoption. But it is also unwise to ignore the fact that the adoptee has had experiences in her life that children who have been raised by their biological parents do not have. The effect of these experiences may become apparent long after the adoptee's initial adjustment to the adoptive home and attachment to the adoptive parents.

Psychological Problems

Psychiatrist Marshall Schechter is often credited with starting the controversy more than thirty-five years ago in an article in which he noted that he had a higher percentage of adoptees in his practice than were in the general population. He apparently received more publicity than his critics who challenged his statistics. Other critics have wondered if he took into account that he might have had a large number of adoptees because he had a reputation for working on adoption issues. Yet some studies since then have also found that adoptees are overrepresented among children referred to mental health clinics and residential treatment centers. (Some adoptees have used these findings to justify the opening of their sealed adoption records. The higher incidence of psychological problems, they believe, is due to their lack of information about their biological relatives.)

Other studies have found that adoptees do not seek mental health counseling any more frequently than do nonadopted persons. And some experts have suggested explanations other than a greater degree of psychological problems for whatever overrepresentation of adoptees in clinic populations there may be. Adoption is generally a middle class phenomenon, as is the practice of consulting mental health professionals. Perhaps a higher percentage of adoptees use counseling services because they come from a class of people who value the use of these services. In addition, people who adopt are accustomed to consulting helping professionals. If they are infertile, they have had to enlist the aid of the physicians to help them become pregnant or may have had counseling to help them resolve their feelings about infertility. With an agency adoption, they have been assigned a social worker who has probed their reasons for adopting and their parenting skills. Even with an independent adoption, parents have needed the assistance of a physician or lawyer. It is, perhaps, easier for these people to turn to a counselor for help than it is for someone who has never been in a state social services office or discussed parenting issues with a professional. While some people have no idea whom to call for needed therapy, the adoptive parents may know a social worker by name or belong to an adoption support organization that refers families to counselors who specialize in adoption issues.

The intensity and concern that adoptive parents bring to their roles may also cause them to intervene sooner than other parents. Parents who have unrealistic expectations of themselves and their child may see anything but near-perfect behavior in their child as a sign of psychological problems. Or perhaps, having been influenced by family members and friends who believe they are going to have more than their share of problems with their adopted child, adoptive parents seek help at the first sign of trouble.

Other studies have looked at children outside mental health facilities to evaluate whether adoptees have more behavioral problems than do nonadopted children. Here, too, the results have been conflicting. Some studies have failed to find differences between adoptees and nonadopted children, while others indicate that school-age adoptees—including those who were adopted as infants—have more behavioral problems. There is also some indication that adopted boys have more problems than adopted girls. Some of the discrepancies among the results of various studies can be explained by poor research methods—not all of which are the fault of the researchers. The secrecy that surrounds adoption has made it difficult for social scientists to obtain representative samples of adoptive families and adequate information about adoptees' biological backgrounds. Nevertheless, some studies are worth looking at.

One large study in Great Britain, which followed children from birth, found that the behavioral problems of adoptees increased between ages seven and eleven—the period when adoptees begin to comprehend that their birth parents placed them for adoption, but before they understand the legal system that makes adoption permanent. This study also found that boys had more problems than girls. In a study that deserves attention because of the way its sample was selected and compared to a control group, David Brodzinsky and his colleagues at Rutgers University found that adopted children aged six to eleven were rated by their mothers and teachers as having more psychological and school-related behavioral problems and more difficulty getting along with their peers than did nonadopted children. Both boys and girls were equally at risk for behavioral problems.

Other studies have had similar findings. The Swedish adoption study by Michael Bohman and his colleagues studied boys who were available for adoption, some of whom were adopted, some of whom were raised in foster families, and some of whom were returned to their birth parents. It found more behavioral problems in all three groups around age eleven, compared to those children who had never been available for adoption; however, by age fifteen, the problems among adoptees had diminished, and by age eighteen, there was no significant difference between the adoptees and the control group.

William Feigelman analyzed data collected in a large national study in the United States comparing the behavior of adopted children in two-parent families to that of children in two-parent biological families and children who were raised in other situations (such as single-parent families or stepfamilies). He found more drug and alcohol problems and juvenile delinquency among the children in adoptive and other families than in those in intact biological families. He also found a higher incidence of running away from home among teenagers who had been adopted, but no higher incidence of teenage pregnancy among the adoptees than among those raised in two-parent biological families. However, the problems were not as great among children in adoptive families as in children reared in a stepfamily or a single-parent household.

As in the Swedish study, by adulthood, Feigelman found virtually no differences between the adoptees and those raised in intact biological families, while those in the third group had lower educational attainment, more unemployment, and more clinical depression.

The findings of yet another study seem to confirm those that indicate that adoption is more troubling during adolescence than during adulthood. That study, which looked at all patients registering for their first psychiatric services at a particular clinic, found that 5 percent of the children, but less than 2 percent of the adults who were seen, were adopted.

While many studies have tried to determine whether or not adoptees have more psychological problems, most have not looked at the reasons some adoptees have more behavioral or psychological problems during adolescence. When Ruth McRoy and her colleagues looked at adopted teenagers who were so troubled as to require treatment in a residential setting, they found *no common denominator.* They did find, however, that *all* the parents, including those in a control group of nonadoptive families, had ineffective parenting skills and that 40 percent of both the adoptive parents and the biological parents were either alcoholic or abusive.

David Brodzinsky speculates that adopted children, particularly during early adolescence, may appear to have more behavioral or psychological problems because they are distracted by the issues adoption raises for them. As was discussed in Chapter 4, normal developmental issues—from understanding how children join families to the formation of identify—are more complicated for adoptees. Dealing with the additional dimension adoption brings may distract children from their schoolwork, cause them to withdraw to reflect or grieve, or lead to agitation that makes it difficult for them to sit still.

Feigelman is inclined to agree. The additional weight adoption brings to normal adolescent issues may leave children feeling overwhelmed and isolated, he says. They're not sure how they fit in at a time when belonging is crucial.

The fact that the vast majority of adolescents change their behavior by adulthood may indicate that whatever issues are raised by adoption are resolved as part of normal development, just as the issues of adolescence tend to be resolved by growth and maturity. Feigelman also suggests, however, that unlike single-parent or other nontraditional families, adoptive families may have the resources and connections that help troubled teenagers get back on track.

What does seem clear are the following:

· The vast majority of adoptees do not have serious problems.

· Adoptees as a group are at somewhat higher risk of having school-related problems, behavioral problems, and psychological problems than children who are raised in two-parent biological families, but their behavior would usually still be considered to be within normal limits. When problems are severe and there is no history of abuse or neglect, it is possible that there are additional factors unrelated to the child's adoption, such as dysfunctional parenting.

· Adoptees as a group have fewer behavioral and psychological problems, less teenage pregnancy, less clinical depression, more professional success, and higher educational attainment than do those who were in similar circumstances at birth but who remained in those circumstances, indicating that the adoptive environment has a positive impact.

· When adoptees do have problems, it may be because they are struggling to make sense of the issues raised by their adoption, rather than because adoption itself is psychologically damaging. The fact that most problems seem to disappear by adulthood indicates that whatever vulnerabilities adoptees have are manageable. That possibility, however, should not be interpreted as meaning that any problems can be ignored or that they will take care of themselves.

· The fact that adoptees as a group are statistically more likely or less likely to have problems under certain situations is interesting, but the most important factor for parents is how *their* child is responding to the challenges of her life. We can spend so much time looking for an explanation for our children's behavior that we forget to intervene. Sometimes, of course, pinpointing the cause of a child's problems helps parents or professionals deal with those problems. We have to be careful, though. We may be searching for a cause—particularly an adoption-related cause— as a way to absolve ourselves of responsibility for our child's embarrassing actions or emotional pain. Not only does that search distract us from helping our child, but it may add another layer to the problem for her: She has to work on her behavior while dealing with the idea that she's having problems because of her birth parent's drinking, irresponsible prenatal care, or genes (this topic is explored in greater length in Chapter 7).

Adopted Child Syndrome

The idea that adoption is psychologically traumatic has gained credence in recent years through the use of the term *adopted child syndrome.* Coined by clinical psychologist David Kirschner of New York and not a recognized psychiatric disorder, the term received widespread publicity after Kirschner used it in testimony he gave in the defense of a young man charged with murdering his adoptive parents in 1984. Since that time, the term has been used—and misused—to explain any deviant behavior among adoptees and to support the notion that all adoptees suffer psychological damage because they were adopted. However, in an interview, Kirschner told me that the term is not intended to apply to adoptees whose birth parents had no obvious pathology and who were placed as infants with emotionally healthy adoptive parents. "I don't think you'd get adopted child syndrome in that situation," he said.

According to Kirschner, adopted child syndrome is a pattern of behaviors that includes antisocial acts, disrespect for authority, lying, stealing, and running away, along with learning disabilities and attachment problems. Those adoptees who he concluded have this syndrome were adopted later in life, had traumatic placements before they were placed with the adoptive parents with whom they grew up, and have had pathological relationships with their adoptive parents who had problems of their own. Although the feelings of rejection and identity confusion that are common to all adoptees to some degree may contribute to adopted child syndrome, this syndrome is not simply an outgrowth of grief or a description of all—or even most—adoptees.

Attention Deficit Hyperactivity Disorder and Learning Problems

Adoptees have been found to have a higher incidence of attention deficit hyperactivity disorder (ADHD). Although true ADHD is said to affect 3–5 percent of the general population, studies have found a much higher incidence among adoptees. The reason for this higher incidence is unclear, partly because the causes of ADHD are still unclear. However, most researchers believe that ADHD is caused by a malfunctioning of certain areas of the brain owing to heredity, the prenatal or perinatal environment, or injury to the brain caused by illness, trauma, or exposure to toxins. So it is unlikely that adoption itself causes ADHD. More likely causes are poor maternal health during pregnancy, alcohol or tobacco use during pregnancy, or genetic factors.

However, it is also possible that ADHD is misdiagnosed in adoptees. Some people suggest that the additional psychological issues adoptees must deal with can be distracting. An adoptee who is trying to figure out why she had to lose her birth parents may be distracted or agitated, much like a child with ADHD. In his book, *When You Worry About the Child You Love,* Edward Hallowell suggests that other conditions, such as depression, can be mistaken for ADHD. Furthermore, he says, some children have "pseudo-ADHD" as a result of the high-tech stimulation in their lives.

Adoptees are often said to have more learning disabilities than nonadopted children. Technically, learning disabilities are disorders of the basic psychological processes involved in understanding, perceiving, or expressing language or concepts, as well as disorders resulting from visual processing. They include such conditions as dyslexia, but do not include learning problems that are the result of visual, hearing, or motor handicaps or those that are due to mental retardation.

Why adoptees may be at greater risk for these problems is not known. The origins of specific learning disabilities are still unclear but include such genetic, emotional, and environmental factors as chromosomal anomalies, metabolic abnormalities, neurological damage, maturational delay of the neurological system, nutritional deficiencies, and sensitivity to environmental substances. Again, adoptees may be showing a higher incidence of problems that result from poor prenatal care or birth trauma. Prenatal exposure to tobacco and other drugs is connected to low birth weight or prematurity, which places children at risk for learning, attention, and behavior problems. Learning problems may also be a sign that the adoptee is grieving.

Parents should not be overly concerned that their adopted

child will develop hyperactivity or learning disabilities. However, because the adoptee may be at a greater risk for these problems, the parents who suspect their child is having them should have their child evaluated periodically. Diagnosis of learning problems or ADHD will be aided by information about the child's biological relatives as well as about complications the birth mother may have had during her pregnancy and delivery. (The importance of a complete history is discussed in Chapter 7.)

Parents who want their child to be evaluated should first consult his physician, who may refer the family to other community resources. Parents of a school-age child can also use the resources of the school system, such as a school psychologist and learning disability specialist.

With early diagnosis and intervention, most children can be taught ways to compensate for and cope with their learning difficulties.

Although getting help for their child is essential, adoptive parents may also need help to understand the child's limitations and prognosis. Learning disabilities often run in families, and when, for example, the father has had a learning problem, he can not only empathize with his child's problem, but may be able to show how he was able to compensate for it or how it has not impeded his success as an adult. If the adopted child is the first person in the family to have a learning disorder, the parents may be more anxious about the long-term effects of the disorder or may not understand the child's frustration. In addition, adoptive parents who place great emphasis on the ability of environment to overcome problems may think that with the right diet, tutor, or extra help at home, they can compensate for the learning disorder. Adoptive parents should also take care to communicate to the child that they are satisfied with the progress the child is making. Adoptees shouldn't feel they are a disappointment to their parents just because the parents asked for a "healthy child" and received a child with a learning disability.

It is advisable for parents who adopt an older child to wait until the child has adjusted to her new school and her new family before deciding whether any problems she is having at school represent actual learning problems or temporary adjustment or grief reactions. Even if her history indicates she has had learning disabilities in the past, her parents should not be overzealous about having her evaluated immediately. She could get the idea that remaining in her adoptive family is somehow tied to overcoming her learning problems.

Long-term Effects of Drug and Alcohol Exposure

Some children who are diagnosed with learning problems or even attention deficit disorder (ADD) with or without hyperactivity may be showing the long-term effects of prenatal drug exposure. According to Ira Chasnoff and his colleagues, who have been studying drug-exposed children for more than twenty years, about 35 percent of children whose parents were heavy drug users showed some degree of difficulty concentrating and staying on task or increased distractibility. Some of these also showed aggressive or impulsive behavior. These children are sometimes diagnosed as having ADD either with or without hyperactivity. However, it isn't known if prenatal drug exposure is responsible for the apparently higher incidence of ADD in adoptees.

Although researchers do not know exactly how drugs and alcohol affect unborn children, Chasnoff suspects that the neurological system's ability to send and receive messages is affected in the developing fetus. Consequently, exposed children have difficulty regulating their behavior or state in response to messages. In a school-age child, it may mean difficulty blocking out classroom distractions or settling down after recess.

Despite these findings, the long-term outlook for drug-exposed children is not as grim as some early predictions, particularly if the children are raised in healthy, stimulating environments. While it is difficult to predict which children will be most severely affected by prenatal drug exposure, the best prognosis seems to be for children who were born full term with a normal birth weight and normal head circumference and those whose growth catches up within the first six months of life.

Any child at risk due to prenatal exposure to drugs, or who was premature or had low birth weight, should have early and periodic screening for developmental and learning problems. Early intervention techniques seem to be effective in mitigating the effects of prenatal drug exposure.

Fetal Alcohol Syndrome and Fetal Alcohol Effect

Children exposed prenatally to alcohol are not only at risk of having low birth weight and learning problems, they are at risk of being born with Fetal Alcohol Syndrome (FAS) or Fetal Alcohol Effect (FAE). Children with either FAS or FAE may have neurologic dysfunctions that can result in behavior problems, learning problems, and difficulty concentrating and comprehending. The most severe effect can be mental retardation. FAS is more severe than FAE and includes physical abnormalities. While FAE tends not to have the severity of symptoms of FAS, it can still result in significant problems. Without the physical abnormalities of FAS, however, it can be difficult to associate a child's symptoms with prenatal alcohol exposure.

For more resources on prenatal drugs and alcohol exposure, see Resources and Organizations at the end of this book.

Academic Expectations

Despite evidence that adoptees have more school-related behavioral problems and are at a greater risk of certain types of learning disabilities than are nonadopted children, research indicates that as a group, adoptees' school performance is acceptable. Studies have found that while adoptees' school achievement is slightly below that of nonadopted children in comparable environments, adoptees do as well as or better than children in the general population.

Studies in Britain and the United States that examined thousands of children at birth and continued to evaluate them for many years found that the adoptees did as well as or better than non-adopted children, particularly in such areas as reading and language use, but that the results for mathematical ability varied.

But when adopted children have been compared to children who were raised in similar environments, they appeared to be performing less well academically. In the British study, for example, adopted boys were not doing as well in mathematics, and the adopted group as a whole was doing slightly less well than children in comparable environments. In a Rutgers University study of 260 adopted and nonadopted children aged six to eleven, the adopted children were rated somewhat lower in academic achievement than were closely matched children who were not adopted. This finding could reflect genetic differences in intelligence or a preoccupation with adoption issues associated with preadolescence that distracts the adoptees from their schoolwork. In any case, although there may be some statistical differences between the academic performance of adoptees and nonadopted children raised in comparable environments, those differences may not be meaningful to most families. That is, we may be talking about the difference between a B-plus and a B average in school.

In the analysis conducted by William Feigelman, adopted men had attended college at the same rate as those in intact biological families, although the rate of college graduation among adoptees was lower. Among women, there was no difference in the graduation rates of adoptees and those raised in biological families.

Resilience

Although children who have experienced neglect, abuse, or other deprivations early in childhood are at risk of psychological or behavioral problems, we have all heard stories of children who have overcome such adversity. Why are some people apparent "victims" of their life experiences while others are survivors? Some people learn coping skills and defense mechanisms or are otherwise able to mask the effects of early deprivation. However, some people have truly achieved emotional health and competence despite a history of adversity. Researchers are finding that both organic and environmental factors protect some children from the adverse effects of early stress. Children who are more "resilient" have average or better intelligence. They can make sense out of a chaotic family environment and reason that they were not the cause of their problems. Intellectual ability also helps children develop skills to take care of themselves and seek help when they need it. Children who overcome adversity tend to have a good-natured, easygoing temperament. When they ask for help, people generally want to oblige them. They have an adult—a parent, neighbor, older sibling, or regular baby-sitter—consistently available to them during the first two years of life whom they can trust. They are independent, but seek help when they need it; are involved in hobbies or jobs (that enable them to escape from their home life); and have an affiliation with a faith community which provides them with a community, a sense of purpose, and a sense of good self-esteem. Resilient children, researchers have found, remain resilient as adults. And some children who develop problems during adolescence overcome them when they have informal supports at critical times, such as a teacher who takes an interest and a spiritual community.

Putting Research into Perspective

It is important to look at research on adoption issues, but it is also necessary to put scientific findings into perspective. If adoptees make up 2 percent to 4 percent of the population, but researchers find that, for example, 10 percent have psychological and other problems, they are going to conclude that adoptees are more likely to have problems than nonadoptees and, therefore, that adoption caused the problems. Even if that figure is correct, it still leaves 90 percent who are well adjusted. An increased chance that an adoptee will have behavioral problems during childhood may be one of the risks of adoption, but it may not be a great risk.

Furthermore, the factors in adoption that put adoptees at risk of greater problems do not doom them to those problems. For example, just because the birth parents decided not to raise their child does not mean that the child must go through life feeling rejected. The way that adoption is explained to her, the degree to which she is allowed to discuss her feelings about being placed for adoption, and the amount of information she has about her birth parents can help her understand and accept the decision.

Thanks to adoptees who are now adults and have shared their feelings about growing up, adoptive parents now have a much better idea of how children react to being adopted and know the kind of information and support adoptees need. Years ago, the fact that a child was adopted was often hidden, and the child was not encouraged to talk about it. It makes sense that the child who couldn't ask a question about her birth parents without her adoptive parents responding, "Why do you want to know that? Don't you love us?" may have had more difficulty reconciling her adoption than the child whose parents were open and not threatened by discussions about adoption or birth parents. Years ago, adoption workers gave parents the advice that they thought was best, and parents followed it believing it was best for their families. We now have other theories about adoption, based on research and experience, that seem to result in healthier families. There is certainly evidence that the more comfortable parents are with infertility (if that is an issue), adoption, and parenting in general; the more support they receive when adopting; and the more open and empathic they are in discussing adoption with their children, the better adjusted the children will be. Furthermore, some people suggest that the process of working through the issues raised by adoption can lead to positive personal growth.

Strengths Drawn from Adoption

Although there has been no research on the beneficial impact of being adopted, some people suggest that certain adoptees not only may overcome adversity, but may grow as a result. Having learned how to feel comfortable in a family in which they do not share genetics, physical characteristics, temperament, or perhaps race and culture, some adoptees find that they also know how to adjust to new situations or to feel comfortable in a wide range of situations and with a wide variety of people.

Joyce Maguire Pavao, a therapist specializing in adoption issues who is an adoptee herself, has been intrigued by the large number of adoptees who pursue individual sports, such as swimming, diving, ice skating, and track. Peter and Kitty Caruthers and Scott Hamilton, Olympic medalists in ice skating; Greg Louganis, Olympic medalist in diving; and Dan O'Brien, Olympic champion decathlete are among the adoptees who have achieved international recognition in individual sports. Although some have speculated that some adoptees may be "overachievers" as a way to prove themselves worthy of having been adopted, Pavao thinks that some adoptees unknowingly turn to activities like sports or music that require a high degree of concentration and discipline or have meditative qualities as a way to help them deal with the distractions that adoption issues can create. These distractions arise from adoptees wondering about their origins, the circumstances of their conception, the reasons they were placed for adoption, their genetic heritage, and what it means to them and to society that they have been adopted. In addition, by developing a high degree of skill in a particular discipline, adoptees may develop a sense of identity that comes from nurturing their innate abilities, which can be important as they struggle with their sense of self-concept.

It is also conceivable that by learning to deal with the uncertainties of their own origins, some adoptees become more comfortable with ambiguity. By coming to peace with their feeling that their lives are not within their control, some learn how to let go of the need for control; by searching for answers to which parts of their identity are influenced by heredity and which by environment, some learn to see issues from several points of view; and by struggling to understand how their birth mothers could have relinquished them, some may learn how to develop empathy with other people, even when they have been hurt.

Adoption is Complicated

Some people may describe adoption as *difficult;* others simply describe it as *different.* I am inclined to think of it as complex. The human experience itself is complex, and being adopted is just one variation. As adoptive parents, we sometimes wonder why raising children by adoption has to be complicated. Why do we have to read all the child-rearing manuals, *plus* the adoption manuals? Why can't we just take our children home, love them, and have that be enough? I suspect that no parenting experience is simple or easy. We may be fortunate to face parenting issues that are so unique that we are clearly aware of them. We are fortunate to have looked so hard at why we wanted to become parents and to have concluded that we want to be nurturers. We are fortunate to realize that attachments between people develop as a result of positive interactions. We are fortunate to know how important environment is in raising children—as well as how imperative it is not to think that we can mold our children into some predetermined ideal. We are fortunate to begin parenting with the understanding that children have losses that they will feel deeply and to know that sometimes we cannot prevent their pain, but that we can be there to comfort them. Yes, other parents may simply take their children home and love them, but all this reflection that we do as adoptive parents—all the questioning and examining of ourselves and of the concept of family and all our effort to see the world through the eyes of our children, rather than through our own childhood experiences—will make us more effective parents and bring us closer to our children.

7

The Important Family History

Ellen developed vaginal cancer at the age of twenty-four. An adoptee, she did not know until later that her birth mother had taken the synthetic estrogen diethyl-Stilbestrol (DES) during her pregnancy and, consequently, that she should have the more thorough screening for cervical and vaginal cancer recommended for daughters of DES mothers. She believes her cancer could have been diagnosed earlier had she known her medical history.

Adoptive parents should have a complete medical, social, and psychological history of their child, including information about the pregnancy of the birth mother and the child's birth. There should also be a way to update this information when new conditions in the birth family are discovered. In some cases, the information in the family history is vital to diagnosing disease or providing genetic counseling. More commonly, the information is helpful, but not essential. Perhaps the most important reason for having a complete family history is peace of mind for the adoptee and his parents.

Nonetheless, adoptees have a moral right to information they would have had if they had not been adopted, especially when the information is related to their physical or mental health.

The Medical History

Physicians and hospitals typically request that patients provide their family medical histories on lengthy forms. But when an adoptee or adoptive parent indicates that such information is unavailable, the health professional may be quick to reassure the patient or parent that the history probably won't be needed. One is left wondering why such a long form is provided if there really is so little need for it.

Most health care personnel are trained to take a complete medical history. In practice, though, some use such histories more than others, depending on their style of practice, the complaint of the patient, and the physician's specialty.

Inherited Medical Conditions

Most people recognize the importance of a family medical history when there are inherited diseases in the family, such as sickle-cell anemia, Tay-Sachs disease, cystic fibrosis, hemophilia, or Huntington's chorea. Fortunately the incidence of inherited diseases such as these is relatively small. Although a physician should be able to diagnose these problems without a family history, it is helpful to the physician to know whether the condition he suspects the patient has has been diagnosed in other members of the family. Even when the person does not have the disease, he may want to know if he is a carrier.

People with a chance of inheriting a medical condition should know how the disease is transmitted, what their chances are of developing the disease or being a carrier, what their chances are of passing the disease on to their children, if there are tests to determine whether the person is a carrier or whether the person has the disease before developing symptoms, and if the disease can be detected in the fetus.

—*Dominant genetic traits.* If either parent has a gene for such a disease, the child has a 50 percent chance of having it. Since symptoms for some dominant traits, such as Huntington's chorea, do not show up until middle age, a person should know whether he is at risk for developing the disease before he reproduces and possibly passes the trait on to his children. Although screening tests are not available for all dominant traits, a person who knows that he has a fifty-fifty chance of developing the disease is in a better position to make reproductive decisions than the person who does not.

—*Recessive genetic traits.* Children of parents who both have a recessive gene for a disease have a 25 percent chance of having the disease and a 50 percent chance of being carriers without having any symptoms of the disease. With some diseases, such as sickle-cell anemia, a test can be performed to determine if the person is a carrier—information that may influence that person's decision about whether to have children. It is also possible to detect certain diseases, such as Tay-Sachs disease, in an unborn fetus using amniocentesis if a parent is known to be a carrier.

—*Sex-linked recessive traits.* With such conditions as color blindness and hemophilia, the male offspring of a carrier mother and noncarrier father will develop the condition, but the female offspring will not. For the daughter to have the disease, she must be the offspring of a carrier mother and a father with the disease.

If there are inheritable genetic conditions, both the birth family and the adoptee need to know. For example, if an adoptee is discovered to have cystic fibrosis, a recessive trait, his birth parents should be told that they are carriers for the sake of other children they may have. And even though an adoptee may not develop a genetic disease, he should know if there is a possibility of his being a carrier for one, for the sake of his children.

Familial Medical Conditions

Some medical conditions are not directly inherited, but run in families and have genetic components. For example, certain forms of breast cancer result from gene abnormalities that tend to run in families. Some forms of lung cancer, ovarian cancer, and pancreatic cancer are also more prevalent in certain families. With some of these diseases, a known family history indicates specific early screening techniques or treatments that would be unnecessary for people without that risk factor. Although only a small percentage of people have family histories of such diseases, for them, thorough, up-to-date family histories could save their lives. More often, knowing that there is a family history of diseases that run in families, such as diabetes or heart disease, may help a physician make a diagnosis, but would not be essential.

A family medical history is helpful, but not essential, in determining the cause of learning problems, including language and hearing disorders. Some learning problems are genetic or familial. Knowledge about the mother's pregnancy, such as whether she consumed alcohol or took certain drugs, can also help determine the cause of some learning or behavioral problems.

Sometimes the absence of a family medical history of rare or inherited diseases is not as frustrating as the absence of common knowledge about the birth parents. For example, if a child appears to be growing slowly, it helps to know whether both birth parents were short. Without that information, the physician is more likely to order tests to discover if some disease is retarding the child's growth.

A pregnant adoptee is often curious about her birth mother's experience with pregnancy. Although decisions about the care of the pregnant adoptee will be made on the basis of her individual physical and medical condition, it can help to know, for example, if the birth mother had a narrow pelvis or a history of short labor.

The family medical history is most useful in preventive health care. For example, if a family has a history of heart disease, a physician may be more aggressive in ordering annual tests that could predict future heart problems and in advising the patient on diet and exercise that could prevent heart disease. Once a person has a heart attack, however, knowing that the family has a history of heart attacks doesn't alter the treatment.

Children of an Incestuous Relationship

Adoptive parents should be told if their child's parents were closely related so they can have their child evaluated for genetic abnormalities that may result from incest. Some of the problems can be diagnosed before any signs or symptoms appear if geneticists know to look for them. Since the diagnostic and evaluation procedures are the same whether the parents were first cousins or father and daughter, it isn't necessary to know the exact relationship between the birth parents.

Geneticist Barbara McGillivray believes that a history of incest should be suspected more often than it is when a girl decides to place a child for adoption, particularly if she is young and not clear about the identity of the birth father. Agencies should probe for a more definite indication of the relationship of the birth parents whose child is being placed for adoption so the adoptive parents can be told if a medical evaluation is needed. While there are no statistics showing that children who are born of an incestuous union are more likely to be placed for adoption, the family of a pregnant girl is probably less likely to welcome a child born of a brother-sister or father-daughter relationship than a child born under other circumstances.

McGillivray and Patricia A. Baird, also a geneticist, found that of twenty-one children referred to them by an adoption agency because of a history of incest, nine had serious abnormalities that were thought to be genetic, including mental retardation, cleft lip and palate, congenital heart defect, neurofibromatosis, and delayed development. This is a much higher proportion than would be expected in the general population. Some of the nine had no outward symptoms of the problems. Three of the twenty-one had abnormalities that were not thought to be genetic, and nine were normal.

Children born of an incestuous relationship have a greater chance of having an abnormality because their parents have a greater chance of having the same recessive gene for an abnormality. If parents have the same recessive gene, their children have a 25 percent chance of being affected.

Parents with a child who is suspected of being the offspring of an incestuous relationship should have the child evaluated by a geneticist. The family physician or pediatrician can refer them to the closest medical center for a genetic evaluation of the child. Such an evaluation should be done soon after birth, and the child should have more thorough medical tests as he grows. Most of the children in McGillivray and Baird's study appeared normal, and some diagnostic tests would not have been done on them had it not been known that their parents were closely related.

When the Family History Is Not Available

Heather's pediatrician told her parents to bring Heather in each year for extensive laboratory tests because her family medical history was unknown. While some physicians advocate more vigorous screening tests, others think that no screening is necessary. Still others advise parents to have inexpensive tests for hearing, vision, anemia, and urinary tract disorders done on their children, but to save the time-consuming and expensive tests until there is some sign that they are needed. Certainly a physician should be more suspicious if there is no medical history on a patient and should not dismiss the possibility that the person may have a rare or unusual condition.

Adoptive parents may want to set up an appointment with their physician aside from their regular visits just to discuss how the physician intends to deal with the lack of a medical history—how important he thinks it is, whether he is willing to contact the agency for additional information, and whether he thinks some screening tests are indicated periodically.

Inheritance and Behavior

In recent years, magazines and newspapers have been filled with stories about the inheritance of conditions such as alcoholism, schizophrenia, and depression, and behaviors or personality traits such as "criminality," "thrill seeking" or even "happiness." Although there is certainly evidence that some mental illnesses and behaviors have genetic components, no one is saying that children are "doomed" to develop in a certain way because a birth relative had a particular psychological condition or behavioral trait.

It is unlikely that a single gene is responsible for any one mental illness or behavioral trait. When genetics is a factor, it is likely that many genes, each with a subtle effect, combine to produce a recognizable trait. Biological relatives may be more likely than biological strangers to inherit all the genes needed to develop a particular behavior, but it is obviously much less likely that the same *combination* of genes than a single gene will be passed on. Even then, scientists believe that environment still plays a major role—that some genetic effects must be "triggered" by the environment. For example, if one twin has schizophrenia, his identical twin has a greater risk of developing schizophrenia, but actually develops the disorder less than half the time. For people who are biologically related but not identical twins and are raised in different environments, the risks are much less, although they may still be higher than in the general population.

It is also important to remember that researchers are finding different forms of many illnesses. Just as some forms of breast cancer are familial and some are not, some forms of alcoholism or depression may have genetic components, while others may not.

Simply knowing that a biological relative was alcoholic isn't enough information for a parent to determine an adoptee's risk of developing alcoholism. At the same time, just because an adoptee is at a greater risk of developing a disorder does not predict his behavior.

Many mental illnesses can be treated and controlled if they are diagnosed correctly. A good family history can be helpful in making a correct diagnosis, but it isn't essential. Furthermore, information is not helpful unless it is accurate, complete, and up to date.

Genetic Counseling for the Adoptive Family

Even if they are willing to do so, most social workers, lawyers, and even physicians are not qualified to obtain the kind of history of the birth parents that is needed. There is more involved than just asking the birth parents if there is any mental illness in the family. Ask a fifteen-year-old girl if anyone in her family has ever been depressed, and she will be likely to answer yes. But that doesn't mean there is anyone in her family who has been diagnosed as having a clinical depression, as psychiatrists use the term; nor does it differentiate between depression and the depressive phase of manic-depressive illness. An alcoholic is not likely to admit his problem to himself, much less to a social worker. The first requirement of a genetic counseling program is that there be accurate diagnoses. Therefore, adoption agencies that want to provide genetic information will need the assistance of geneticists, psychiatrists, or both. Geneticists also have to be available to explain the diseases and the risks of diseases to adoptive families. It isn't enough to provide information; parents need help interpreting that information.

Obtaining a complete history of the adoptee is an ongoing process. Most of the psychiatric problems and many physical diseases that have genetic components do not develop until after adolescence. The teenage parents who placed their child for adoption may not have shown signs of schizophrenia or heart disease, for example. That is one more reason why it is so important for adoptees and their birth families to have a means of communicating.

Attitudes and Expectations

The adage *A little knowledge is a dangerous thing* can be particularly true with regard to genetics and adoption. Some people, including some psychiatrists, believe that adoptive parents should not know if their child's birth parents had a history of mental illness. They are concerned that the adoptive parents will hover over the child and worry about every unusual behavior, creating psychological problems when there may be none. They are also concerned that adoptive parents may expect certain behaviors or traits in their children on the basis of what they know about the birth parents, and that a child who grows up with parents who are fearful that he will become an alcoholic, for example, will fulfill his parents' expectations.

Furthermore, too much emphasis on the *cause* of a child's behavior can distract us from dealing with the problem itself. For example, Attention Deficit Disorder (ADD) seems to run in families and to have strong biological components, so it may be helpful in diagnosing a child to know that his birth father had ADD. At the same time, when it comes to helping the child get treatment or learn strategies for coping with ADD, it makes little difference whether he "got" his ADD from his birth father, from his birth mother, or in some other way.

Social workers are concerned that the growing emphasis on genetic influences will return us to a time when adoptees were considered "bad seeds," doomed to grow up like their "undesirable" birth parents. While it is unreasonable for adoptive parents to think that genetics will have no influence on their children and that they can "mold" their children to be like them, it is also unreasonable to blame genetics for any characteristics in their children that they don't like. The outdated idea that traits, abilities, and behaviors are influenced solely by the environment in which children are raised is an appealing concept when children develop exactly as their parents want them to. When they do not—which is usually the case—an environmentalist position can be a tremendous psychological burden for parents. When there are serious behavioral problems, such as a conduct disorder; a condition that carries social stigma, such as mental illness; or even a physical illness that causes pain and suffering, there can be a powerful temptation for parents to absolve themselves of responsibility by blaming genetics. As human beings, it is natural for us to want to know *why* something happens. We are curious, and human behavior gives us much material to think about. Nonetheless, as adoptive parents, we have to be cautious about compartmentalizing our children. Each one is a unique individual, and we must be sure we communicate to our children that we love each one as an individual and as a whole human being—not just the parts that we influenced.

8

Contact with Biological Relatives

When the first edition of this book was published in 1986, the idea that adoptive families and birth families would communicate with each other—perhaps even know each other's identities—was relatively new and highly controversial. Since that time, it has become commonplace for birth parents to select the parents they want to adopt their children; for birth parents to request and receive periodic updates on the children, including letters from the adoptive families and photographs of the children; and for birth families and adoptive families to exchange identifying information, have direct contact with each other as the children grow up, and, in some cases, to develop close relationships. Even people who have adopted from overseas in recent years have made efforts to establish or maintain contact with their children's birth parents.

Within the adoption community, these practices are seen as beneficial to adoptees, birth parents, and adoptive parents. Many adoption facilitators who once had misgivings about *open adoption* (in which the birth family and adoptive family communicate directly) and *semiopen adoption* (in which communication is handled through an intermediary) have had sufficient experience with them to see their many advantages and to learn ways of overcoming the disadvantages. Many adoptive parents who approached openness with reservations have become advocates of the practice after finding that their worst fears did not materialize. Even adoptive parents who have had difficult experiences with the birth parents seldom denounce the practice, but look for ways in which their relationship with the birth parents could have been different.

Those who do not have much experience with open adoption, however, are often skeptical of the wisdom of it. Prospective adoptive parents, as well as their families and friends, often have misgivings about having contact with their child's birth parents, but are willing to consider it if that's what it takes to get a baby. Adoptive parents and those who are close to them worry that if the birth parents know the child's whereabouts, they will kidnap the child. They're afraid that if the child knows her birth parents, she will be confused about who her parents are, have divided loyalties, or love the birth parents more than her adoptive parents. Even birth parents and their friends and family members can be skeptical. They worry that the birth parents will not be able to move beyond this profoundly deep loss if they continue to see their child or that they will regret their decision and want the child back, but not be able to get her back.

Adoptive parents should not agree to open adoption if they view it just as a way to get a baby. Nor should birth parents consider open adoption as a kind of compromise—a way to mitigate the pain of relinquishment. Before entering into open adoption, the adoptive parents and birth parents need to understand that while there are benefits to them, open adoptions should be entered into because there are benefits for the adoptee. Both adoptive parents and birth parents need to be committed to maintaining their relationship even when it is complicated or difficult because they are committed to meeting the child's needs.

Disadvantages of Confidential Adoption

To understand the benefits of open adoption, it is first necessary to understand the history of confidential adoption and its limits. Confidential adoptions began in the first quarter of this century as a way to protect birth mothers and adoptees from unforgiving public attitudes toward them. Sealed adoption records kept birth parents and adoptees from suddenly appearing in each other's lives to reveal the truth.

As society's attitudes changed, the fact that a child was adopted became common knowledge in the community. Birth parents stayed in their communities through their pregnancies. The original need to keep the birth parents away from the adoptee so the secret of her origin would not be revealed became unnecessary.

At the same time, we began to learn more about what it was like for children to grow up having been cut off from their origins. We learned that this was a significant loss unrelated to how much adoptees loved their parents. We learned that adopted children sometimes felt abandoned, unwanted, and rejected by their birth parents; that it was more difficult for them to form a personal identity when they had little information about their genetic origins; and that they developed fantasies—sometimes troubling ones—to fill in the missing pieces in their personal histories.

Although many adoptees in confidential adoptions worked through these challenges successfully, some people began to wonder whether it was necessary for adoptees to have these challenges when the original reason for keeping adoptions confidential was no longer valid. Open adoptions have developed as a result.

It would be a mistake to suggest that open adoption is a cure-all for the deficiencies of confidential adoption. Open adoption provides adoptees with the opportunity to know they are loved and valued by the people who gave them life. But there is nothing about exchanging letters, photographs, or names and addresses that will guarantee this feeling. Only a relationship can accomplish it. For open adoption to be effective, both the adoptive and birth family have to understand that its primary purpose is to benefit the child. This means that even when the relationship is difficult, each person makes an effort to work through the problems.

There is no question that in most families, open adoption is going to add complications because relationships are complicated. But that doesn't justify avoiding or discarding it. When we adopt, we sign up not only for a different way of *forming* a family, but for a different way of *being* a family. Our children have unique needs that nonadopted children do not have, and we must make a commitment to do whatever is necessary to meet those needs.

The same is true for birth families. Open adoption, as an ongoing responsibility of the birth family, is more complicated than relinquishing a child. Birth parents have to figure out what their role and relationship are with the child whom they are not parenting but are still involved with. It is not similar to being a noncustodial parent after a divorce. Nor is it just another relationship in their lives—one they can participate in when they feel like it and let lapse when they don't. Becoming involved in an open adoption is a commitment to the child, and it is as important ethically as providing a complete medical history and naming the correct birth father.

The Open Adoption Relationship

In our book, *The Open Adoption Experience*, Sharon Kaplan Roszia and I describe the open adoption relationship as being like the relationship people have with their in-laws. This comparison has been echoed by many people who are familiar with open adoption. The birth family and the adoptive family may not share the same lifestyle or political views. We may find each other exasperating. We may have different values or not enjoy the same jokes. However, we make the effort to build a relationship because we have in common the love of a single person. In marriage, our spouses are connected to their families, regardless of whether we like them or not. Their families fill a part of their lives that we can never fill. They have a connection that precedes ours and is independent of ours, whether we acknowledge it or not. Usually, however, we recognize that it would be a tragic and unnecessary loss for our spouses to have to give up the relationship with their family of origin to form a new family with us.

Similarly, our children have a connection to their birth parents that precedes their connection to us and is independent of their relationship with us. Although adoption law says that when the birth parents relinquish their parental rights, it is as though their relationship never existed, that is not possible biologically, psychologically, or spiritually. It is a tragic and unnecessary loss for the adoptee to have to give up honoring her connections to her family of origin to gain adoptive parents and a family. Adoptive parents and birth parents validate the adoptee when they acknowledge this reality and make the effort to maintain those connections.

When we get married, we are looking more for a partner than for in-laws. The idea of in-laws may even be intimidating. We've heard stories of the interfering mother-in-law or the spouse who couldn't let go of the apron strings and commit to the relationship.

These are many of the same worries prospective adoptive parents have with open adoption. They worry that the child will be confused about who her parents are or play one set of parents against the other. They worry about losing their privacy if the birth parents call or visit. They worry that the birth parents won't be able to let go of the child—that they will want the child back. They worry that they will be constantly competing with the birth parents for their child's love.

All adoptive parents, whether in a confidential adoption or an open adoption, fear that they will someday lose their children physically or emotionally to the birth parents. They fear that if they are measured against the birth parents, they may be found inadequate. With confidential adoption, however, adoptive parents did not have to confront these fears. They could ignore their own insecurities because confidentiality ensured that their children would never be able to know the birth parents and therefore love them or compare them to the adoptive parents.

Many adoptive parents have gained the confidence to overcome these fears by experiencing the closeness that grew between them and their children, having faith that this was genuine and not a temporary substitute for the "real thing": love between children and their birth parents. They felt their relationship grow through the challenges and crises and joys and pleasures of family life and realized that however imperfect they might be as parents, their relationships with their children were real and strong. They watched their children grow and develop and realized that to honor their children, they had to honor everything about them, including their connections to the other people who helped shape them. Once afraid of the birth parents, these adoptive parents yearned for a way to let their children's birth parents know what wonderful children they brought into the world and what wonderful human beings the children were becoming. Some felt that by knowing the birth parents, they might come to know their children better. Many felt spiritually connected to the birth parents, realizing that they all had a part in the children's development. From the spiritual connection they felt, they began to recognize what that connection is like for adoptees.

Prospective adoptive parents, however, do not yet have a relationship with their children. Many of them are particularly vulnerable to the possible physical or emotional loss of their children to the birth parents because they may have already suffered infertility, pregnancy loss, or potential adoptions in which the birth parents decided to raise the children themselves. They still want an experience that is as close as possible to what they can't have: giving birth to a biological child. To accept open adoption, they need to acknowledge their fears and go about gathering information that will mitigate those fears. They need to learn, for example, how adoptive parents and their children form attachments and why these attachments are every bit as strong as those in families that are formed by birth (see Chapter 3). They need to realize that although confidential adoption was begun to protect birth parents and adoptees from society's attitudes, the barrier of it came to be interpreted as necessary to protect adoptees from the birth parents and the birth parents from the adoptees and hence was believed to be necessary for adoptive families to feel secure and authentic.

Prospective adoptive parents need to understand that by adopting they are taking on a parenting experience that differs in significant ways from those of parents who give birth, but is deeply satisfying in its own way. They need to understand the importance of entitlement (discussed in Chapter 1), recognizing that their authenticity as parents of their children comes from their commitment and relationship, rather than from biology, but is every bit as valid. Once they see that this is not a second-best kind of parenting or parenting experience, but a unique experience all its own, the presence of the birth parents in their children's lives is no longer as threatening, nor are they resentful of the "complications" that come from including the birth parents in their lives. They have achieved the kind of change of heart that is essential not only for successful open adoption, but for successful adoption.

Birth parents also have to understand what their role will be in an open adoption. Some birth parents think that open adoption is a way to avoid completely "losing" the children. Although the birth parent who can see her child blossoming as a result of receiving the kind of loving care that the adoptive parents give certainly gains peace of mind, there is still an enormous loss involved in not being the parent who is raising that child. Birth parents who do not realize this may not be prepared for the grief that is part of an open adoption.

Whether the birth parent who continues to see her child has more difficulty grieving is something that we need to learn more about. Janelle, a birth mother who saw her child regularly during the first year after the placement, said when she was alone and grieving, it was easy to fantasize about being able to take care of her daughter. However, when she saw her daughter thriving in her adoptive family, she knew she could not give her daughter what she needed. Mariel, however, had a different experience. Seeing her daughter was too painful. It may be an individual matter—some birth parents may grieve more while others find it helpful in resolving the loss to see the child thriving in the adoptive family. Perhaps those who have more difficulty grieving were expecting less of a sense of loss. Or perhaps birth parents who are in contact with their children after placement are forced to confront their feelings rather than suppress them as birth mothers in confidential adoptions were often encouraged to do, so it may seem more difficult. In fact, it may be more difficult in the short term, but healthier in the long run. More research needs to be done in this area.

Sometimes open adoption is viewed as a kind of "bonus" that is given to birth parents—they are allowed to have contact with their children if they want it and if the adoptive parents are gracious enough to agree. As a result, when birth parents find that seeing their children is difficult, either emotionally or logistically, or when adoptive parents find it inconvenient to maintain the relationship, there is sometimes a presumption that it is all right to discontinue the contact. It can't be emphasized enough that birth parents and adoptive parents have to be committed to open adoption for the benefits it will provide children over their lifetime.

While some birth parents choose open adoption as a kind of compromise, and some as a bonus, others recognize that there is an overwhelming loss with open adoption, but that they will be able to bear it if they are able to have contact with their children. Their fear is that after trusting the adoptive parents to maintain contact with them, the adoptive parents will betray them, cutting off contact.

It is true that in most states, open adoptions are not legally enforceable. Their preservation depends on the commitment of the adoptive parents and birth parents. Open adoption tends to be successful when adoptive parents and birth parents:

- are committed to openness for the sake of the children
- understand, respect, and affirm their own roles and that of the other family
- have a unified, understood vision of how the open adoption will proceed, but recognize the need to be flexible as situations change
- see open adoption as a relationship that will have ups and downs and will grow and change, but is not fundamentally different from other relationships.

Setting Rules for Contact

Adoptive parents sometimes wonder how to set limits with members of the birth family who are intrusive, who do not recognize their boundaries, or who request more contact than the adoptive parents want to have. When the adoptive parents have a clear sense of entitlement and understand that the birth parents relinquished their parenting role, but not their connections to the child, they do not feel powerless to set limits with members of the birth family. They realize that open adoption is not coparenting or joint custody. They view open adoption as an ethical obligation to their child, not some kind of "compensation" to the birth parents for entrusting their child to them, or "gift" that they are giving and can withhold if they like.

Adoptive parents may feel they can't say no to birth parents who visit at an inconvenient time because *these birth parents gave them their child.* They can never "repay" the birth parents for their gift—how can they begrudge them a visit . . . another photograph . . . a simple phone call. But the adoptive parents do not need to go beyond what they feel comfortable doing to accommodate the birth parents because they feel guilty. Furthermore, they cannot "repay" the birth parents for the child, and to equate compensation with a photograph or a phone call trivializes the relinquishment.

Open adoption relationships take many forms, just as relationships with in-laws do. Some are reserved and polite while others are intimate. Just as we do in our own families, some adoptive parents have a closer relationship with some members of their children's birth families than with others. Marianne and Larry include their child's birth mothers in their family; they have even gone on family vacations together. Julie and Chris don't have a lot in common with their son's birth parents and live too far apart to get together often enough to get to know each other well; they work hard at the relationship, but it still feels awkward.

There are no "rules" for the relationships in open adoption beyond those that we have in any family relationship—to be respectful, communicative, and forgiving. When the birth parents or adoptive parents do not even follow these basic rules, the adoptee suffers. Unfortunately, that sometimes happens. Adoptive parents who agreed to open adoption because they saw it as a necessity and have not worked through the fears that open adoption raises sometimes cut off contact with the birth parents after the adoption is finalized. This becomes an additional loss for the birth parents and ultimately for the adoptees. Birth parents who have faced this situation have sometimes been successful in getting the adoptive parents to live up to their responsibilities by engaging an intermediary, such as a social worker or therapist, who can help them negotiate what is basically a crisis in the relationship.

However, sometimes it is the birth parents who threaten the future of the relationship by unacceptable behavior, including, in rare cases, behavior that could be damaging to the children's welfare. Of course, sometimes there is a fine line between behavior that is annoying and behavior that is intrusive. Sometimes the adoptive parents argue that the birth parents are upsetting the children when it is the adoptive parents who are upset. Sometimes a child who is withdrawn or sad after a birth parent's visit is having a normal grief reaction to issues that are part of the adoption experience, rather than a negative reaction to the birth parent. It is important for the adoptive parents to determine how disruptive or harmful the birth parent's behavior actually is and be creative about ways to set limits without ending the relationship.

When the relationship is harmful and adoptive parents have exhausted the resources available to people who are trying to improve their relationship, the adoptive parents may determine that the relationship cannot be maintained—at least at this time. They can let the birth parents know the conditions for a relationship, such as that they remain drug-free. If necessary, they can take steps to protect themselves, such as getting a restraining order. In most cases, however, the mechanism for staying in contact with one another can remain in place until some time in the future when contact is again reasonable.

When Interest in Contact Wanes

It is not unusual for the birth parents in an open adoption to communicate frequently with the adoptive parents during the first year or so after placement. They may find that frequent contact helps them work through their grief. They need reassurance that they made the right decision, and they get it when they see the child growing and thriving in his adoptive family. It is also not unusual, however, for the birth parents' involvement with the child to begin to wane after a time as they move on with their lives. This can be a frustrating and sad situation for the adoptive family, even if they didn't welcome an open adoption at the beginning. Once the adoptive parents have built a strong attachment with their child and gained a strong sense of entitlement, the birth parents are far less threatening and are often viewed by the adoptive parents as the valuable resource to their child that they are.

Adoptive parents need to recognize that, as in any relationship, there will be times when they have more contact with the birth parents than at other times. Because the birth parents may be getting messages from their friends or relatives that they should not "interfere" with the adoptive family, it is important for the adoptive parents to communicate clearly to the birth parents how valuable they are to the adoptee and reiterate that open adoption is primarily for the child. It is also important for the adoptive parents to communicate to the birth parents the importance of staying in touch with each other even when frequent contact is difficult. Adoptive parents often find that other birth relatives, particularly birth grandparents, are more constant, perhaps because they are in a more stable period of their lives than the birth parents. Furthermore, while the birth parents may not be ready to be parents, the birth grandparents may be able and willing to be grandparents. They, too, can be welcomed into the "extended family" of the adoptee, providing information to the adoptive family and maintaining those important ties. Madeline's daughter Beth had run away from home when she was sixteen and called home only when she was in a crisis. Her pregnancy was such a time. Madeline, who had adopted Beth from the foster care system when Beth was eight, knew that her daughter could not raise a child, and although she was willing to help her, she could foresee struggles between them over what was best for the child. She encouraged Beth to make an adoption plan, which Beth did. After selecting a couple in an open adoption, Beth disappeared again. Madeline, however, has stayed in regular contact with the adoptive family and her grandchild.

One of the most difficult concepts that adoptive parents may have to communicate to their child is that their birth parents chose not to have contact with her when they had the opportunity to do so. The child may interpret this information as further rejection or abandonment. The adoptive parents can let the birth parents know how hurtful it may be to the adoptee if the birth parents have no contact with her and can encourage them to stay in touch. If their attempt to maintain contact is not successful, the adoptive parents can validate the adoptee's feelings that the lack of contact is hurtful and affirm her value by saying something like, "Your birth parents sure are missing out on knowing a neat kid."

Sometimes the adoptee is not interested in maintaining contact with the birth parent or doesn't follow through on the interest he has. It may be hard for her to write to someone whom she sees only once a year, for example. The adoptive parents and the birth parents should not expect a minor child to take responsibility for maintaining contact. The agreement to stay in contact was made by adults and should be carried out by the adults involved. The child needs to understand that contract, but it isn't up to her to live up to it. For example, the adoptive parents should let the child know that it is all right for her to send a birthday card to her birth mother, but they shouldn't nag at her to send one. It should be the child's choice, within the limits of the agreement. If she doesn't choose to do so, it's up to the adoptive parents to communicate with the birth parent. The situation is not much different from that of a child and her grandparents. Often the child who lives a great distance from her grandparents and doesn't know them well can't remember to send them birthday cards or a school picture. Rather than nag the child, most parents just sign the child's name and enclose the photograph. And just as they don't interpret a child's lack of interest in the grandparents as a sign that they should cut off all contact between the grandchild and grandparents, adoptive parents shouldn't decide against open adoption just because the child does not maintain enthusiasm about it. It's best to let the child determine how active a role she wants in having contact with the birth parent, but the adoptive parents should maintain the relationship so it's there when the adoptee is ready to take a more active part in it.

Semiopen Adoption

Some adoptive parents believe that semiopen adoption, in which the birth parents and adoptive parents communicate anonymously through an intermediary, offers the best of both worlds—a means of communicating with the birth parents without fear of intrusion or competition. But semiopen adoption does not eliminate the concerns that adoptive parents have with open adoption any more than confidential adoption does. Any fears the adoptive parents have of the birth parents, any misgivings that their child may love the birth parents more or prefer them if given the chance, and any desire to eliminate or minimize the complexities that adoption brings must be dealt with regardless of the kind or frequency of contact between the birth family and the adoptive family. Although semiopen adoption initially gives adoptive parents a sense of emotional safety, a study conducted by Ruth McRoy, Harold Grotevant, and Susan Ayers-Lopez found that four to twelve years after the placement, adoptive parents in semiopen adoption were more fearful of the birth parents, had less sense of entitlement, and had less satisfaction about the amount of control they had than did adoptive parents in either confidential or fully disclosed (open) adoption. It may be that when their children get old enough to begin asking questions about their adoption, adoptive parents realize that semiopen adoption does not have the "safeguards" of confidentiality—it would not take much for the semiopen adoption to become fully open, especially if their child began demanding it. Without the reassurance that parents in open adoption have of knowing the birth parents and trusting them, parents in semiopen adoption may feel more vulnerable.

An additional disadvantage of semiopen adoption is that the child is not always involved in the communication. In the same study, about half the adoptive families involved in semiopen adoption had not yet shared the letters from the birth mothers with their children. When children don't participate personally in the relationship with their birth parents, they don't realize the benefits. They don't have a chance to get their questions answered, to be reassured that their birth parents did care about them, or to grow up integrating their relationship with their birth parents into their lives as their understanding of adoption grows.

Semiopen adoption can be a good intermediate step. Since it is natural for adoptive parents to feel vulnerable early in the adoption, they can use the opportunities for communication in a semiopen adoption to develop a trusting relationship with the birth parents.

Then, as they build attachment with their child and gain a sense of entitlement, it may seem natural to move from communication through an intermediary to direct communication. The adoptee then gains the benefits of having direct contact with her birth parents.

Open Adoption with Older Child Adoptions

Parents are finding that open adoption can have benefits for children who are adopted at an older age. Although it may seem that children would not want to have contact with birth parents who had neglected them or been abusive, we are learning that connections are deep. Children can love parents who are abusive, inconsistent, or neglectful. And even parents who love their children can hurt them. These children sometimes feel disloyal to their birth parents when they are adopted and resist building attachment to their adoptive parents. However, if they are able to maintain connections with their birth parents—and with other biological relatives (who may not have hurt them)—these children sometimes feel freer to accept love and nurturing from their adoptive parents.

For more detailed information on open adoption relationships, including open adoption with relative adoptions, older child adoptions, and international adoptions, see *The Open Adoption Experience.*

Contact with the Adult Adoptee

The adult adoptee is able to make her own decisions about whether to have contact with her birth parents. She does not have to consult her adoptive parents or get their permission. Nevertheless, the feelings of the adoptive parents are important to most adoptees in confidential placements who consider searching for their birth parents. Many adoptees delay searching until after the deaths of their adoptive parents, so concerned are they not to hurt them. Others just do not tell their adoptive parents that they are trying to meet their birth parents.

In some respects, a meeting between the birth parents and the adoptee can be more threatening to us after our son or daughter reaches adulthood than it is when they were young. We often view ourselves as nurturers. Once our son or daughter leaves home, we may be concerned about our future relationship with them. If our grown children no longer need nurturing, is there a need for us? If there is no blood tie, will our son or daughter come home? If an adoptee begins her adult life by searching for her birth parents, these fears can be even greater.

Why Adoptees Search

It isn't unusual for adoptive parents to wonder why their children want to find their birth parents, particularly if there is no medical emergency requiring information from the birth parents. We wonder if the adoptee has been dissatisfied with her life all along or if she doesn't really love us. We wonder if the desire to search reflects a psychological problem. We wonder if we have failed her— told her too soon or too late that she was adopted or not explained her adoption in the right way.

Studies have tried to discover why some adoptees search for their birth parents and have come up with a variety of results. Some have found that adoptees who search have psychological problems, whereas others have concluded that the desire to find the birth parents is normal and understandable.

We simply don't know why some adoptees search and others don't, mainly because it is hard to get a good representative sample of adoptees who are searching and a control group of those who aren't. Researchers end up studying people who have replied to an advertisement or letter, perhaps because they want to be studied. It's difficult to draw generalizations from such self-selected populations.

What we do know is that a desire for information about their genetic and social origins is not unusual in adoptees, nor does it reflect an abnormal adjustment to adoption. Many adoptees who are searching for their birth parents are not looking for a father or mother, but for information. For some reason, they have decided that the best way to obtain the information is to talk directly to the birth parents. For some adoptees, the development of a relationship with their birth parents is the goal of the search, although that relationship is not meant to supplant the one they have with their adoptive parents.

There are other, more intangible, reasons why adoptees search, however. Adoptees speak of the need to reestablish connections that every other person has—connections not only to parents but to "clan," to ancestors and siblings. They speak of wanting to fill in the missing parts of their lives so they can feel "whole." They speak of the desire to be "mirrored," to see themselves reflected in people who resemble them. They talk about wanting to know what traits they might have inherited and how they fit into the history of the human race. Those of us who have had these things all our lives perhaps cannot imagine not having them, so it may be hard to understand why adoptees feel that they need them, but they do. Adoptees also search to resolve issues in their lives, particularly to get a definitive answer to the question of why they were relinquished and to be reassured that they were not rejected but were wanted and loved.

An adoptee is most likely to search for her birth parents after a significant life event, such as marriage, divorce, or the death of an adoptive parent. The birth of a child is frequently mentioned as an event that forces an adoptee to think about her genetic makeup and what she may be passing on to her children. Pregnancy and childbirth cause a woman to wonder about her birth mother's experience. Questions from her physician may point out to her the importance of knowing whether her family has a history of early labor or twins. In addition, adoptees say how profoundly aware they are of meeting someone for the first time to whom they are genetically connected when they have their first children. That often causes them to think about meeting other biologically related people. Losses, such as divorce or death, may cause the adoptee to seek out as many sources of comfort as possible. And at some point, the adoptee's awareness of her own advancing age reminds her that if she delays her search, her birth parents may die before she finds them.

A general sense of dissatisfaction with life may also prompt an adoptee to search for her birth parents. We all have periods in our lives when it seems that something is missing. We sometimes look for a simple answer to our dissatisfaction—a new job, a new spouse, another child, or a move to a new city. The adoptee may focus on her absent birth parents as the cause of her dissatisfaction. I received a letter from a prisoner who was inquiring about how to undertake a search because he thought that meeting his birth parents might somehow explain why he couldn't stay out of trouble with the law.

Supporting the Search

Adoptive parents sometimes react to a search by feeling inadequate or betrayed. Carol Demuth, an adoptee and counselor, says that the institution of adoption implies that adoptive parents completely supplant the birth parents. Adoptive parents are led to believe that if they are loving, nurturing parents and are open with their children about adoption, they will meet all their children's needs. When adoptees search, adoptive parents sometimes feel that either they have not adequately met their children's needs or that they were misled about adoption itself. They may feel they did everything that was asked of them and were not "rewarded" with the loyalty or affection that goes with being the children's "only" parents. The betrayal was not by their children, but by an adoption system that, with good intentions, tried to deny some realities of the human existence. By loving and nurturing our children, we meet all the needs adoptive parents can meet, but our children have needs that cannot be met by us, and we needn't feel inadequate or guilty about that.

In her book, *Adoption Reunions*, Michelle McColm says that it isn't unusual for adoptive parents to feel vulnerable and threatened by a search. Their old fears about attachment may resurface—especially if the fears were never fully resolved. They remember when the angry adolescent adoptee would tell them: *I hate you. I wish I'd never been adopted by you. I wish I lived with my birth mother.* The adoptive parents wonder if their attachment will be strong enough when other parents are available—parents who were there first and who have a connection that reaches into every cell of their child's body. This feeling can be intensified if the adoptee is in the process of emancipating from her family and the adoptive parents are already wondering what kind of relationship they will have with their child after she leaves home.

Others feel secure in their relationship with their child but wonder if they will have to "share" her with the birth parents. Will the adoptee's energies be directed away from the adoptive parents and toward the birth parents? Will the adoptive parents have to compete with the birth parents for phone calls or visits on holidays? Demuth says that some adoptive parents who feel that their relationship with their children is solid nonetheless wonder if they will have to compete with the birth parents for the role of grandparents to their grandchildren.

Of course, sometimes the actions of the adoptee do seem to confirm the adoptive parents' fear that they will have to compete with the birth parents for the time and energy of the adoptee, if not for her feelings. It is not unusual for an adoptee to become obsessed with the search—spending all her energy on it and talking about nothing but finding her birth parents. After a reunion, the adoptee may continue to spend an inordinate amount of time with her birth family as they attempt to catch up on the years they've missed.

It's natural for adoptive parents to feel jealous or hurt when the adoptee directs all her energy to the search or her newfound birth family. Adoptive parents should be patient—the high level of energy adoptees devote to the search or reunion process cannot be kept up indefinitely. Adoptive parents frequently express their fear that their son or daughter will want to spend holidays with his or her birth parents after a reunion. Spending holidays together is considered to be a "family" experience, and the adoptive parents' fear that they will lose this experience may symbolize their fear that they will be replaced by the birth parents.

Demuth, an adult adoptee who successfully searched for her birth parents with the blessing of her adoptive parents, says that adoptees may want to spend holidays with their birth parents to see what their traditions are like or to try to fulfill their fantasies of family holidays. "One of the sad realities is that every adoptee and birth parent has to realize they will never have what might have been," says Demuth. No matter how close the adoptee and birth parents become, spending holidays with them will not feel like "going home," she says, because it isn't. Some of them know that intuitively, but others need the experience to realize the truth. Once again, patience on the part of the adoptive parents is required, along with faith in the relationship they have built with the adoptee.

Adoptive parents may feel jealous of birth parents who get the benefit of a close relationship with the adoptee without having done any of "the work" to raise her. They need to remind themselves that the birth parents also missed the joys of nurturing the child and watching her grow—and that both experiences contribute to the attachment parents and children feel for each other.

In other situations, adoptive parents who are struggling to help their grown son or daughter assume adult responsibilities may feel their efforts are being undermined by birth parents who are responding to an adoptee's "neediness" in inappropriate ways. For example, adoptive parents who have decided it's necessary to charge their grown son room and board in an effort to get him to take responsibility for himself may feel frustrated when the birth parent agrees to let the adoptee move in with her free of charge. This kind of experience can also feed the myth that the adoptee was searching because of inadequacies in his adoptive parents. Adoptive parents need to have faith in their parenting decisions, relying on their past experience in determining that, in the long run, children respect parents who set limits.

One reason adoptive parents may be concerned about their son's or daughter's plan to search is that they are afraid the adoptee will uncover an unpleasant truth or be rejected by the birth parents. Their desire to protect their child from any pain that may result from a search is a typical parental reaction. But Demuth notes that no matter how much parents want to protect their children, part of their job is to help their children learn to cope with the adversities that come with life. If they have been doing their job as parents, they have been helping their child develop these skills.

Adoptive parents should be available to listen to the fears of their son or daughter—which are probably similar to their own—without sending the message that they don't think the adoptee can handle disappointment or rejection. Instead, Demuth advises, parents can point out the difficult situations the adoptee has handled in the past and assure her that they will be there to support her if the outcome is disappointing.

One of the most important ways adoptive parents can support adoptees who are searching is by working through their own fears. Adoptive parents' fears can intensify the anxiety the adoptees already feel when embarking on a search. When the adoptees' parents are not supportive, the adoptees feel isolated. They need to know that they are not going to lose an important connection—to the family they grew up in—just because they have chosen to search for their birth parents. Demuth tells adoptive parents to continue to express their love to their children during this time; they shouldn't assume that the adoptee knows.

Adoptees who search would like to have the blessing of their adoptive parents, but this is different from adoptive parents giving the adoptees permission to search. Adoptive parents do not *allow* their adult sons or daughters to search, but acknowledge and honor the adoptees' right to search.

Adoptive parents also have to maintain a delicate balance in expressing their support for the search. They need to be able to offer support and express an interest without prying or seeming to take control of the search. Searching brings up personal issues, and adoptees may not be able to share everything as it unfolds. Adoptive parents can express their support by providing relevant documents or bits of information and by listening when the adoptee wants to talk. They can let the adoptee know that they are interested in hearing about the search but respect her right to choose what she wants to share. At the same time, the adoptive parents have the right to ask for time and privacy to process the information they are being given.

Unfortunately, it may be difficult for adoptive parents to find the support they need during what is often a challenging time. Most search groups are composed of adoptees and birth parents, rather than adoptive parents, although these groups can be useful in helping adoptive parents understand the process that adoptees go through as well as the adoptees' feelings. The best healing for adoptive parents comes from time and the reassurance of their adopted children, although sometimes an adoptee is too caught up in her own feelings or the details of the search to be attentive to her adoptive parents' needs. In the meantime, some of the many books written about the search process or about the adoption experience may be helpful to adoptive parents (see *Selected References and Resources* section at the back of this book).

The purpose of finding the birth parents is to get answers to questions and to integrate the divergent parts of the adoptee's life into a whole. Even when the information received from the birth parents is negative or the birth parents reject a reunion, the adoptee is likely to emerge from the search in better shape than she started. This is not to say that adoptees who search are better adjusted than those who don't. But people who have a need, identify it, and take action to fill it are likely to feel better than they would if they denied that they had that need.

Part III

Special Issues in Adoption

9

Ethnic and Cultural Identity

തൟ Some years ago, a television commercial showed a Korean American girl who was valedictorian of her high school graduation class reminiscing about her life with her adoptive parents. The advertisement captured the hope of parents who adopt transracially—that despite our differences, we will grow and thrive as a family. Indeed, the great majority of transracial and intercountry adoptions have been highly successful in terms of the quality of attachments parents and children form and the children's development of positive self-images. Problems that do arise are due more often to the age of the child at the time of adoption, the number of moves a child had prior to being adopted, or previous trauma than to differences in racial or ethnic backgrounds. Nonetheless, transracial and intercountry adoption is not without its challenges—for the adoptee, the parents, and other children in the family. Some of these challenges are discussed in other chapters: the reaction of relatives to the child, the difficulty both infants and older children have in adjusting to new foods and customs, and the effects of spending formative years in orphanages in Chapter 2 and why attachment may take longer for infants and mothers who are racially different in Chapter 3. However, it is other issues—racial identity and racism—

that have made transracial adoption controversial and led to federal laws affecting it. We do our children a disservice if we minimize the fact that there are some real trade-offs when children of color are adopted by parents who are members of the culturally dominant white race—the most common form of transracial adoption—or when children leave their homeland to be adopted by parents in another country with different cultural traditions. This does not mean we should abandon transracial or intercountry adoptions, for I believe the benefit to the children of having stable, loving families outweighs the disadvantages. However, it is important to acknowledge that most parents of white, European ancestry will find it difficult to provide their children with the same degree of cultural and racial awareness that the children would have if they were growing up in families of the same racial or cultural makeup. This is not because parents are unwilling to, but because they understandably lack the sensibility themselves. By acknowledging this, we become aware of the need to find others who can compensate for our deficiencies. Perhaps more importantly, by acknowledging this we also acknowledge the reality of our children's lives.

Developing a Sense of Ethnic and Cultural Identity

Children as young as three or four are conscious that they belong to a group distinguished from other groups by physical differences. Somewhere between four and seven years of age, they become aware that more than physical characteristics distinguish the races—that there are attitudes and expectations associated with people of different colors. Children acquire their racial attitudes as preschoolers, generally through observation and indirect messages; they see the kinds of jobs people of different races have and the neighborhoods they live in. They overhear conversations and learn there are social implications to membership in different races. They read books, hear their friends talking, watch television, and observe their parents' interaction with people of different skin colors. As a result, they may see whites as superior to blacks or consider race unimportant, a problem, or a stigma. In adolescence, each person will evaluate the racial attitudes he acquired early in life and make conscious choices about them, just as he evaluates other values with which he was raised.

The first difference children notice is skin color. When reading a multiracial picture book to her three-year-old Asian son, Marge asked him if he saw any children who looked like him. She was surprised when he pointed to a picture of an African boy instead of an Asian boy. But children are aware of slight differences in skin color even before they are aware of the differences in eye shape or hair color.

Some people believe that the transracially adopted child will understand that he is not the biological child of his adoptive parents as soon as he notices the racial differences. However, the inheritance of physical characteristics is a fairly advanced concept for children. They will know that they belong to a particular racial group before they understand the genetic explanation. Consequently, although young children are aware of the physical differences between them and their adoptive parents, they may not realize that these differences are evidence of their adoption.

Parents should not try to develop racial awareness in their child by pointing out his differences or those of other people, by saying, for example, "Do you see that woman in the sari? She's from India, too. See how she has brown skin like you?" Such remarks only make a child self-conscious of his differences. Discussions of the child's physical differences should be held when the child brings up the subject. If the child notices the woman and remarks that she must be from India, parents can ask, "What clues did you have that she is from India?"

Parents should take the opportunity to make positive comments about the child's physical features whenever it is appropriate and natural to do so, but these comments don't have to be made in racial terms. A mother can comment on how nice and thick her child's hair is while she is combing it or how good a particular shirt looks with the child's coloring. Parents should resist the pitfall of trying to make up for the cultural view of white supremacy by implying that a child's racial characteristics are superior, such as by saying, "Aren't you lucky your skin is brown—you can have a tan all year round!" However beautiful each person's racial characteristics may be, children sense that parents are trying to overcompensate for the cultural view that nonwhites are inferior.

It isn't unusual for transracially adopted children sometimes to wish they were the same color as their parents. Most likely, this is not a rejection of their racial identity, but a desire to be like the people around them. It's not that they want to be a different race; they simply don't want to stand out. Sometimes children say they want to be the same color as their parents because young children idolize their parents. They want to think that when they grow up, they will be as beautiful as their mother or as handsome as their father. Saying, "When I grow up, I'll have hair like yours" may not be so much a statement that the child thinks being blonde is more attractive as an expression of the fact that he finds his mother or father attractive.

Children occasionally express a dislike for their skin color or other racial characteristics. While this is normal, parents should take the opportunity to let the children know that they like that feature. A child may just be dissatisfied with one of his physical characteristics, or he may be wondering if his parents would love him more if he looked like them. The child needs reassurance that he is valued as he is. If a child is persistently dissatisfied with his racial features, though, he may be having difficulty with self-esteem or his racial identity.

Parents of Asian children, in particular, need to remember that their children are physically different from the majority of the American population and need to reassure them they are attractive. Although other minority children are also physically different, the increased racial awareness of African Americans in the United States has resulted in attractive role models being portrayed in magazines, television shows, and movies. The Asian child's features are obviously different, yet he does not have the "heroes" the African American child has to help him feel good about his racial identity; he is not going to find many Asians depicted on posters of movie stars, rock singers, and television actors. Latino children face some of the same issues, particularly since they may be racially white, but seldom find that white role models are Latino.

Researchers tell us that transracially adopted children have no difficulty understanding which racial or ethnic group they belong to by virtue of their physical characteristics. However, racial and ethnic identity is more than skin deep. A real challenge for parents who adopt transracially is to help their children develop a sense of ethnic identity.

Ethnic and Cultural Identity

Before embarking on a plan to help our children have a sense of ethnic and cultural identity, it's important to know what those terms refer to and how ethnic and cultural identity is acquired. *Ethnicity* has come to mean belonging to a group that shares characteristics, such as national origin, language, religion, ancestry, and culture. Because ethnic groups sometimes cross political boundaries and even groups with the same name practice different religions or have different histories, we should think of ethnic groups narrowly, like *Irish Catholic immigrants,* rather than broadly, such as simply *Irish.* Ethnicity is a matter of biological and historical fact and is not changed by the culture in which a person grows up. A child from the Ukraine, for example, will always be a member of a group with a particular history, unique physical characteristics, and rich traditions that grew out of the beliefs and experiences of the group. However, if the child is raised in the United States, immersed in the culture of this country, he may not identify with that group of people—even if his parents try to teach him the history, songs, and traditions of his people. He may understand that his ethnicity is Ukrainian, but not have a Ukrainian ethnic identity.

A person's *ethnic identity* is a person's sense of *belonging* to an ethnic group. Ethnic identity is drawn from the realization that part of one's thinking, perceptions, feelings, and behaviors are consistent with those of other members of that ethnic group. It is recognizing that one belongs to a particular group that shares not only ethnicity, but common cultural practices. *Culture* is used to describe what people develop to enable them to adapt to their world, change their world, and survive in the world. It is the language and gestures people develop to communicate with each other, tools used to enable them to survive and prosper, customs and traditions that define values and organize social interactions, religious beliefs that make meaning of their world and rituals to express those beliefs, and dress, art, and music to make symbolic and aesthetic expressions. Culture determines the practices and beliefs that become associated with an ethnic group and give it its distinctive identity. Even if a Ukrainian child knows about the Ukrainian culture—its language, customs and rituals, and dress and music, if he does not use them regularly or draw on them as the basis for looking at the world, his ethnic identity will not be Ukrainian, although his ethnicity will be. If he is raised in a white, middle-class, midwestern Protestant family, his cultural identity is likely to be similar to other white, middle class, Midwestern, Protestant people, while his ethnic identity is likely to be similar to that of other Ukrainian children adopted by white Americans.

This reality is a loss for the adoptee. The adoptee has lost important ways of connecting with his ancestors and with contemporaries with whom he shares ethnicity. It can be hard for parents to understand that in place of his own cultural values, traditions, and practices, he has theirs—which they may view as adequate or even superior. That's not the point. Although a girl who was adopted from Korea may not want to have grown up in a culture in which she would have to defer to her younger brother; she has still lost significant cultural connections.

Even parents who recognize the importance of these connections will have a difficult time maintaining them for the adoptee. They may make the effort to acquaint their child with the customs, music, and dress of their child's ethnic origins, but it is far more difficult to transmit the values and beliefs that gave rise to those customs or expressions. For example, if the parents haven't been reared as Buddhists, how can they adequately convey the subtle ways in which Buddhism has influenced the thinking and practices in a Buddhist country? If they have grown up with a linear concept of time typical of Europeans, how can they convey the circular concept of time that is essential to some cultural groups? Furthermore, people transmit cultural beliefs and practices in subtle ways. Why do African American girls have less concern about being thin than do European American girls, despite efforts to communicate to European American girls that they do not need to diet and the exposure of African American girls to the same fashion advertisements? Obviously, some more powerful messages are being given, though probably in quite subtle ways. If transracially and internationally adopted children are going to grow up with a cultural awareness of their ethnic groups, they will need to be part of communities in which those cultural values are transmitted. They will have to live in neighborhoods or attend schools or churches in which their ethnic group predominates, where the cultural values of that group influences daily life, and where they have mentors— teachers, ministers, or respected elders—who can transmit those values and practices. An open adoption relationship with a child's birth family can be enormously helpful in this way, but only if the birth and adoptive families have sufficient contact. What's more, the adoptive parents will have to be open to the idea that their child is being exposed to values that are different from those in their family. For example, in some cultures, children would learn that their actions bring shame on their parents, while Americans would say we are each responsible for our own actions. Parents have to be prepared to help their child sort out the different messages he is getting, being respectful of other cultural values while not compromising their own. Ideally, by expanding their cultural awareness, both parents and children will learn that no one culture has the "right" answers to how we should relate to the world around us. Rather than be torn between conflicting cultural values, transracially adopted children will have additional viewpoints to draw on in developing their own worldviews.

Some adoptive parents may question the idea that transracially and internationally adopted children need to attend integrated schools or live in integrated neighborhoods. They note that many families of color live in predominantly white neighborhoods and attend neighborhood schools and churches. Other parents may point out that *they* don't immerse themselves in their own ethnicity, so why should their children?

The answer to both questions is that culture is transmitted subtly. African American parents in a predominantly white neighborhood still transmit their cultural identity to their children, as we all do, regardless of whether we realize that we are doing so. A person who is part of the dominant cultural group is less likely to be aware of communicating cultural values because those values are all around; the contrast is not as evident.

At the same time, it is important to recognize that the child's immersion in his cultural origins through daily exposure is an ideal—not a necessity. Perhaps this is a personal bias, having raised two children who were born in Korea in a predominantly white community in Idaho (although with the liberal and international flavors of a college town); however, I don't think parents should avoid or be denied transracial or international adoption because of where they live or the cultural resources available in their communities. Nonetheless, parents should make an effort to expand their cultural horizons out of a sincere belief that other cultures are valuable. Children can have dolls representing a variety of ethnic groups—not just their own; they can be read folk tales from many countries—not just their own; they can learn about different religions, different foods, and different historical perspectives. This effort should be a routine part of family life, not a special event. For example, making certain Indian foods part of the family's regular mealtime fare does more to show how valuable and accepted that culture is than having a special "Indian meal" once a year and avoiding curry the rest of the time. More than one adoptive family has driven many miles to an international food festival only to have their internationally adopted children opt for the hamburger booth.

Parents should be cognizant, however, that these explorations of other cultures are in no way comparable to a child's daily exposure to his cultural heritage. That gap can be bridged somewhat if they make an effort to get beyond the symbolic expressions of culture to find the underlying cultural values. For example, parents who adopt an African American child will probably want to celebrate Kwanzaa, a holiday developed to remind African Americans of their African roots. However, the celebration will be far more meaningful in helping the child develop a sense of ethnic and cultural identity if, as part of the occasion, the child becomes more aware of the struggles of the African people who were brought to America.

It isn't unusual, despite parental efforts to acquaint their child with his cultural heritage, for the child to reject anything related to his ethnic origins. Indeed, even immigrant parents struggle to get their children to value their own ethnic heritage in the face of the dominant culture. When that culture is not only pervasive, but equated with financial success and social status, it's natural for children to value it over other cultures. However, a child's lack of interest in or resistance to learning about his ethnic heritage should not discourage parents. Parents need to keep in mind what their goal is in exposing their child to his cultural and ethnic heritage. According to Joseph Crumbley, an adoption therapist, the goal is to raise a child who can identify and interact with people of his own ethnic group and not be embarrassed to have been raised by white parents. The goal is for the child to appreciate his ethnic and cultural heritage enough not to feel alienated from others with the same heritage and to want to explore it and draw on it. William Cross, Jr., Ph.D., author of *Shades of Black,* says that ethnic identity helps people who are likely to experience racism or discrimination feel that they belong to a group that values the very qualities that are being reviled. An ethnic identity gives a person a feeling of being wanted, accepted, and appreciated by people who share a particular history and culture, even though they may vary in their beliefs, preferences, and affiliations.

In an essay in *Ethnic Identity,* George Devereux differentiates between *ethnic identity* and *ethnic personality.* A person's ethnic personality is his display of behavior that is typical of a particular ethnic group. Not only does the person identify with that group, but others can identify him by means of his behavior. Some members of ethnic groups seem to demand that individuals demonstrate an ethnic personality to be considered an authentic member of that ethnic group. The terms *oreo, apple,* and *banana* have been used to describe African Americans, Native Americans, and Asian Americans whose ethnic personality is more consistent with that of European Americans despite their skin color. Adoptees probably will not develop the ethnic personality of their ancestral group, particularly if they do not grow up in a family or neighborhood in which those characteristics are demonstrated. However, they can still have a healthy ethnic identity. Sometimes, transracially adopted children who do not have the opportunity to explore their ethnic identity take on the ethnic personality of their ethnic group in an attempt to belong without necessarily understanding the cultural values. Sam, an African American boy who was adopted by a white couple living in a predominantly white community, began dressing and talking the way he saw African American rap singers do on MTV. Devoid of true mentors, he saw only the superficial aspects of his ethnic group. As a young adult, however, he was able to go beyond this ethnic personality to explore his ethnicity in greater depth.

Identity Development in Adulthood

Ethnic identity is only part of a person's overall sense of identity. Religion, gender, sexual orientation, physical characteristics, abilities, talents, and personality all make up one's overall identity. Sometimes or in certain situations, one facet of a person's overall identity may be more important than another. Often a person does not have much of a sense of ethnic identity until, as a young adult in college or in the workplace, he experiences an event that reminds him that he is part of an ethnic group at the very least because of his ancestry. An Asian American may experience someone speaking slowly to him, as though he does not understand English. An African American may suspect that a job or apartment was denied to him because of his race. A Latino may be exposed for the first time to the rich tradition of Latin American literature. Whatever it is, it may take the young person by surprise, shocking him into the realization that he does not see himself as others see him or has not fully explored who he is.

Frequently, a young adult who has had such an encounter will be motivated to immerse himself in his ethnicity. For a time, he may become completely absorbed by anything related to his ethnic group and see those cultural traditions as superior. The adoptee may want to visit his homeland, learn the language of his country of origin, or major in college in the study of his ethnic group. Eventually, he will be able to go beyond a simplistic view of his ethnic group to a more serious understanding of his people. When he does, he emerges with a new ethnic identity.

Latino Identity Issues

Adopted children of Latin American heritage face many of the same identity issues as do transracially adopted African American children or children adopted internationally. Yet in some ways, the identity and ethnicity issues of children of Latin American heritage are unique, particularly for those living in the United States. *Latino/Latina*, the term often preferred by people of Latin American heritage because it is more accurate and less pejorative than *Hispanic*, is not a racially descriptive term. Some Latinos are white, but they do not share the ethnicity of European Americans, which, along with African Americans, is the national image of an American. Even though many Latinos can trace their ancestors to people living in the continental United States before the arrival of Europeans, Latinos are often asked *Where are you from?* Nor do all Latinos have a common culture. Indeed, there is a historical animosity among some Latino ethnic groups, and many identify themselves in terms of national origin—such as Cuban, Puerto Rican, or Mexican—before they identify themselves as Latino or Latina. However, they have found commonality with each other in the need for more political and economic power and in the way they are treated by Anglos and accept the use of the terms *Latino/Latina*, *Hispanic*, and *Chicano/Chicana* for that reason.

To understand his ethnic identity, the Latino adoptee will have to understand that he is a member of two ethnic groups: the specific group of people from whom he is descended—Colombian, Guatemalan, European, or indigenous people—as well as the ethnically artificial, but politically important, group called Latino/Latina.

Mixed Racial Identity

The ethnic identity of a child of mixed racial heritage remains controversial, particularly when the child has one white birth parent and one black birth parent. Some people emphasize that the child should identify himself on the basis of his physical appearance, regardless of his racial heritage, because that is how other people will view him. However, others suggest that a new racial category—*biracial*—should be acceptable. Certainly, children should have factual information about their racial heritage and should have opportunities to learn about and cherish it. They should know that if their physical appearance does not immediately classify them by race, others will be confused, though that they are not obliged to clear up the confusion (see page 84). They should know that there are conflicting views about how they should classify themselves and that they have a choice; they are not being disloyal to their white adoptive parents if they choose to emphasize their African American heritage, for example. Most important, they should be aware that their physical appearance may result in their being treated with bigotry or discrimination. Being biracial does not mean that they can "choose" to be white or black or that they have the best of both worlds. Children must be armed with enough realism about the world to understand that people of mixed racial heritage encounter the same kind of racism as do people of color and that their efforts to explore their white heritage may be seen by people of color as disloyal. Ultimately, these children must do what we all must do—reconcile the way society sees them with their own view of themselves.

Ethnic Identity and Self-esteem

The response to those who argue against transracial or international adoption because they fear the children will not grow up with a true sense of racial identity is obviously complicated. Studies show that transracially and internationally adopted children clearly understand to which racial or ethnic group they belong. However, the other question is whether the ethnic identity of these adoptees is as strong as those of children who were raised in their racial or ethnic groups. When transracially or internationally adopted children are asked to which group they belong or identify with, they probably are likely to name the group with whom they have a common cultural upbringing, rather than or before the group with whom they share ethnicity. This is evident in the fact that studies have found that African American teenagers who were adopted by white parents have more white friends than black friends and date whites more than blacks, although they also tend to have more black friends and more black dates than their white peers do.

Some people see transracial adoption as a way to blur color lines and bridge cultures. The fact is that regardless of a person's ethnic identity, when he is living in a country that is dominated by the white, European culture, he must know how to function in that society without sacrificing his own ethnic identity. Transracial adoption may give adoptees an edge when it comes to functioning comfortably in the white society, but not necessarily because they have learned how to bridge the two cultures. Opponents of transracial adoption fear that if a person does not have a healthy racial identity, he will be unprepared to deal with discrimination and racism. When he is confronted with racism and realizes that other people do not see him the way he sees himself, he may feel isolated, confused, or vulnerable.

Dealing with Prejudice and Racism

Many parents who adopt transracially start out "color-blind," says therapist James Mahoney. They believe the best way to counter racism is to adopt the attitude that race doesn't matter. Though well intentioned, that approach denies the actual experience of people of color. Race "doesn't matter" to the people whom race favors. When race results in someone being treated as second class, it does matter. Eventually, most adoptive parents see that race does matter to other people. When their children are the victims of racial slurs, are stereotyped, or are treated more harshly by the police than the white children in the community, the parents realize that the world is not color-blind and they cannot protect their children from both overt and subtle forms of racism. The first is easy to recognize; the second may not be, especially in ourselves.

Dealing with Our Own Prejudice

One form of prejudice among white adoptive parents of minority children is the attitude that they have "rescued" their children from what would have been a disadvantaged life—given a homeless child a home, a malnourished child an abundant diet, or an improverished child middle-class advantages. All adoptive parents are vulnerable to feeling that they have rescued their children by adoption, but it may be easier to resist falling into this trap when they adopt healthy white babies because parents know that their infants would not have waited long for other families. But when they adopt a child who has lived on the streets, who has been neglected, or who was otherwise disadvantaged, parents can believe that the child's life would have been much worse had he not been adopted. In many cases, it's true. But sometimes there is underlying racism or nationalism in that belief. We may think that being raised in the United States, in a traditional Judeo-Christian religion, or in a middle-class white family is automatically better than being raised in Colombia, being raised Buddhist, or being raised in a working-class African American family.

Children do not benefit from being cast as victims in need of rescue. In the first place, a victim is a victim only a until he is removed from his life-threatening predicament. Once removed, he does not continue to need to be saved; he is no longer helpless. More important, being cast as a victim implies that the child owes his parents something for saving him—a debt he can never repay and that he may one day come to resent, since he did not choose to be saved by these parents. We also send our children confusing messages when we display sensitivity to any bigotry regarding our child's ethnic heritage, but continue to display subtle intolerance of other groups.

It is not enough for parents to be tolerant of the differences between them and their child; they need to be tolerant and accepting of other differences. The family who refrains from telling jokes about Asians after adopting a Chinese child but continues to tell Polish jokes is saying that they do see some ethnic groups as inferior to others. Allowing some racial slurs—even though they do not refer to the child's race or ethnic background—tells the child that racial, religious, or ethnic differences do matter and that nonwhites, non-Americans, or people of other religions are inferior.

As children grow up, parents should consider whether their expectations are in any way tied to the child's race or ethnic background. Do we expect our Asian daughter to be a whiz at math? Do we think our tall African American son is more likely to enjoy basketball than our tall white son? We have all been bombarded with racial and ethnic stereotypes throughout our lives, and though parents generally do not adopt transracially or transculturally unless they reject these stereotypes, they may be more influenced by the society than they think. The conscious rejection of stereotypes is an ongoing task.

Dealing with the Prejudice of Outsiders

We often become aware that our child will encounter prejudice when the child goes to school for the first time and is clearly a minority in the classroom. Before children enter school, parents can, to some extent, structure their environment so the children are not exposed to prejudice. Once a child is in school, however, parents cannot protect him from misinformed people.

Most transracially adopted children encounter prejudice in the form of teasing, comments, or insults. A few experience more violent racism or nationalism. And the teasing and insults can come both from white children who view minorities as inferior and from members of the child's own ethnic group who view the child living with a white family as disloyal to his race or ethnic group. One boy decided to go to a racially integrated high school because he was teased about being the only African American in his junior high school. But having been raised in a white neighborhood by white parents, he was taunted by the other African American at the high school for not "dressing black" or "acting black." He became embarrassed to be seen with his parents. It was not until he was successful on the football team that he felt accepted by his peers. A Chicana found that every time Central America was discussed in her history class, her teacher expected her to be more knowledgeable than the other students. Although she wasn't being insulted, she quite rightly thought she was being singled out because of her ethnic background. Not only did she feel conspicuous, she felt disloyal because she did not know more about her country of birth.

Children know that their parents will be hurt when their children are teased because of their race or ethnic background, so they do not always share these incidents with their parents. Consequently, it is important for us to prepare our minority children when they are young to deal with prejudice. That means helping them develop a healthy ethnic identity and survival skills for a racist world.

Margaret Beale Spencer, an authority on identity development in African American youths, says that teenagers who do not have an ethnic identity—a sense of belonging to an ethnic group—tend to experience racism as being directed at them personally, rather than as part of a group. Therapist Joseph Crumbley points out that when children who have been raised color-blind are confronted with negative stereotypes of their own race, they have little option but to accept the stereotypes and feel bad about themselves. They feel alienated from the culture in which they were raised because others don't see that they belong in it, as well as alienated from the culture of their own ethnic group because they don't feel they fit in it—or may not want to because they see only the negative stereotypes. As a result, they are at risk of feeling isolated; experiencing rage; or developing poor self-esteem, self-hate or depression.

In addition to providing their children with enough knowledge of their ethnic origins so they do not have to depend on stereotypes to know what it means to have their ethnic background, Crumbley says parents must consciously provide children with a repertoire of responses to the racism and prejudice they will encounter. The unfair experiences that children of color are likely to encounter must be discussed openly if the children are to be prepared to deal not only with the experience, but with their feelings of anger at the injustice.

It is not unusual for children in the primary grades to focus on the differences among them, which sometimes leads to hurtful comments or teasing. Often, the child will tell his parent about these incidents. Parents may be outraged by incidents like these and be tempted to get on the phone and call everyone, from the other children's parents to the school board. Although doing so may make the parents feel better, it probably doesn't address the child's feelings of hurt and confusion. What's more, a child is unlikely to continue to tell his parents about incidents like these if the result is that they get upset. Rather, the parents can use the incidents to help their child develop healthy boundaries. For example, if a child comes home and tells his mother that a classmate said his brown skin makes him look "dirty," the mother can ask, *Is your skin brown because it's dirty?* When the child says that it isn't, the mother can then reply, *Then I guess your classmate was wrong.* The goal is for the child to realize that some people say things that are wrong and that he does not have to accept opinions that he knows to be false, including the one that nonwhite people are inferior to whites. Eventually he will learn to make these assessments on his own. In addition, parents should take the time to explore the child's feelings about the incident. He may have bottled up his emotions so as not to let on how hurt he was. He needs a chance to express them.

The parents can also ask their child how he responded in the situation, whether he thought his response was effective or whether he would try a different strategy in the future. If the child doesn't know how he could have responded, the parent can offer to do some "brainstorming" to figure out some possible approaches the child could use in the future. By approaching the situation in this way, the parent is empowering the child to respond rather than be a passive victim; however, the parent also starts a dialogue in which the advantages and disadvantages of different strategies can be explored. When the child reaches adolescence—and is viewed as threatening simply because of his skin color—this knowing which strategy to employ in which situation can be even more important.

For example, children of color need to know that if they are loitering in a convenience store, they are likely to be treated differently from white children. They need to know how to communicate that they are not threatening and how to handle any confrontation with the store manager that may arise. They need to understand that an outraged attitude by a white person who is accused unjustly will be viewed differently from a similar attitude by a person of color. Therapist James Mahoney recommends, for example, that parents of young African American men make sure their sons have complete emergency car repair supplies in their cars—and cellular phones if possible—so if they have car problems, they do not have to risk going to the door of a house where the owner may view an unexpected African American male as a threat to his family's security.

Therapist Joseph Crumbley says what stops adoptive parents from discussing these issues is not only their lack of experience with them, but their aversion to destroying their children's innocence—especially when having to lose this innocence is itself unfair. This same dilemma comes up in other ways as parents try to prepare children for the realities of the world. For example, it destroys a child's innocence to learn that adults sometimes sexually abuse children. Parents want their children to be free of such worries and to view adults as helpers in their world, rather than as potential victimizers, but they also want their children to have enough awareness and skills to keep from being victimized. When it comes to racial issues, parents would like to believe that their children will be evaluated on their own merits, rather than by their skin color. However, they need to understand that the attitude that *Life is good, life is fair, and if you are the best you can be, people will judge you appropriately* is more true for white persons than for persons of color and therefore may not serve their children. Parents may also be concerned that their children will begin to approach life with a "chip on their shoulders"—believing that people will discriminate against them—and that they will use this belief as an excuse for not doing their best. But even highly successful minority business executives have had to learn survival skills for interacting in a racist society.

Crumbley adds that children of color must learn to recognize situations in which racism and prejudice may occur. Called "protective hesitation," this is an ability to observe a situation for clues that racism may be involved or a potential conflict may arise. Children must also develop a sense of "selective confrontation" and "selective avoidance"—that is, knowing when to back off from a situation and when to deal with it directly. Once they decide on confrontation, they must also learn various appropriate ways of confrontation. Children also need to know their legal rights and the institutional resources that are available to help them when they are the victims of racism, including the courts and community organizations. Perhaps the best way for transracially adopted children to learn ways to cope with racism is the same way other children of color do—through contact with older generations who can pass on what they have learned. Again, teachers, ministers, elders, and other mentors can help our children learn what we may not be able to teach.

When Our Own Child Is Racist

One year during my daughter's elementary school years, she experienced frequent racially based taunts from one particular boy. The most difficult part of the experience for her to understand was that the insults were coming from someone who was Asian like she. Sometimes teasing is an effort by children to find another child's vulnerabilities and exploit them to gain a sense of power. A child who has experienced bigotry himself knows that's a vulnerable area for others like him. However, sometimes children of color express hostility toward each other, says Joseph Crumbley, when they have not developed a positive racial identity and experience self-hate as a result of being part of a group that isn't valued in our society. Children who have been transracially adopted may also express racism because they feel a sense of divided loyalties. They want to feel part of their white family and may think that to show them allegiance, they must show allegiance to their parents' race.

If a child is expressing racism, parents should be sure the child feels good about his racial identity. They also need to help him know that he can love himself without being disloyal to his adoptive parents and love his adoptive parents without being disloyal to his own race.

10

International Adoption

⤙⤚ The adoptive parent who has been to the grocery store or the playground with a child who was adopted internationally knows that raising a child from overseas is a different experience. If adoptive parents are "wonderful" to have adopted, the parent who has adopted a child from a developing country is a saint. (Conversely, if parents who adopt take a big risk, the parent who adopts internationally is thought to be entering into the unknown.) If strangers feel compelled to comment on the red hair of a child adopted by two brunettes, they have no hesitation about pronouncing little Asian babies "adorable." This is just a sample of what it is like for the adoptee herself. Children who were adopted internationally face many of the same ethnic and cultural issues that other transracially adopted children face. However, they also face additional issues. They have not only lost the opportunity to be raised in their ethnic culture, but they have lost a homeland and perhaps a language. They have not only had their connections to their birth parents severed, they seldom have much, if any, information about them. Even less often do they have ongoing contact with their birth relatives. Even those who are able to maintain or establish contact with their birth relatives find that geography, culture, and language have put more distance between them and their birth relatives than the adoption itself.

Despite these challenges, international adoption has been remarkably successful. In their book, *International Adoption: A Multinational Perspective,* sociologists Howard Altstein and Rita J. Simon present data indicating that internationally adopted children adjust well—whether adopted in the United States or in European countries. Far more significant than the fact of international adoption in how well children do is how old they were at the time of placement and whether there was a history of previous abuse. When a child is already stressed for those reasons, the additional stresses of international adoption can be exacerbated. Another factor in the outcome of international adoptions that has become more prevalent in recent years is whether the children spent a significant portion of their formative years in an orphanage.

Parents who adopt internationally can expect more scrutiny, a more complicated adjustment (see Chapter 2), and more identity issues than can other adoptive families, but they can also expect great satisfaction. I have often wondered if the obvious differences in families with internationally adopted children leads to a greater awareness of the issues and ultimately a greater openness about discussing them, with the result that parents and adoptees address the issues and work through them, rather than ignore them.

Language, Customs, and the Homeland

When a child older than three is adopted internationally, parents should not try to "Americanize" their child as quickly as possible. While that may seem to be in the child's best interest, what is communicated is that her past is something that should be discarded because it isn't worthwhile. Parents should not fear their child will be stigmatized if she isn't Americanized quickly—she will quickly abandon her language and customs on her own. The grief she is experiencing for the loss of her country and culture and the loss of being similar to those around her will paradoxically motivate her to assimilate her new culture.

The first stage of the grief process is denial. The transracial adoptee denies she's different from those around her by hiding those differences. Eventually, says psychologist H. Sook Wilkinson, she will experience a reawakening of her ethnic heritage, acknowledge it, and seek people of the same background with whom she can identify. Ultimately she will accept her ethnic background (see Chapter 9).

Children move through these stages at different rates. And the child who was adopted as an infant may go through them when she is old enough to understand that her racial or ethnic background sets her apart from others. It is difficult for a child to perceive her ethnic background as positive when she is in the denial phase, and she is unlikely to want to associate with people of her race or ethnic background. Parents should remember that her lack of interest in her ethnic heritage is temporary and try to preserve as much as possible of the child's cultural background, so when she is ready to embrace it, it is there. For example, they can save any mementos of her country, even though she may say she doesn't want them anymore.

Bilingualism

Children who are speaking their native language when they arrive in the adoptive family should be encouraged to speak their language, or at least should not be discouraged from speaking it. The child who is pressured to speak only English may not be able to express her feelings during the critical adjustment period because her grasp of the language is too limited. In addition, she may feel that her cultural past is not valued.

Since most of us cannot provide our children with adequate opportunities to speak their first language, all but those who were adopted after the age of nine or ten are likely to forget it. That is not going to be detrimental to the child as long as she is allowed to use her first language for as long as it is helpful to her.

There are educational as well as psychological benefits to allowing a child to use her first language while she learns English. Researchers have found that bilingualism enhances a person's intellectual and educational abilities because it increases opportunities to use and analyze language. Obviously, there is more to learning a language than learning words and grammar; there are concepts involved. For example, the difference between *on* and *over* is subtle, but the two year old just learning to talk does not get the concepts confused. She learns the difference in those concepts before she learns to talk. If she is forced to suppress her first language, she also suppresses much of the conceptual basis she developed before she learned to talk. On the other hand, if she is allowed to use her native language, her early language skills can be used to process concepts that are not clear to her in English. This does not diminish her capacity to learn or use English, but enhances it, although parents should not expect great jumps in academic achievement as a result. The child who continues to use her native tongue may take longer to learn English, but she will have a greater awareness of language, an increased capacity for creative thought, and greater conceptual development.

Of course, the child's ability to transfer language skills from her first language to English is dependent on the quality of her early language development. The child who had poor language skills in her first language is not going to have much to draw on conceptually.

It is not easy for parents to communicate with a child who speaks a different language, particularly when the child is scared and confused by her new surroundings. Bilingual dictionaries; language tapes; introductory word books, such as those used by toddlers who are just learning to talk; and interpreters are all used to bridge the communication gap. We should keep in mind that the communication problems we are having are due as much to our lack of ability in the child's language as to the child's lack of skill in ours. The child should not feel responsible for misunderstandings that are based on language differences.

Some parents have sought out native speakers to help their children communicate or feel more comfortable, only to have terrified youngsters on their hands. For some children, hearing their native language or seeing people from their country of origin is frightening. Though familiar, these sights and sounds may remind them of painful times, and some may be worried that they are about to be sent back. If the children become frightened, it can be helpful for parents to give reassurance concretely, such as by saying *This is still your bed; this is still your house; we are still your parents.*

Culture Camp and Homeland Visits

Even years later, children may have a similar reaction to being sent to a "culture camp" or taking a family visit to their homeland. Betty, a single woman who adopted a girl from Russia, was helping her daughter pack for "Russia Camp." Like culture camps for children adopted from Korea, China, India, and other countries, Russia Camp would bring together adoptees from Russia to spend time learning about the culture of their homeland, often from immigrants. Betty was surprised that her daughter seemed reluctant to go to the camp until her daughter revealed that she thought going to Russia Camp was the same as going back to Russia—and she didn't want to leave her mother. Betty explained the difference and reassured her daughter that she was going to stay with her at the camp and that they were both going to return home after the camp was over.

Culture camp can be an excellent experience for internationally adopted children, but not just because it exposes them to the culture of their homelands. As Chapter 9 points out, brief cultural explorations tend to be superficial. What is valuable about culture camp is that it brings together children who have had a common experience not shared by most people. After the cooking class and dance rehearsals, these children can talk with each other about the teasing they get at school or other common experiences and know that they will be understood. One mother said that the biggest benefit her eleven-year-old son gained from going to Korea Camp was that he found out that his fear of being too short to date white girls was shared by other Korean adoptees. All the boys were reassured by the counselors—all of whom had also been adopted from Korea—that they would get dates.

Some culture camps are residential camps, while others are day camps. Agencies that specialize in intercountry adoption, as well as adoptive parent organizations, are good sources of information about culture camps. Some of these camps were started by parents who could not find culture camps in their areas. They contacted the immigrant communities in their region for help in putting together a cultural experience for their children.

As valuable as a culture camp can be, it is no substitute for the real thing. Many parents look forward to taking their children back to their homelands for a visit one day. While that can be a memorable and valuable experience, it is not without its pitfalls. Some adoptees—especially those who are still concrete thinkers—will confuse "going back to Guatemala" for a visit with "going back to Guatemala" for good. Again, concrete reassurance can be helpful: Tell the child explicitly that you are all returning to your home; show her the return airline ticket with her name on it; leave a task undone at home and tell her she is to do it when she returns—something she knows you will insist that she do, such as clean her room—and have her bring a "transitional object" with her—something from home that gives her comfort.

Even when a child is old enough to understand that the trip to her homeland is temporary, the visit can bring up issues that are not always anticipated. One family went to Korea and visited their son's orphanage. They asked to look at his records, not expecting to find anything, and found the name and address of his birth mother. Since they had no idea when they would be able to afford another trip to Korea, they decided to look for their son's birth mother. Although they were delighted to have found her, none of them had prepared emotionally for the experience. It was several months after the visit, and some visits to a therapist, before the young boy was able to process that unexpected development.

For an adolescent or young adult, a trip to the homeland can clarify as well as confuse identity issues. If the adoptee has been questioning how she "belongs" in her family or her country—perhaps being treated as a recent immigrant—she may expect that she would feel more comfortable in a place where she is surrounded by her "own people." In some ways, a trip to the homeland results in a heightened awareness of one's ethnicity—a sense that *these are my people.* At the same time, however, adoptees often realize that despite their physical similarity to people in their homeland, there are significant differences—some subtle and some overt. Each adoptee will process this information in her own unique way. Some may return to their country of residence determined to immerse themselves in learning about their ethnicity (see Chapter 9). Others may grieve for the realization that they have lost their ethnic identity. Some may be confused. Parents who are planning a trip to their child's homeland must consider these possibilities, help their child prepare for them, and provide assistance in the aftermath.

In addition to these issues, there are practical considerations in planning a trip to the child's homeland. Young children may not be able to sustain an interest in the trip, preferring the hotel pool to temples or museums. Parents who have spent a lot of money on what may be a once-in-a-lifetime trip may be frustrated with their young child's lack of interest. Traveling with teenagers is also challenging in its own way. Because of their intense concern with privacy and control, they may grumble about their parents' itinerary, but not express what they are really interested in seeing. Children of all ages may have difficulty adjusting to differences in food, water, and sanitary facilities or find the practices of bartering for goods or being solicited for handouts uncomfortable.

For these reasons, parents who are enthusiastic about taking their children back to their homeland may want simply to let their children know of their interest and willingness, but let the children indicate their readiness.

Images of the Homeland

Although adoptive parents generally try to convey to their children that their homeland is rich in beauty and tradition, the image that their children get from the news media or hear about from other people may be different. From the media, they may get the impression that Korea is a country where they eat dogs, the Chinese do not value girls, crime is rampant in Russia, and Colombians are all drug lords. Until late in middle childhood—around the age of ten—children have a hard time integrating two widely disparate views of the same thing. A child of this age may think that if her country is full of crime and poverty, as shown on television, it can't have the beautiful costumes and dances the child experiences at culture camp. Rather than simply present the counterview to the media's images, parents need to present the integrated view. They need to let the child know that she came from a country that has made many wonderful contributions to the world, but also has its share of problems. They should be sure to point out that this is true of all countries, including the United States. With this basis, when a child is presented with evidence of problems in her homeland, she will understand the context. Then her self-esteem as someone who came from that country will not suffer an unnecessary blow.

Parents who adopt transracially often explain to their children that the poverty of the birth parents—in what is frequently a developing country—led to the children's availability for adoption. This is not always true. Children are sometimes placed for adoption in other countries because the birth mothers are middle- or upper-class and will not be able to marry within their class if they have borne children out of wedlock. In some cultures, men do not want to raise another man's child, so even widows may place their children for adoption in order to remarry. In China, the restrictive reproduction policies apply to the rich and poor. Parents cannot assume that their children's birth parents were poor, even when the children were born in developing countries. They need to learn the circumstances in which children in a particular country are relinquished for adoption. They also need to understand the cultural context of those circumstances so they can explain them to their children without being judgmental. For example, it may seem selfish for a widow to place her children for adoption so she can remarry, but in some cultures women are still dependent on men for economic security; thus, a widow may not be able to support her children—or herself.

Sometimes an adoptee who has been told that her birth parents were poor expresses concern about their welfare. Occasionally, she may even feel guilty that she "escaped" that fate. Therapist Holly van Gulden says that the adoptee's concern for her birth parents may be the way the adoptee is expressing the "yearning and pining" typical of the early stages of grief. It could also be part of the bargaining phase. That is, if the child was told that her birth mother couldn't raise a baby because she was too poor, then the child may think that if she could "fix" the poverty, she could undo the loss. Psychiatrist Robert Jay Lifton says that as adoptees reach adolescence, they want to know about their birth parents in far more personal terms than they have in the past. In addition, they are able to conceptualize their birth parents existing in the present, not just as they were at the time of relinquishment. Concern about their birth parents' welfare can be a way for them to try to identify with their birth parents. Lifton also notes that adoptees who know their lives would have been much more difficult had they remained with their birth parents do not have true "survivor guilt" because they probably were not in a life-or-death situation. However, almost everyone who experiences a loss feels some guilt or self-blame. Trying to determine what we did to cause the loss or how we might have prevented it is a way to gain a sense of control over a situation that was out of our hands.

Because the adoptee's expression of concern for her birth parents' welfare may reflect complicated issues, it is important that parents not rush to reassure the child, but listen carefully to what she is saying and deal with the issues that surface. The parents of adolescents can ask their teenagers to consider what difference it would make to them if they knew the present circumstances of their birth parents: Could they realistically do anything to help them? If they believe they could do something, the parents can suggest that they take some kind of action—raising money or collecting clothing for an overseas charity, for example. Indeed, with a child of any age, giving them something to *do* gives them a sense of control. Children also need to be clear that they were not responsible for the decisions that led to their being adopted while others remained behind. Their parents can ask them to look at the choices that were made for them and whether they made those choices or whether other people did. If a child seems to be experiencing guilt or concern about her birth parents to the point of depression or another harmful emotional state, professional counseling may be necessary.

Medical Considerations in International Adoption

The 1997 Benchmark Adoption Survey found that nearly half of all Americans believe that children who are adopted from abroad are less likely to be physically healthy than children adopted domestically. Indeed, children from other countries may have parasites, skin diseases, or venereal diseases or may have been exposed to tuberculosis, measles, hepatitis B, or other diseases. Children adopted internationally may develop diseases or medical conditions—some of which are not familiar to many physicians in the United States—long after their adjustment period is over. On the whole, however, the long-term prognosis for the health of internationally adopted children is good. Good nutrition and access to high-quality health care make significant differences in children's lives.

Prior to Arrival

Jerri Ann Jenista, M.D., a pediatrician and specialist in infectious diseases and international adoption, says that waiting adoptive parents' anxiety about their child's health increases in direct proportion to how far away they are from the child. Medical reports from the child's country should not be presumed to be accurate. Sometimes the medical condition of a child is understated in the hope that the child will be more readily adopted. Sometimes a medical condition is overstated to enable a child to meet governmental regulations that require a child to have a "special need" to be adopted internationally. Sometimes a diagnosis or condition is stated in terms not used in Western countries. While there are screening tests that can be done prior to a child's placement to determine the presence of some diseases and conditions, the reliability of assessments, tests, treatments, and medical records in other countries is so variable that parents should not depend on them. Parents should expect children who have been living in crowded conditions or orphanages to have impetigo, lice, scabies, and vitamin and iron deficiencies, Jenista says, and points out that these are all treatable conditions. The main categories of conditions to be considered for screening tests before adoption, Jenista notes, are *neurodevelopmental disorders,* including cerebral palsy, fetal alcohol syndrome, and mental retardation, and *chronic medical disorders,* such as congenital heart disease and hepatitis B. However, if the condition is not obvious on physical examination, it may not be possible to diagnose it prior to the child's arrival. Videotapes of the child can be a way to diagnose developmental delays or fetal alcohol syndrome or to otherwise confirm or refute a written medical report. However, in an article in the *Journal of Pediatric Health Care,* Jenista and Marie A. Sills Mitchell, R.N., say, "Sometimes the best (and only) question a prospective family can ask is, *Do the workers in the orphanage or foster care system see this child as any different from others of the same age in the same situation?"*

After Arrival

Jenista recommends treatment for any acute or unstable medical condition within twenty-four hours of the child's arrival in her new country. Children with known medical conditions, such as a cleft palate, can be seen within a week, just to make sure the parents are coping until more thorough evaluations can be given. Children who appear healthy can be seen at a physician's office within a few days after arrival to obtain baseline growth data and perhaps begin immunizations and screening tests. A more comprehensive medical evaluation should take place two to four weeks after the child's arrival, to allow the child and parents time to recover from travel and to adjust to a new time schedule and routine. By that time, the parents should begin to have a sense of what is "normal" behavior for the child. According to Mitchell and Jenista, during the thorough examination, the child should have:

- A complete "clothes-off" physical examination.
- A complete "well-child" screening including dental assessment, vision tests, and hearing tests.
- Updated vaccinations. With the exception of children arriving from more developed countries, such as Korea and Taiwan, parents and physicians should not assume that any vaccination records are accurate or that the vaccine was of good quality. In addition, vaccines given to severely malnourished or chronically ill children may not have been effective. When in doubt, the vaccination should be repeated.
- Screening tests including urinalysis, blood count, tests for Hepatitis B, VDRL or any serologic test for syphilis, stool ova and parasite examination, HIV-1 and HIV-2 screening tests, Mantoux

test and chest X-ray for tuberculosis. Other tests, such as screening for hepatitis C or cytomegalovirus, are not routinely recommended. However, the child's ethinic background, history, risk of exposure, or physical examination may prompt evaluations for these and other conditions, such as hepatitis D, malaria, iodine deficiency, hypothyroidism, hemoglobinopathies such as sickle cell anemia, rickets, lead poisoning, intestinal pathogens such as salmonella and shigella, genetic disorders, Fetal Alcohol Syndrome, and Helicobacter pylori.

For more on the health care of internationally adopted children, including the specific tests that should be ordered, consult Jenista's excellent monthly newsletter *Adoption/Medical News* and the other resources listed at the end of this book.

The Malnourished Child

Some children from developing countries are malnourished or undernourished when they arrive in their adoptive homes. Most studies have connected malnutrition with retarded mental development, but the children in these studies remained in deprived situations. One study found that when malnourished children receive adequate nutrition and stimulation early enough, the effect of malnutrition on their growth and intellectual development may be reversed.

Pediatrician Myron Winick, an authority on the effects of malnutrition on mental development, studied malnourished and undernourished Korean children who were adopted by the age of three and found that their growth and intellectual development four to thirteen years later was normal. Malnourished children adopted after the age of three did, however, have achievement levels below norms for children in the United States.

Although the effect of malnutrition seems to be reversible if the child's environment is enriched soon enough, the change may not be immediate. Pediatricians in Latin America who studied the effect of an enriched diet and proper stimulation on malnourished infants adopted before the age of two did not see the dramatic improvement in the children after one year that was seen in the Korean children after several years. They suggested that it may take longer than one year for the effects of adequate nutrition to be seen.

Parents whose child has been undernourished, malnourished, or understimulated should expect to see a significant weight gain within weeks to months after she arrives in her adoptive home, reflecting the more adequate nutrition and care. Eventually, the child's growth will stabilize in a normal pattern.

Measuring Growth of the Internationally Adopted Child

Tom and Lucy took their daughter, who arrived from India at three months of age, to the physician for her twelve-month checkup. The physician was concerned that she was still only in the fifth percentile for weight. Yet she was eating well and seemed healthy. Tom and Lucy suggested that perhaps it was not appropriate to compare her against a growth chart designed for North American children. Perhaps on a growth chart for Indians, she would be average.

It isn't necessary to measure a child from another country against a growth chart developed for people in that country to determine whether the child is growing adequately. But it is also unreasonable to expect the child to achieve the same standards for height and weight as North American Caucasians.

An infant's size is determined by in utero conditions and postnatal factors, such as diet, exposure to infection, and stimulation, but the effect of genetics on a child's size is not seen until the infant is about nine months old and does not dominate until the child is two years old. In other words, differences in the size of babies younger than two years are due to prenatal and postnatal environmental factors. Consequently, all babies can be evaluated using the same growth chart. If an infant is unusually small, it is not because her mother and father were small, but because conditions for the child in utero or immediately after birth were not optimal. If a six year old is small, though, it can be because her parents were small.

Even after the age of two, it may not be appropriate to evaluate a child against a growth chart developed for her race or country if the child has been living in North America and eating a North American diet. Growth charts reflect not only constitutional factors for a group but environmental factors for that country. If people in the country typically have inadequate nutrition and high exposure to disease, expectations for their growth will be lower than if they were receiving adequate nutrition and health care. In other words, a child may have a predisposition to be small, but if she is raised in the United States where there is proper immunization, use of antibiotics to treat infection, and a nutritionally sound diet, she is likely to be larger than she would have been had she remained in a developing country.

Parents and physicians should not be as concerned about where the child falls on the grid for height and weight as long as her growth remains consistent and the child's height is proportionate to her weight.

The Child of Unknown Age

In her practical guideline, *Parenting the Ageless Child*, Joyce Kaser relates how a child development clinic gave her son a thorough examination before saying he was about eight years old. Their pediatrician, orthodontist, and dentist, however, fixed his age at somewhere between eleven and thirteen. Shortly after the evaluation, the boy reached puberty.

A child adopted at an older age may not have a record of her exact date of birth. Parents may assume that fixing an exact age for a child is relatively simple, given today's sophisticated medical diagnostic techniques. In fact, assessing a child's age is more complex than examining her teeth or taking an X-ray of her wrist. The process may take several evaluations by different specialists. Even then, there may be conflicting results. The best the specialists may be able to come up with could be a three- to five-year age range. Factors such as nutrition, emotional health, and illness can all influence dental, musculoskeletal, and sexual development. It can be extremely difficult to assess the age of a child if the heights and weights of her birthparents are not known; if the child has emotional problems stemming from abandonment, separation, or trauma; if the child had poor nutrition or inadequate dental care; and if the child's formal education was nonexistent, sporadic, or interrupted.

An assessment of age should include measurements of height, weight, and head circumference; developmental screening; a bone-age evaluation; a dental assessment; and a genital examination, with an estimation of testicular size in boys and an assessment of sexual maturity in children older than five years. In her article, "Estimating an Unknown Age of a Child," Jerri Ann Jenista, M.D., says that in addition to these medical assessments, families should review the child's paperwork for clues to the child's age. For example, by adding up the number of years the child was in an orphanage or with foster families, parents can establish a minimum age. Jenista also recommends asking the child how old she thinks she is or if she remembers certain significant events, such as an earthquake in her country. Parents can ask the workers who determined the child's age what factors they were using. One family discovered that their child's birth date was not arbitrary at all, but had been left with the child when she was "abandoned."

It may be necessary to follow the child's development over time to establish patterns of growth. Parents of a child with an undetermined age are understandably anxious to establish a precise age as quickly as possible. However, the process may take a long time, may not be conclusive, and may be very expensive. Parents should remember that other aspects of a child's adjustment, such as attachment and the correction of immediate medical problems, are more important than knowing exactly how old the child is.

A child whose age cannot be precisely determined faces some unique situations. The child should be placed in a grade at school appropriate for her academic and emotional levels. But if she has an academic age of eleven and a musculoskeletal age of fourteen, the parents and the school may be criticized for allowing her to play sports against other eleven year olds—even though they are in the same grade. Emotionally, the same child may prefer to play with nine- or ten year olds. Parents of a child with a presumed age will need to get involved with the school system, as well as with groups sponsoring extracurricular activities, to act as an advocate for their child. Ultimately, they will have to determine what age the child will be considered.

When parents discover that the age on their child's birth certificate is inaccurate, they may want to change it. Birth dates can be legally changed and new birth certificates issued, but parents should be cautious about changing a date of birth. An initial evaluation of a child's age may not be consistent with assessments made later. And birth dates are used not only to verify a child's age, but to determine when she can vote, buy alcohol, drive, retire and collect social security benefits. Since changing a date of birth is a legal process that varies from state to state, an attorney should be consulted. A birth date can be changed at any time, even after the adoption is finalized and after the child becomes an adult. Although there is no limit on the number of times a birth date can be changed, common sense dictates that parents should take the time to think about all the consequences before rushing into court.

Jenista reports that some parents use different "informal" ages, depending on the activity and the child's abilities, for example, a younger age for school but an older age for sports. When in doubt, she recommends assuming a younger rather than older age, so the child has more years in school to develop academically and emotionally.

Other Medical Considerations

- Because children in some countries are given antibiotics too frequently, bacterial infections that are resistant to certain antibiotics may develop. Therefore a physician should culture the site of an infection and test it for sensitivity to a number of antibiotics so the most effective treatment can be given.

- Infants whose bottles are propped, which may have been the practice in an orphanage, often develop ear infections as a result of milk draining from the back of the nose into the eustachian tubes. If not treated promptly, the eardrum may perforate and hearing may be lost. Parents who suspect a hearing deficiency in their child should have her tested.

- Poor nutrition or dental hygiene or a diet high in carbohydrates and low in calcium can result in dental problems in children adopted from other countries. Some children arrive with bleeding gums, deficient enamel on their teeth, or many cavities. Parents should be aware of the possibility that their child will need dental work, but save trips to the dentist, other than for emergency treatment, until the child is settled in her new home.

- Ninety percent of Asians, 75 percent of African Americans and Native Americans, and 50 percent of Latinos develop lactose intolerance by their teens. This means they have an insufficient amount of the enzyme lactase in the lining of the small intestine to break down lactose, the principal carbohydrate in milk. Babies as young as a year old may show signs of lactose intolerance, but it is more common for the symptoms to appear when children are eight to twelve years old and to worsen as children reach adolescence.

- Some children who were undernourished or malnourished have an early onset of puberty, perhaps because their sudden growth mimicked the growth spurt typical of adolescence.

- Children who were premature or who had a low birth weight, who were undernourished, who lacked vitamin D-fortified milk or formula, who were confined indoors for many months, or who were consistently heavily swaddled or overdressed may be at risk of rickets.

· Many parents who have adopted children from China have discovered a small scar on the children's bodies, usually in the abdomen or chest area, that sometimes resembles a cigarette burn. These scars are believed to be "marks of love" to let the children know they have a spiritual connection to their ancestors. The marks are made either with tiny acupuncture needles or with a lighted plant used in Chinese medicine. Rather than signs of abuse, the scars are apparently intended to let the children know that their birth families loved them. This practice may have been an ancient custom that fell out of favor until recent events caused its resurgence.

· Other medical conditions in children adopted internationally include exposure to radiation in children from parts of the former Soviet Union; the risk of hypothyroidism because of severe iodine deficiency in some parts of China; resistant strains of malaria in children from Cambodia, southern China, and Africa; gastrointestinal problems caused by *Helicobacter pylori;* lead poisoning; and vitamin A deficiency.

Even conscientious physicians sometimes fail to consider a diagnosis of a disease or medical condition seldom seen in Western countries. Therefore, adoptive parents need to educate themselves, as well as their health care providers, about the special medical concerns of internationally adopted children. Dana Johnson, M.D., operates a clinic for internationally adopted children at the University of Minnesota Medical Center and is an excellent source of information. Both Jenista and Johnson have published numerous articles on the health care of internationally adopted children in professional medical journals, which are good resources for health care providers. In addition, the Manitoba College of Physicians and

Surgeons has developed physicians' guidelines for assessing children adopted internationally, and the Adoptive Parents Association of British Columbia has prepared a brochure for parents to give to physicians on the children's first visit outlining the medical tests appropriate at that time. (For addresses for these organizations, see the Resources section at the back of this book.)

Development and Attachment

Although parents who adopt children from overseas often expect their children to have medical problems, they often do not expect problems in the area of developmental progress, attachment, or behavior. The majority of children adopted internationally—including those adopted from orphanages—progress well in these areas. However, some children have severe problems, and most of these are children who have been in orphanages. Furthermore, children who are having the most serious behavioral problems also tend to be the ones with attachment and developmental problems. It is not surprising that parents of these children tend to be the most stressed, particularly if they were unprepared for these problems.

Most of the recent research on the outcomes of internationally adopted children has focused on children from Romanian orphanages. However, the findings are consistent with earlier studies and can probably apply to children from orphanages in China, Eastern Europe, Latin America, and other places.

Perhaps the most interesting findings from a long-term study of Romanian children adopted by Canadian families are the factors that seem to be correlated with the most problematic outcomes. The researchers looked at children from Romanian orphanages shortly after their arrival and again three years later. Three years after the adoption, they found that roughly one-third of the children had no serious problems. (Serious problems were defined as an IQ below 85; behavioral problems severe enough to require professional help;

atypical insecure attachment; or the persistence of repetitive behaviors, such as rocking.) Another third had one or two of these problems, and the remaining third had three or all four problems.

It was not surprising that the longer the child spent in an orphanage, the more problems she had. However, this seemed to be the case *regardless of the conditions in the orphanage.* Nor did the characteristics of the children at the time of the adoption predict which children would have serious problems later on. Neither birth weight, weight at the time of the adoption, nor the parent's impression at first meeting of the child's general health or responsiveness or the parent's impression of the child's abilities was related to the number of serious problems the child would have later on.

In addition to the length of time the child had been in an orphanage, the following factors seemed to be related to the child's long-term prognosis:

- The number of Romanian children adopted. Romanian children with siblings adopted from Romania had more serious problems, particularly if they were adopted at the same time. It may be that when there was more than one child in the family with special needs, the added stress was more than the parents could handle.

- Higher socioeconomic status and family income. Parents with more financial resources seemed to have children with fewer long-term problems, perhaps because they had an easier time getting the children the interventions that were needed.

- Age of the adoptive mother. Children whose mothers were older at the time of adoption seemed to do better than those whose mothers were slightly younger, although still mature. The reason for this difference isn't clear, although it could be that the slight difference in experience made it possible for the older mothers to advocate more effectively for their children.

- Which parent traveled to the country to select the child. Although the characteristics of the children did not seem to predict which children would have more problems, children who were selected by the mothers or both parents had fewer problems than children selected by the fathers alone.

When Victor Groza, Ph.D., a social work researcher at Case Western Reserve University, looked at Romanian children brought to the United States for adoption, he, too, found that only about half the group had any kind of problems. However, a high percentage of children with problems had been in orphanages. Groza found that:

- 30 percent of children had delayed language development
- 29 percent had delayed development of fine motor skills
- 26 percent had delayed social development
- 24 percent had chronic medical problems
- 22 percent had delayed gross motor skills
- 21 percent had abnormally high levels of activity
- 19 percent wet the bed
- 18 percent were oversensitive to sensory stimulation, such as touch, sights, and sounds (see Chapter 2)
- 16 percent rocked themselves.

Attachment Behavior

The Canadian study of Romanian adoptees found that three years after placement, all the children from orphanages had formed attachments to their parents. About a third of them were *securely attached,* and another third were *insecurely attached* in commonly found, mild ways that do not usually lead to problems. The final third, however, showed *atypical insecure attachment,* which put them at risk of later problems. The children who had the most behavioral or developmental problems (as defined earlier in this chapter) also tended to have the most attachment problems. It may be that their lower IQ made it harder for them to communicate their needs or that their other behavioral problems made it more difficult for the parents to respond to them.

Many parents also reported that their children were "indiscriminately friendly." That is, they were affectionate and friendly to all adults and didn't seem to have the caution when meeting strangers that is normal. It appears that they learned to be indiscriminately friendly to become more privileged in the orphanage environment. Although parents initially think that their children's friendliness is charming, when the behavior persists, they become fearful that their children will be endangered by their own lack of fear. Some people have suggested that this behavior is actually an attachment disorder. However, the Canadian researchers did not find a clear relationship between indiscriminate friendliness and attachment. They did find that children with insecure attachments were more likely to show extreme forms of indiscriminate affection, such as wandering away from home without distress or being willing to go home with a stranger. Victor Groza says that because indiscriminate friendliness is a survival behavior, it can persist long after the original need for it is gone.

Considerations for Parents

Although the vast majority of children from orphanages do well, particularly if they have not spent much time in them and receive good intervention once in their adoptive families, when there are problems, they severely stress the family. Consequently, many professionals recommend that parents who adopt children from orphanages assume they are adopting children with special needs that will probably require professional services. They should get good preadoption counseling and preparation and have access to postplacement services, including early childhood development intervention, remedial education services, speech and language therapy, and occupational therapy. The workbook *With Eyes Wide Open* was developed by the Children's Home Society of Minnesota to help parents who adopt children from overseas who are older than twelve months get a realistic perspective on the challenges they may face, as well as their ability to meet those challenges.

11

Serious Behavioral Problems

Sometimes serious behavioral problems last beyond the typical "testing" phase of the adjustment period and challenge even the most capable and patient parents. These problems may include bed-wetting, soiling, temper tantrums, inappropriate sexual behavior, lying, stealing, running away, arson, truancy and other school problems, and the inability to form close relationships.

Experts, such as therapists and physicians, should be consulted for help with specific problems, yet many parents have found effective ways to modify some of their children's behavior and to live with the behavior they cannot change.

Dealing with Serious Problems

There are many possible explanations for serious behavioral problems in children, but experts do not agree on which physical or emotional traumas cause which problems if, indeed, there is a simple cause-and-effect relationship involved. Certainly, there are adopted children who have been traumatized, and the list of possible traumas is long: separation from the mother when the child was old enough to have formed a strong attachment; multiple homes and caretakers; failure to grieve for the significant losses; physical, sexual, or emotional abuse; malnutrition and neglect; and failure to experience a permanent, trusting relationship with an adult.

Most children who have been in the child welfare system for more than a year will have experienced more than one kind of emotional or physical trauma. These children will have emotional scars, but not all will react to their early trauma in the same way. Many will demonstrate serious behavioral problems; on the other hand, early deprivation and trauma seem to spur some children to high achievements (see Chapter 6). Still others develop behavioral problems without any apparent history of early trauma or neglect. It is imperative that we as adoptive parents recognize that while early life experiences may help explain a child's behavioral problems, they cannot predict them. In particular, we cannot say with certainty that a specific trauma results in a specific behavioral response.

Although most of us would like to know why our child is behaving the way he is, knowledge of what happened in the child's past may be only marginally helpful in living with a child who is exhibiting serious, perhaps even dangerous, behavioral problems. What is important is that the child change his behavior at least enough to function appropriately in the family and in society.

Much of the behavior that parents find most difficult to deal with can be categorized as follows:

- Lack of conscience—the inability to tell right from wrong or to feel remorse or regret when he does something wrong. Often a lack of conscience is the result of the child's failure to make attachments. The child who doesn't care about his parents is not motivated to behave in a way that will please them. Some children fail to develop a sense of conscience because values have never been clearly spelled out or because they have lived in many places with conflicting values.

· Inability to differentiate and express feelings. The child who has experienced early trauma may not know any other feelings besides pain and the lack of pain. He may not be motivated to improve his behavior because as long as he isn't in pain, he is experiencing the most "happiness" he has come to expect in life. Or a child may have been discouraged from expressing his emotions and so does not know how to express his feelings of anger, fear, grief, or love.

· Attachment disorder—the impaired ability to form a close, reciprocal relationship with an adult based on trust. Attachment disorders show up as a variety of behavioral problems, including inappropriate dependency or autonomy, demanding affection without reciprocating, difficulty showing affection at appropriate times or in appropriate ways, lack of trust, difficulty building and maintaining relationships, lack of conscience, poor impulse control, inability to consider consequences, and difficulty recognizing or expressing feelings, as well as cognitive problems and developmental delays.

· Oppositional defiant disorder—a pattern of negative, hostile, and defiant behavior without the more serious violations that are seen in conduct disorder. Children are argumentative with adults, frequently lose their temper, swear, are angry and resentful, and defy rules, beyond what might be considered common among children of that age.

· Conduct disorder—a persistent pattern of violating the basic rights of others, as well as societal norms and rules. Children with this disorder are commonly physically aggressive and may be cruel to other people or animals. They destroy property, sometimes through fire-setting, and often steal.

While oppositional defiant disorder, conduct disorder, and certain attachment disorders are all specific psychiatric diagnoses, many have behaviors in common.

Children with such problems, along with their parents and perhaps other members of the family, should be seeing a therapist regularly. But parents can use some techniques on their own. If these techniques seem to conflict with the treatment the therapist recommends, the parents may want to consider selecting another counselor.

We cannot give our child a conscience—that is a choice the child has to make. But we can show our child why a conscience is important and give him a framework or model for developing his own standards of behavior.

Past and Future

The adoptee who has been in several foster or adoptive homes may have behavioral problems because he has not completed his grief process. (Helping a child grieve is discussed in Chapter 5.) The child may need to make a life book or otherwise reconstruct the places he's lived and the people he's known before he can begin to care enough about his new parents to want to please them.

We should take care to remind our child of past events with our family. We should take pictures of the child and the family engaging in activities and put them in a permanent album. Children who have lived with many families have never experienced the thrill of looking through a photograph album and seeing the development of the family. A scrapbook, or perhaps the child's life book, can contain mementos of past activities and events.

Children need a sense of the past, but they also need a sense of the future to realize there is more than "living for today." Adoption specialist Barbara Tremitiere says we should talk about future events and plan for them so that our children begin to think in those terms. Discussions of Halloween costumes, summer vacation plans, Christmas celebrations, and other events can begin months in advance. Activities, such as 4-H, Junior Achievement, and scouting, in which children work on projects with specific goals in mind, should also be encouraged.

Talking about the future and reliving the past tell the child that he is a member of the family and that the family has a shared history and a future to look forward to.

Physical Contact

Touching is essential to the development of attachment, and attachment is essential to the development of a sense of conscience. Abused children often avoid physical contact at all costs, and while parents may have to proceed slowly with these children, they should not let the children prohibit physical touch. We know we do not intend to hurt our children by touching, so we can proceed slowly, starting with a slight touch on the shoulder and progressing to longer expressions of love. As was described in Chapter 2, children who spent an extensive amount of time in orphanages may not have received adequate sensory stimulation during their early years and may be hypersensitive to touch. Social worker Linda Katz points out that parents may have to be creative about finding nonthreatening ways to touch children who are especially sensitive to physical contact, for example, by brushing a child's hair, or helping a child swing a bat. Although these examples may not seem like significant forms of physical contact, touching is so powerful that even casual contact conveys an important message. It may take years for some children to lose their fear of physical contact, but a foundation of trust should be built from the beginning.

One way that child psychiatrist Gerald Nelson recommends for parents to get close to their child and build attachment is the "M&M game," in which the parent sits close to the child, while the child closes his eyes and sticks out his tongue. The parent places an M&M on the child's tongue and asks him to guess its color, pointing out that he won't be able to tell until the M&M melts. While the child is concentrating on the taste of the candy, the parent quietly tells him positive things about himself. Since the child cannot distinguish colors by taste, any color he guesses is "correct," and the child is rewarded with another candy. The parent and child can continue this way for about ten M&Ms. In effect, the child is rewarded for sitting calmly—both with candy and with the good things he hears about himself—and the parent and child have a pleasant, close experience. Even if the child catches on to the game, it can be fun.

Neutral Language

Children with chronic behavioral problems have been disciplined so often that they no longer listen to people saying they are "bad" or "naughty" or going to be "punished." These emotionally loaded words are also belittling and diminish the child's self-concept, which, in turn, leads to continued misbehavior. After all, if the child thinks of himself as worthless, he will behave that way.

Neutral terms, such as *unacceptable, inappropriate, intolerable,* or *provocative,* may challenge the child to stop and think about what is being said, but not convey a negative message about the child. Of course, the parents must be sure the child understands the words before they are used.

Josephine Anderson recommends that parents use a neutral word, agreed upon ahead of time, to "cue" the child that he is starting to behave inappropriately. For example, the parent and child could agree that when the parent says the word *cantaloupe,* it means the child's behavior is inappropriate and, if continued, will result in predictable consequences. The word is nonjudgmental, doesn't embarrass the child in front of his friends because only the child and parent know what it means, and can keep the situation from escalating. It is important to let the child choose the word, that it be a neutral term, and that the child clearly understand what is meant when it is said. The child can also use the word when he thinks his parents' behavior is starting to provoke him.

Expressing Feelings

Children may have to be taught appropriate ways to express their feelings—a difficult task for parents who were not encouraged as children to express their negatives feelings. Having grown up hearing "Big boys don't cry" or "Don't talk to your mother like that," parents are often unsure how to encourage children with a lot of anger and sadness to ventilate those emotions appropriately.

We should encourage our children to express their anger verbally, but within limits. For example, parents can permit a child to yell at them or a sibling as long as the child does not use vulgar language or personally attack the other person. In other words, the child should be taught to express what he is feeling, not what he thinks of the other person. He can be told that it is all right to want to hit someone, and even to think about it, but it is not permissible to hit someone. He may, however, punch a pillow, slam a tennis ball against a wall, smash empty aluminum cans, chop wood, or otherwise channel his negative feelings into acceptable physical activities.

Many children who are adopted after experiencing physical or emotional trauma do not cry readily, so the problem for parents is letting them know they can express their sadness or grief. One way to help children express themselves is to suggest how they appear to be feeling, for example, by saying, "You look sad. I think it's because . . . " Even if that doesn't result in an emotional release by the child, he will know that being sad is all right. Many counselors have posters or charts that depict different feelings through facial expressions. Parents can use these charts or posters to help their children learn what the emotion they are experiencing is called. Since children are sometimes reluctant to cry in front of other people, in her book, *Helping Children Cope with Separation and Loss,* Claudia Jewett Jarratt advises, that parents suggest that the child cry after he goes to bed or in the shower where no one will hear.

Natural Consequences

Crucial to the development of a conscience is the understanding that actions have logical and natural consequences. The child without a conscience has little sense of the future and, consequently, can't see why doing something right now will benefit him later. Teaching a child that there are consequences to his actions requires that the child be allowed to make choices, and this can be difficult for parents. For example, if the child does not take his dirty clothes to the laundry room, they do not get washed; hence, he doesn't have clean clothes to wear to school. To allow the child to make this choice, parents must be willing to let their child go to school in dirty or wrinkled clothes. Parents must decide what is more important: that their child look clean and neat or that he have the chance to make the choice and take the consequences. In this case, they may need to remind themselves that looking unkempt affects only the child and refuse to accept responsibility for his appearance—even though some people will think that the boy is untidy because his parents are neglecting their responsibilities. The child's refusal to take care of his dirty clothes may seem like a minor problem compared to his other behavior, such as truancy or drug abuse, but by being forced to accept responsibility for his actions in these small areas, the child learns the idea of accepting consequences for his actions, which he can apply to more important situations.

An excellent example of allowing children to take the consequences of their actions was described in the advice column "Dear Abby." Children who had been suspended from the school bus for misbehavior were required by their parents to walk the several miles to school for the duration of the suspension. The parents followed the children in their cars to make sure they went to school and were safe. Though many readers wrote in to criticize the parents, the parents' actions allowed the children to realize that if they did not follow the rules of the school bus, they would not be allowed to ride it, and if they could not ride the school bus, they would have to walk to school.

In some cases, the natural consequences of a child's actions may be serious, and the parents should let the child know that they are not going to "protect" him from those consequences. For example, the parents can say, "We don't want you to take the car without permission because we care about you and want to know where you are going and how you are getting there." The parents should let the child know that they expect him to make the right choice by saying, "We know you wouldn't deliberately cause us concern, so if the car is missing, we will assume it is stolen and report it to the police."

Behavior Diary

It may be helpful for parents to keep a "behavior diary" about their child. Each day, the parents can note actions or events that got out of hand, as well as actions that were potentially explosive, but kept in control. The time of day and events leading up to the situation can also be recorded. The diary can help the parents chart their child's progress, since when the child is in a period of difficult behavior, it sometimes seems that he has always behaved that way. It also helps to look back and see that a certain behavior had a definite starting point and that there have been similar periods in the past. In addition, by keeping track of what led up to the behavior, the parents may be able to see patterns. For example, conflict may seem to occur immediately after the child comes home from school. Knowing when behavior is likely to get out of hand can help prevent it. Perhaps the child explodes after school because he is having trouble at school or because he is hungry then. Identifying the school problem or sending a snack with him to eat on the way home may prevent or minimize further conflict. Each parent should keep a separate diary, since each parent has different interactions with the child, and the child can be encouraged to keep his own record. The diary should be used to chart improvement and never be used against the child to remind him of past misbehavior.

Parents in Charge

To discipline our children effectively, we must believe in our right to act as our children's parents, though developing this sense of entitlement can be particularly difficult with a child adopted at an older age who has severe behavioral problems. The adoptive parents and child will not share a history, and the child may remember his birth parents or foster parents and have contact with them. As a result, the adoptive parents may feel like outsiders. In addition, the child with behavioral problems is likely to have a therapist, a social worker, and perhaps a special education teacher or counselor at school, all of whom have opinions about how the child should be cared for. Thus, the parents may feel like members of a therapeutic or caretaking "team," rather than parents. We must remember that even though the child has had other parents and has other people who care about him or who play a significant role in his life, we are the only people who can or should act as his parents. Important as professionals are, the social service personnel dealing with the child are not in charge; parents do not have to defer to them. In fact, parents should act as though they are employing these professionals even if they aren't paying the bills. In a real sense, the helping professionals are working for the family, not vice versa.

While many children have "survivor" skills and give the impression they can take care of themselves, Barbara Tremitiere reminds parents that these children want strong parents so they can act like children. Chances are the child entered the child welfare system because he, rather than his birthparents, was in charge. The child who has been in control is likely to try to hang onto that control, but down deep he wants to be the child he is, and that means having parents who are willing to set firm, consistent limits and follow through to ensure they are not exceeded.

Setting and enforcing limits is not an easy task for parents of children without consciences. Such children are not likely to follow directions for the same reasons other children do—because they like to please their parents, obeying their parents is the "right" thing to do, or they fear the consequences of not following the directives. These children do, however, respect someone stronger than they are. Demonstrating who is in charge may seem more authoritarian than many of today's parents would like, but reasoning with a child without a conscience or without an emotional attachment is unlikely to be effective.

Parents who attempt to show they are in charge should select a situation they can have some control over. It also may be wise to take the initial stand on a situation that is not important to the child, such as hanging up his coat. Then, when authority has been established, more important issues can be settled. Parents show they are in charge by following through on a directive; when the child is told to wash the dishes, the dishes must be washed—and washed well. If they aren't, the child must do them again. Obviously, this situation can turn into a test of wills. It may seem easier to allow a mediocre job to pass for the completion of a chore, but it is important for the children to learn that they cannot manipulate their parents.

A primary goal of a therapist working with families with unruly children should be to help the parents take charge, set limits, and follow through. Developing insight into why problems developed and allowing children to express their feelings are valuable benefits of therapy, but parents who live with children with severe behavioral problems need to work out tolerable living arrangements. Some methods that behavior-oriented therapists use to empower parents may be unusual. Parents should find out from other clients whether the techniques are effective before rejecting them.

When setting limits, parents should try to keep the number of rules in the family down to a manageable number. More important, they should not make rules they cannot enforce. For example, parents cannot enforce a rule prohibiting the child from using drugs because they cannot be with the child all the time. They can, however, enforce a rule that prohibits the child's use of drugs at home. To do so effectively, we need to decide what values are critical in our family and perhaps let go of some that are desirable, but not critical. In deciding on rules, parents should take into account their personal values, not just what will help maintain order. For example, they may require everyone to eat dinner together each evening in addition to prohibiting physical violence or alcohol abuse in the home.

The Abused Child

The child who has been abused often will seem to elicit additional abuse, and the parents must take great care not to fall into this trap. The child isn't eliciting abuse because he likes it; he is reproducing an anxiety-producing event in the hope that the next time he will be in control of it. Children who have been sexually abused may be flirtatious or openly seductive. The child who has been physically abused may provoke parents to the point where they either strike the child or come close to hitting him. Besides reproducing the abuse to gain control of it, some children may provoke abuse because it is the only pattern of parent-child interaction they know. Children who were sexually abused may be seductive because it is the only way they know to be close to an adult. Some children may believe, on the basis of their experience, that all parents hit their children and want to find out the limits in this family before abuse occurs. Often, the more the parents resist, the more the child escalates his provocative behavior, in effect negatively reinforcing the parents for their self-control. As one boy said to his adoptive mother after she hit him, "I finally gotcha. I knew I would— it just took you longer than the rest."

Child abuse can be prevented by proper preparation by the adoption agency. Being told the child's history and patterns of behavior can help prepare parents for what to expect. Any parent has the potential to abuse his child. Just because we have never been tempted to abuse other children and have been "approved" as adoptive parents does not preclude the possibility that we will be pushed to the brink of abuse. Parents should analyze their own emotional limits, capacity for anger, and attitudes toward disobedience and rule breaking so they can anticipate a potentially abusive situation and head it off. If they feel they are becoming abusive, they should enlist the services available to abusive parents; that is, they should have some kind of respite child care available and may even want to participate in Parents Anonymous, a self-help group for abusive parents. Parents should also have a social worker or counselor who understands their potentially explosive situation and who is willing to work with them. Ideally, the parents should find out whom they can work with before they need to call that person, having questioned their social worker or therapist ahead of time about her attitudes. Obviously, if the social worker or therapist does not understand the potential for abuse, calling her at a time of crisis could result in the child being removed from the home. Parents will want to be sure that the person they call on for help is as committed to keeping the adoptive family together as she would a biological family in similar circumstances.

The provocative child is adept at finding the parents' vulnerable points. A recently divorced mother, who cares deeply for her children, was told by her son: "You don't know how to take care of me and you didn't know how to take care of dad." She slapped him; he had found her most sensitive area, and she learned what her emotional limits were.

Adoptive parents who succumb to the temptation for abuse should keep in mind that the child has probably escalated his behavior for the purpose of eliciting abuse. There is no defense for child abuse—adults have the responsibility to maintain control of themselves. But a parent should not give up his role just because he equates hitting a child with failure as a parent. If the parent is willing to continue parenting the child and willing to work with a therapist to prevent further instances of abuse, the abusive incident alone is not sufficient reason to disrupt the adoption. Naturally, the parent will feel guilty. He will probably feel he is "no better" than the birth parents who beat the child. What is critical, however, is that the parent must be willing to try to prevent abuse from recurring.

Social worker John Boyne pointed out at a national adoption conference that the child who has been abused may understand the problems an allegation of abuse creates for parents and how to manipulate the child welfare system to make such a report. Some adoptive parents have false claims of child abuse filed against them by a child who is trying to gain control over his parents or who wants to put distance between himself and the parents he is starting to feel close to, having learned from previous placements that feeling close to someone results in pain when separated from that person. On occasion, adoptive parents will be falsely accused of child abuse by a teacher, medical personnel, or a neighbor who misinterprets the bruises of a hyperactive child or the Mongolian spot that resembles a bruise on Asian and Indian children.

Although most child protection workers are fair and want to work with the family, they may not all understand the manipulative child or take into account the child's psychological and social history in investigating the child abuse claim. In addition, child protection workers are trained to believe that children do not lie about abuse—and for the vast majority of children, that is true. But a child who lacks a conscience, does not care about people, has a history of lying and manipulative behavior, and who is sophisticated in the workings of the child welfare system may lie about child abuse.

Adoption and child advocacy groups are encouraging child protection workers to become more informed about adoption and to take into consideration all historical information about the child, as well as statements from psychological, educational, and medical resources, in investigating a child abuse claim. Pediatrician and adoptive parent Jerri Ann Jenista recommends that during the first medical examination after the child's placement, any signs of previous trauma, including previously broken bones and signs of prior sexual abuse, be clearly recorded. If a claim of child abuse is later filed against the adoptive parent, it can be important to have evidence of the child's medical condition at the time of the placement. Adoption specialist Josephine Anderson recommends that parents of children with behavioral problems write a statement outlining the child's historical and current behavioral patterns and have the document signed by a juvenile court judge, pastor, physician, psychiatrist, psychologist, and social worker. The parent who has a verified statement in hand when a child protection worker begins investigating a claim looks less like a defensive parent and more like a parent who understands and recognizes her child's problems.

The parent who has a false claim of child abuse filed against her, especially by the child, is likely to be devastated, especially if the child has been provocative and the parent has resisted the urge to hurt him. Even if the case against the parent is dismissed, it is likely first to become public, causing embarrassment with friends, relatives, and coworkers. Parents who are having a difficult time with their child may reevaluate their decision to adopt and wonder if the pain is worth the small difference they seem to be making in the child. They will need a firm support system—friends, a minister, a therapist, a social worker, or an adoptive parent group—to help them through what will be a traumatic experience.

Effect on the Family

While serious behavioral problems are not limited to children who were adopted after infancy, most parents who adopt older children who have been in foster care, residential treatment centers, or other adoptive homes expect their children to have some emotional problems. Agencies today are taking greater care to prepare children for the move to their adoptive families and to prepare parents for the kinds of behavior they can expect from the children. They have found that parents are willing to adopt emotionally troubled children as long as they know what to expect and that many of the difficulties families have faced in the past have been the result of inadequate preparation of the children or the families.

Being prepared helps, but it is not the whole answer. Although parents who decide to adopt a child with known behavioral problems have the advantage of realistic expectations, both of their child's behavior and of the rewards of parenthood, they are not immune to the effects of that behavior on themselves or the family.

Maintaining a Positive Self-Image

Living with a child with chronic, serious behavioral problems is a strain, no matter how much the parents understand their child's behavior or how committed they are to raising the child. Furthermore, parents are not completely altruistic in adopting a child—they have their own needs and expectations. Usually people adopt because they want to love a child and feel love in return. The child who does not express affection, whose affection is only superficial, or who seems to demand affection from strangers while rebuffing his parents' emotional overtures is not meeting the parents' needs. Parents whose child defies parental, community, and school authorities because he does not care whether he does right or wrong can cause them to wonder what effect they are having on the child or will have in the future.

It is not unusual for parents in these circumstances to feel like failures—to feel that they have let down themselves; the agency; and, most of all, the adopted child. They may be frustrated by the slow progress or lack of progress that their child is making. They may even despair at times that the situation will ever improve. Linda Katz says that parents do better under these circumstances if they are able to delay gratification—if they don't expect to "get anything back" from their efforts immediately. This is contrary to what most of us expect from raising children. We expect a smile in response to ours or the "reward" of seeing development proceed as a result of our efforts. It may be years before parents of children with serious behavioral problems see any sign that they are having any effect. It may be difficult for parents to realize or be comforted by the fact that the child might be doing far worse in another environment.

Parents often have more difficulty living with a child with serious behavioral problems if he is the only child or if he was adopted as the second child to provide a playmate for a first child. They may have unrealistic expectations of that child and not enough parenting experience and self-confidence. Parents who adopt a difficult child after raising several other children seem to draw on their previous successes to keep their self-image strong. Those with one or two children can focus on the child with behavioral problems—perhaps over-doing it—while in a large family, the behavioral problems are diffused, to some extent, by the number of children in the family who require attention.

Parents in the helping professions may be particularly susceptible to feeling like failures. More than one social worker or psychologist has said something like, "I thought I would be the ideal parent for this child. Living with him has helped me do my job better, but my profession hasn't made it easier to live with him." Those in the helping professions should remember that they cannot be both therapist and parent to the same child. Nor does the success or failure they experience as a parent reflect on their professional life.

Some parents are most vulnerable when the child's behavior seems directed at them—when the child openly rejects the parents' affection, attacks them physically or verbally, or seems to be deliberately embarrassing them. It is difficult, but important, to remember that the child would be behaving the same way with any new parent; it is not a personal rejection or statement of contempt. While most of us think that a child in an abusive or temporary situation would prefer to be in a permanent home with loving and caring parents, Barbara Tremitiere says that children often prefer what is familiar, even if it means suffering.

Isolation

Parents of children with serious behavioral problems frequently feel isolated, like they are the only parents having such serious problems. Parents of a child whose behavior has resulted in his being suspended from school or arrested by the police or that has had other public repercussions may be embarrassed and not want to face their friends. Parents who are highly visible in their communities and are expected to have children whose behavior is beyond reproach, such as ministers and probation officers, may be particularly susceptible to feeling that their children's behavior has cut them off from their community. Parents need to separate their child's behavior from themselves and not allow themselves to feel judged for the child's actions.

Adoptive parent support groups can be helpful because people in them are experiencing similar problems. Nevertheless, some parents find it difficult to be open about their problems even with other adoptive parents. Consequently, people who could provide each other with emotional support hold back, each thinking that theirs is the only family with such problems. One solution is to form a subgroup of adoptive parents with the criterion for membership being an emotionally troubled child. Such groups have found it helpful to meet apart from the main group; to require attendance at meetings, rather than have people come just when they are having a crisis; and to set some rules for confidentiality.

But there are also times when what is needed is a break from parenting. Parents should give themselves a chance to do something successfully, such as their jobs, church work, or other nonparenting activities. This will not only counteract some of the feelings of failure they may experience as a result of their interaction with their child, it will also give them time away from the child and from parenting.

Strong Emotions

Parents are likely to have conflicting feelings about a difficult child—loving him and wanting him to love them, but sometimes feeling so hurt, angry, and frustrated that they want to lash out at him physically or verbally. They may be determined to raise the child, but consider disrupting the adoption. Parents should try to identify exactly what is making them feel uncomfortable—the child's behavior or their feelings about the child. Linda Katz says that many parents are not prepared for the strong, negative feelings their child's behavior will elicit, and what they may want is an end to their unpleasant feelings, rather than an end to the relationship with the child. Most of the time they dislike what the child is doing, not the child himself. But sometimes parents may feel that they hate the child. At those times, they can give themselves permission to feel that way, but set limits on how long they will feel that way and what the consequences will be, saying, for example, "I'm going to let myself hate him until he goes to bed, but I will not hurt him physically or verbally, and I will not hate him in the morning."

The Role of the Father and Husband

Because the mother tends to be the primary caretaker, much conflict takes place between her and the child. Consequently, she is at a greater risk of feeling guilty and like a failure. She sometimes hides these emotions from her husband, not wanting him to know she is a "failure."

The marital relationship may also suffer from the strain of having a child with behavioral problems, in part because the family is under a lot of stress, and in part because some children are skilled at playing one parent against the other, having learned that if the parents are arguing with each other, they are not paying attention to the children. Vanessa's son would verbally abuse her and physically attack her when they were alone, but when Vanessa's husband John was there, the boy was calm and pleasant. John thought Vanessa was exaggerating her descriptions of the boy's behavior and that she just needed to learn how to handle the boy as well as he did; after all, even Vanessa agreed that the boy wasn't a problem when his father was home. Eventually, through counseling, John learned that his son was being selective and manipulative in his behavior and gave his wife the support she needed.

When there are two parents, the husband needs to do more than provide his wife with emotional support. In a small study, Joyce S. Cohen found that adoptions were less likely to be disrupted when the husband could give his wife relief—time to refresh and rejuvenate herself outside the home while he took over the primary parenting role. When the husband sees his job as merely sustaining the wife emotionally—listening to her express her feelings—he is likely to get worn down by the complaining and may even demand that the source of her problems be eliminated; that is, that the child be returned to the child welfare system.

Realistic Expectations

Parents who do well raising children with serious behavioral problems are those who can take small bits of progress and see them as major successes. They aren't expecting miracles or drastic changes overnight. They are happy to see any improvement at all and to know that they may have made a little difference or, at the least, kept the child's situation from becoming worse. For example, the parents may like their daughter to quit using drugs completely, but can see progress in the fact that she is no longer prostituting herself to get money to buy drugs.

Parents should celebrate the successes they have. In some cases, it is appropriate to celebrate as a family with a special meal or other pleasant activity. At other times, the parents may want to keep their sense of success private. It would not be appropriate, for example, to have a party honoring the daughter who is no longer selling her sexual favors, but together the parents should somehow take note of the progress and let it revitalize them for future challenges.

Obviously, parents who are expected to find something to feel good about in what is probably a grim situation must have a sense of humor. Perhaps more than anything else, the ability to laugh will help them through the dark times there are bound to be when raising children with serious behavioral problems.

Effect on Siblings

Many of the situations that arise when a child with serious behavioral problems joins the family may continue after the adjustment period. Parents should be prepared to continue to deal with the issue of fairness—that they have different standards for different children—as well as be aware that the other children in the home may be embarrassed by the behavior of the child, particularly at school. Siblings may be the object of inappropriate sexual overtures, and parents should take care to protect them (see Chapter 2).

Siblings should be given permission to express their feelings about the child with behavioral problems. A sensitive child will recognize that his parents are having a difficult time and may think that if he complains about the child's behavior, he is adding to his parents' burden. One mother reported that her son burst into tears one day, saying about his sibling, "I've tried and tried to like him but I just can't." He clearly felt he had let his parents down by not doing his job—liking his sibling. The mother reassured him that there were days when she didn't like the boy either and let him know his feelings were both normal and acceptable.

Like their parents, brothers and sisters of the child with serious behavioral problems may need respite—a place to go when the situation at home becomes too difficult. A relative, friend, or parents of one of the children's friends could be enlisted to keep them overnight or for a weekend when they need a break from the turmoil at home.

In addition, the siblings may be involved in counseling. Many therapists believe it wise to include all family members in counseling, even though one child in particular may be having problems, not only because that child's problems affect the entire family, but because it is less stigmatizing to the child with problems if everyone is in therapy. Rather than the child being isolated as "the problem," the problem is the family not functioning smoothly.

Living with a sibling who has serious behavioral problems often contributes to the maturity of the other children, especially those born into the family. The children learn tolerance, compassion, and how to interact with people with different values and attitudes. Though the experience is sometimes painful, the children are much less isolated from the problems of the world than are other children and grow as a result.

Residential Treatment

When a child's behavioral or emotional problems reach the point when he can no longer be managed with outpatient treatment, parents sometimes must place the child in some form of out-of-home care—a psychiatric hospital, structured school, therapeutic foster home, or residential treatment center or group home. Placing a child in residential care is often an intense emotional experience for everyone in the family. The parents and other children in the family may not be prepared for the broad range of feelings they will have, says Vera Fahlberg, M.D., author of *Residential Treatment: A Tapestry of Many Therapies*. Family members feel both relief and grief, fear as well as safety, despair mixed with hope, and peace on top of anger.

By the time parents decide to place a child in out-of-home care, everyone in the family is usually physically and emotionally exhausted from living with the child who is out of control. Once the decision is made, however, the process is far from over. The parents need to decide what type of treatment to seek and may receive conflicting advice from the professionals they have been dealing with. Not only must they investigate therapy options, but they must look into ways to fund what is an expensive form of treatment. Some parents have had to go to court to get the state to assume financial responsibility for the children's treatment. When it is necessary to do so, it is important for adoptive parents to get good legal advice so that they do not jeopardize their parental rights to get financial assistance.

Parents do not always find the emotional support they need at this time. Some people may think they are abandoning the child, while others may think they should go further and have the adoption set aside. The parents may feel guilty that they "failed" to meet their child's needs; hopeful that the treatment will work; yet fearful that if it doesn't, they have exhausted their options. At the same time, they must deal with the reactions of other children in the family, including the fear that the adoption is dissolving and that they will be the next ones to have to leave the family. During this stressful time, all the family members need to recognize the strain of the situation and take the time to take care of themselves and each other.

Once the child has been removed from the home, the parents and the other children in the family may feel relief—and guilt at that relief. However, the overwhelming feeling, Fahlberg says, is grief. As peaceful as the household may be, there is still an empty place at the table. Families should use the first months the child is in residential treatment to shore up their relationships. The other children in the family may have been neglected while the parents dealt with one crisis after another. The husband and wife may have gotten out of the habit of communicating about anything but their child's latest emergency. The family needs to get back to feeling strong and capable and learn to enjoy themselves again.

When the child's out-of-home treatment is completed and the time comes for the child to return home, Fahlberg says that the family members may experience many of the same emotions they had when the child was placed in residential care. They are hopeful that the treatment worked, but fearful that the child will revert to his old behaviors. Sandra and Jeff's daughter was suicidal before she went into residential treatment, and her unpredictability had scared and disrupted the family's life. After she returned home, it was months before the other children in the family trusted her. She was resentful—she had worked hard in her treatment program to get well and change her behavior, and she didn't want to have to "prove" herself again. Family counseling was necessary to help the family communicate and reintegrate at this critical time. Though it was a rocky time, the daughter improved and the family survived.

The Threat of Adoption Disruption

Sometimes families and adoptees cannot make the adjustments necessary to continue living together. Technically, when this happens before the adoption is finalized, it is known as disruption; after finalization, it is called dissolution. But in human terms, whenever it happens, it is a disruption for the child and for the family. As we learn more about what causes the breakdown of adoptions and as more agencies provide services to help families in crisis, disruptions and dissolutions should become less common.

Causes of Adoption Disruption

Kathryn Donley Ziegler, an expert on adoption disruption, believes there are three reasons why adoptions break down:

- Unidentified factors—factors not recognized as critical at the time of the placement—for example, the adoptive parents live on a farm and the adoptee is used to city life. He may not be able to adjust to the different social atmosphere or smaller school.
- Unpredictable life events, such as divorce or the death of a parent, which place additional stress on the family
- Misassessment of the readiness of the child or the family—that is, either the child or the family (or both) is not adequately prepared for the adoption. This is probably the primary cause of disruptions.

Although the child with behavioral problems is at a greater risk of disruption, it is incorrect to assume that the more difficult the child is, the more likely the adoption will end in disruption. Some adoptions of children with extreme behavioral problems are succeeding, while the adoptions of children who have less serious problems are disrupted. The child must be ready for the adoption—a subjective assessment made by the social worker—and the parents must have the skills and willingness to raise the child who has serious behavioral problems. In general, older children are at a greater risk having a disrupted adoption, especially if they have had a previous adoptive placement disrupt. Disruption does not seem to be related to a child's gender or race, nor does it seem to make a difference whether the child was placed with siblings or whether the other children in the family were adopted or born into the family. Single parents do not appear to be any more likely than married couples to disrupt an adoption.

Disruption often occurs during periods of major change in the child and the family, such as during the adjustment period, when the child changes schools or the family moves to a new town, or during adolescence.

Stages of Adoption Disruption

Ziegler identified predictable stages that families go through when an adoption is disrupting:

- Noticeable family discomfort that does not diminish over time.
- Discomfort that markedly increases.
- Complaints that are out of proportion. Parents may focus on a particular behavior of the child or may have the general complaint that "everything the child does is wrong."
- A calm period during which conflict is not resolved, but appears to disappear. The family can't explain why things have improved because nothing has really changed.
- Resurfacing of unresolved complaints, resulting in a crisis.
- The decision to disrupt the adoption.

Sometimes it is the child who wants to leave, not the parents who want him removed, but the stages are similar.

Families who are in the early stages of adoption disruption need help because the situation can escalate rapidly. Some families do not call the adoption agency for help until they have already decided there is no choice but to disrupt. Rather than seeking help, they are seeking permission to disrupt, saying, in effect, "Look how bad this situation is. There is no solution but disruption." And if they have not had help until that point, their conclusion probably is accurate. Many times, though, a different solution could have been found had the family sought help earlier. Ideally, a family should be able to look to their social worker for help in resolving conflicts. But not all social workers are trained to work with families who are in crisis, and not all adoption agencies offer adequate postadoption services. The social worker may panic and remove the child without first trying to keep the family intact, perhaps because of past experiences with families in crisis. Or she may not understand the commitment and attachment in adoptive families and not realize how important it is to try to help the family stay together. Her own ego may become involved if she sees an adoption disruption as a failure of the person who made the placement. All adoptive families, particularly those adopting children who are at high a risk of disruption, should find out early the attitude of the social worker toward disruption and the services available through the agency for families in crisis. If the services are not adequate, the family can look for another agency that is willing to help them if they are in danger of disrupting or find a therapist with experience in this area.

When Adoptions Disrupt

Once a decision has been made to disrupt an adoption, the parents' first task should be to help prepare the child for the move out of the home. The child should know why he is moving, in terms that do not lay the blame on him. For example, the parents can say, quite accurately, "We found out that we aren't as patient as we thought we could be, and it scares us that you set fires when you get angry. Perhaps your new parents will be more patient or not as easily scared. Or maybe you'll find a way to express your anger that isn't so scary." The child should receive permission from his parents to move on and to love other people. The parents can say, "We care about you and want you to be happy. We'll always remember you, but we hope you will have another family that you can be happy in." The child should have an opportunity to say good-bye to other people who are important to him, such as friends or teachers, as well as help explaining to them why he is leaving, again in a way that does not place the blame on him. He should take with him photographs of the family and other mementos that are important to him. He may be hurting so much that he doesn't seem to want any memories of the home or family. If that is the case, the parents should see that his social worker keeps the items for him because he will need evidence of places he has been and people he has lived with. A ritual can be an effective way of communicating to the child, as well as to other children in the family, that a significant change in the family is taking place. Through the ritual, people who were important to the child can say good-bye, offer good wishes, and perhaps give a gift of remembrance.

Although the parents might expect to feel relieved when the child leaves the home, they are likely to feel grief. In particular, they may feel angry and try to fix blame on someone else — on the agency for not preparing them adequately, on the child for acting the way he did, or perhaps on the therapist who was unable to resolve the crisis. They are also likely to blame themselves, think of the things they should have done, the feelings they might have had, and what could have been "if only . . . " They may feel despondent—that they are failures as parents and as human beings. If the grief process is allowed to run its course, they will ultimately reach the acceptance stage, when they can begin to consider another adoption.

If there are other children in the home, the parents have to make clear what happened in such a way that they do not assign blame. Although parents often begin thinking about disruption when they believe the child's behavior is having a detrimental effect on other children in the family, the other children should not feel responsible. Particularly if there are other adopted children in the family, the parents will have to reassure them they are not going to have to leave, too. The parents may need counseling at this time to help them through their grief, and the other children may need therapy to deal with their fear that staying in the family is contingent on their good behavior.

Resources for the Family

Parents who adopt a child with behavioral problems should not wait for a crisis to develop, but should consider family counseling that is necessary for the success of the adoption. Other community resources also may be needed to help the child or parents, such as special education services or an adoption-support group. If the child has not been adequately prepared for the adoption, for example, if he does not have a life book or another record of his previous placements and significant people, or if he has questions related to where he has been before, that work will have to be done. The social worker, counselor, or adoptive parents can reconstruct the child's past with the cooperation of agencies who have knowledge of the child's history. The family should expect crises in the adoption of a child with behavioral problems and line up ahead of time the resources they can draw on at any time of the day or night, such as other families who can take the child for a period of respite or an emergency number for the therapist.

Working with Professionals

When seeking help from professionals, the parents should remember that although the social worker or therapist may give advice, only they are responsible for the child and should make the final decisions. This responsibility can be particularly difficult before an adoption is finalized because the parents may not have a complete sense of entitlement as long as the agency retains a controlling role in the child's life. But it is important for the parents to make decisions for the child—first, because even if the child has lived with them only for a short time, they probably know the child better than the professionals do and second, because parents must feel completely in charge to be effective with children who have behavioral problems. If the child perceives that the parents do not have the final say in matters concerning him, he may use that fact to undermine the authority they do have.

When possible, parents should work with therapists and other professionals who understand that adoption adds another dimension to many situations in a person's life and in family life. One complaint of adoptive parents is that professionals do not understand that experiences prior to a child's adoptive placement and the adoption experience itself can affect the child's behavior, both immediately after placement and years later. Professionals with insight into adoptive families are better able to identify when a problem is adoption related and when it is not and are unlikely to let misunderstandings or personal prejudices about adoption interfere with the services they are providing. The parents of a child with behavioral problems that are probably related to the number of families he has lived with during his life do not need to feel responsible for all the child's problems.

When parents have no choice but to work with a professional who is uninformed about adoption, they should keep in mind that they are the experts and educate the professional, keeping him from making decisions based on false assumptions about the adoptive family. Too often, in seeking advice from someone, we defer to the person's authority in all areas; we want that person to solve the problem, so we let him be the expert. We must remember that we retain some expertise, particularly about our children and families, even though we seek help from someone else. And the professional who is not willing to consider the parents' viewpoint is not worth the parents' time and effort.

Choosing a Therapist

Parents who adopt children with serious behavioral problems should select a therapist whose goal is to change behavior, not help the child develop insight, says psychologist James Mahoney. These "task-oriented" or "action-oriented" therapists are likely to be considered unconventional by professionals who practice "talk therapy." Indeed, they may use unusual techniques because they will do whatever produces results—by going to the family's home for counseling sessions, for example. The children probably will intensely dislike such a therapist during therapy, but will like him just as intensely when therapy is complete, whereas the therapist will be popular with the parents during the counseling period because results are apparent within a few months.

Mahoney believes that a therapist should have other qualities, such as these:

- accurate empathy—the ability to reflect accurately the feelings the client is having
- unconditional positive regard—the ability to find something she likes about the client
- nonpossessive warmth—enjoyment at being part of the process of improvement, but willing to let go when her job is completed.

Adoptive families who are seeking a therapist should ask other adoptive families for recommendations and interview the therapists to find out their attitudes toward adoption, their approach to therapy, and their experience dealing with children with behavioral problems.

Busy parents who cannot find a therapist who is sensitive to adoption issues in their area may be tempted to use whatever counselors are available, rather than drive long distances to see a therapist who has insight into adoption. If these parents live in an area large enough to have several adoptive families who need the services of a therapist, they may be able to entice the therapist to hold "office hours" in their area once a week or once a month. If not, they should consider that the services of a therapist who is knowledgeable about adoption issues are worth the commuting time.

Books and Other Resources

In recent years, a number of books have been written for parents of children with serious behavioral problems. These books offer more detailed descriptions, treatments, and advice than can be addressed in this book, and parents are encouraged to refer to them for more information. Many of the books are listed in the Resources section at the end of this book. There are also numerous resources on the Internet, including discussion groups and E-mail mailing lists that act as support groups and sources of information for parents of children with a particular set of behaviors, such as ADD.

12

Special Situations in Adoption

🔊 Jim Forderer and Marian Aiken-Forderer met through their mutual interest in adoption. Both were single adoptive parents of children with physical disabilities, and they shared the challenges of adoptive parents, of single parents, and of parents of disabled children. When their marriage merged them into a family with eleven children, they discovered they had much in common with other large adoptive families. Their particular situation is unique, but there are many families today who do not fit the traditional picture of adoptive families.

Parenting the Mentally or Physically Disabled Child

Parents who adopt a child with mental or physical disabilities have much in common with the biological parents of a child with a similar condition. Additional involvement is required of them and other family members. The parents must be advocates for the child in the social service system, the educational system, and the health care system. They must know more than bureaucrats about what state services are mandated for disabled children, more than teachers about the child's educational needs and abilities, and more than physicians about the child's condition.

It is not surprising, then, that adoptive parents of disabled children are often more involved with organizations that deal with their children's particular conditions, such as the United Cerebral Palsy Association or Association for Retarded Citizens, than with adoption organizations, since the disability issues seem more pressing than the adoption issues. Nevertheless, there are some differences between being the biological parents and being the adoptive parents of disabled children.

Preparation and Expectations

Parents who adopt a child with a known disability do not have the same reaction to the child's disability as do parents who give birth to or adopt what they expect to be a healthy child. When a disability is unexpected, parents typically react with shock, denial, anger, and the other stages of grief. They have experienced the loss of the healthy child they expected and respond by trying to find a physician who can "fix" or cure the child or someone or something to blame for the disability. Biological parents often feel guilty for somehow causing the child's disability or for bringing her into the world. They fear how the child's disability will affect their lifestyle and future. They have to modify their expectations of parenthood and the "rewards" they would receive from their children.

Parents who know their child's mental or physical condition prior to adoption have an opportunity to learn what life with the child will be like before they agree to be her parents. They can investigate community resources ahead of time, consider the effect that raising a disabled child will have on other children in the family, and plan for the times that have been found to be critical in the lives of families with disabled children—such as when the child enters school, when the child reaches adolescence, when the child becomes an adult, and when the parents can no longer care for her because of age or infirmity. Without grief or guilt to interfere, these parents can effectively concentrate on the child's needs from the beginning.

There may still be unforeseen aspects of raising a child with a disability, and adoptive parents have to adjust their expectations accordingly, sometimes even going through a minor grief process before accepting the unexpected. Perhaps the medical report on the child was inadequate, or they did not know what questions to ask to get a complete understanding of the child's problem. Jim Forderer points out that parents sometimes are unprepared for conditions that are secondary to the primary disability, such as body odor or bedsores.

The child with a grim prognosis will often rapidly improve soon after placement because she is receiving the love, personal attention, and treatment she has needed. So the child who had been diagnosed as severely mentally retarded advances to where she can be considered mildly retarded, or the child who was not expected to use her hands learns to feed herself. Observing the effect of love and good quality care, parents may expect the progress to continue until the child is fully able. Ultimately, this unrealistic hope may put them in the same situation as the parents who expected a healthy child, and adoptive parents may have to go through the process of accepting their child's limitations.

Occasionally a child who is presented to prospective adoptive parents as being healthy is later found to have a mild or even severe disability. This is more often the case with international adoptions than with domestic adoptions; the diagnosis may have been missed in the child's country of origin, or the adoptive parents may have been intentionally misled in an effort to see that the child was adopted. Sometimes a child's condition is thought to be temporary—the result of being in deprived conditions—and the parents later discover it is not. When this happens, the parents not only grieve for their loss of expectations, but may feel angry and betrayed by the professionals who led them to believe that the child's medical condition was different. Unless they successfully work through this grief and adjust their expectations, the stress they feel as parents will probably be greater.

Children with HIV/AIDS

A child born to a mother infected with HIV will test positive for the infection at birth as a result of the presence in her bloodstream of her mother's antibodies. However, only 20 percent to 35 percent of children born to infected mothers will be infected with HIV themselves, and this risk is even less if the mother received AZT therapy during her pregnancy. Although HIV screening tests which detect antibodies in children may be positive as long as 18 to 24 months, there are other sophisticated tests to determine the HIV infection status of a child born to an HIV infected mother. With these techniques, virtually all perinatal HIV infections can be detected within weeks to months after an infant's birth. Parents who adopt a child who may be HIV infected or who is known to be HIV positive have issues similar to other adoptive families and families of medically fragile children, but these issues are often magnified by the medical and social implications of HIV and AIDS.

Although the developing treatments for HIV and AIDS are extending life expectancy, parents must still be prepared for the likelihood of their child's early death. At the same time, because of medical progress in this area, parents must simultaneously prepare to care for their child for many years. Increased life expectancy also means that many HIV-infected children are living long enough to have questions about their own health and life expectancy, about how their birth parents acquired the disease, and whether their birth parents are still alive. Adoptive parents have to be ready to provide their children with answers to these questions and to help them grieve. Not only must the children grieve for the loss of their birth parents through adoption, but they may have to grieve for the death of their birth parents; not only do they sometimes feel rejected because they were placed for adoption, but they may feel rejected by society because they have HIV or AIDS; not only do they question "why" they had to be relinquished for adoption, but they question "why" they had to be infected with HIV; not only must they deal with the "shame" of being "unwanted," but they may have to deal with the "shame" of having HIV or being born to birth parents who acquired the disease through intravenous drug use or unhealthy sexual practices.

The issues for adoptive parents are also magnified. Some people question why anyone would adopt a child, and even more have reservations about the adoption of a child with special needs. Even less support is available for parents who knowingly adopt a child with a fatal disease that carries a social stigma. Thus, adoptive parents may feel abandoned by friends and family members and need to develop new support systems for the times when they face medical and emotional crises. Even with friends or family members who are supportive, parents who adopt children with HIV may feel isolated because they need to protect their medically fragile children from the risk of infection, such as colds and flu, transmitted through casual contact. They must also make decisions about to whom they disclose the fact that their child has HIV/AIDS. While the risk of contracting HIV/AIDS through casual contact is extremely low, the fear many people have of the disease and the social stigma make the question of disclosure more difficult. However, parents can use the same standards for revealing that their child has HIV/AIDS that they do with other personal information: If the other person has a relevant need to know the information, then she should be told. If she does not have a need to know it, the child's privacy should be paramount.

Developing Attachment

Creative ways to form an attachment to the disabled child need to be found because the usual ways parents and children form attachments may be complicated by the child's disability. For example, physical contact may be difficult with a child who is spastic, and eye contact may not be possible because of a child's visual impairment. The simple satisfaction of feeding a child, which normally contributes to attachment, may be overwhelmed by the child's eating problems. The child may not be able to smile or may smile grotesquely. When the disability is unexpected, attachment can be complicated by the parents' inability to resolve their grief. But adoptive parents who choose to adopt a disabled child often have less difficulty "claiming" such a child.

Some hospitals that specialize in birth defects or in treating persons with disabilities have programs to help parents form attachments to disabled children. Special education programs may offer additional guidance. Many of these programs concentrate on helping parents feel comfortable enough with the child's disability to get close to the child, showing how to hold her and how to develop alternative forms of communication, such as signing. Some parents have found that medical crises and treatments create opportunities to form attachments to their children. Because attachment develops as children learn they can depend on their parents to meet their needs, the child whose parent remains by her side during painful or difficult treatments learns she can depend on this parent. For this reason, some parents of medically fragile children advise other parents in similar situations to be highly involved in their children's treatments and remain with them when hospitalized. Despite modifications that have to be made to facilitate attachment, families often find that living with a disabled child provides a common goal, and as each member of the family does his or her part to achieve that goal, the family is pulled together into a cohesive unit.

Parents sometimes find that their relationship with their disabled child is more intense than their relationships with their fully able children. Intense attachment can reach the point of overdependence for the parent and child. An overly solicitous parent should resist feeling she is the only one who can take care of the child and be willing to call on other people to help, for the parents' sake and the sake of the family.

Acting as the Child's Advocate

Understanding the child's condition is critical to acting in the child's best interest. Parents of mentally or physically disabled children are surrounded by experts—physical therapists, physicians, occupational therapists, special education teachers, counselors, and others. In dealing with this management team, parents act as coordinators of services and must remember that each expert sees only her area of specialty. For example, the person who fits the child's wheelchair does not know what the child's school or classroom is like, so some modifications may be necessary. Parents of disabled children find they often must be assertive about obtaining the services they need, as well as rejecting those they do not. They often become so informed about the various aspects of their child's disability—medical, social, educational, and psychological—that they are truly the experts in her care. Therefore, they should not let their lack of academic credentials keep them from questioning professionals.

Effect on Nondisabled Siblings

Siblings often help care for the disabled child by helping her dress or giving her medications. Frequently, the disabled child also depends on the siblings for recreation, particularly if her condition restricts her recreational opportunities. Some siblings resent the additional demands of a disabled brother or sister, while others take them in stride. In general, most siblings of disabled children have a maturity that exceeds their age and learn to be more tolerant of others. One teenage girl reported that as she prepared to attend her first prom, she suddenly realized that her mentally retarded sister would never participate in dating and dances, and she was saddened by her awareness.

Parents should make sure that other children in the family

understand how to care for the disabled child—not only what she needs help with but what she does not need help with. Some siblings become overprotective of their disabled brother or sister and, by their help, sabotage the independence parents may be trying to foster. Children should also know what their roles are expected to be in the future. The sibling who does not know what the plan is for the disabled child may become concerned about her own future; an adolescent may think she cannot go away to college because she is needed at home, for example.

It is not unusual for the brothers and sisters of a disabled child to feel guilty because they are fully able. They may also feel guilty when they get angry at the child or tease her. It isn't unusual for siblings, particularly teenagers, to be embarrassed by their disabled sibling. Siblings often find they have to explain their disabled sibling's condition to friends more frequently when the disability is mild than when it is clear from the child's appearance that she is disabled. Nevertheless, children usually rally to their sibling's defense, protecting her from the teasing of other children.

Parents should be sure that the demands of raising a disabled child do not blind them to the needs of their other children. Although the other children in the family should be involved in caring for the sibling, their responsibilities should not be so great that they are unable to have full lives themselves. The siblings of disabled children need an opportunity to express their feelings, which are likely to be somewhat confusing and contradictory, and some communities have support groups for brothers and sisters of disabled children. Above all, the parents should be sure not to neglect their children without disabilities because of the time required to care for the disabled child. Because the siblings may feel guilty that they are fully able, they may be reluctant to complain about the degree to which they are expected to care for the disabled child or about the lack of attention they receive from their parents.

The Single Adoptive Parent

Single adoptive parents are raising children with as much success as are married couples, despite the fact that single applicants have traditionally been restricted to the adoption of children with special needs. One reason for their success is that when difficulties arise, single parents have no one to blame for the decision to adopt. Nor do they have conflicts with their spouses over discipline or other parenting decisions. The manipulative child cannot play one parent against the other in single-parent homes, making one-parent homes the placement of choice for certain children. However, single parents do not have a partner to turn to when they are anxious, sick, or otherwise need help. For this reason, it is crucial for them to have a solid support system. Without adequate support, they can become isolated, frustrated, and ineffective as parents.

Support Systems

Single adoptive parents meet more resistance from adoption agencies and intermediaries, from relatives, and particularly from friends when they decide to adopt. This situation is not surprising; although it has become more acceptable in recent years for people to raise children alone, most of the acceptance is directed at those who become single parents unexpectedly—through death, divorce, or unplanned pregnancy. Those who choose to become single parents, either through a planned pregnancy or adoption, often are criticized for taking on an enormous responsibility alone, for raising a child without two parents, or for acting unconventionally. This resistance can be compounded by friends and relatives who typically have reservations about the adoption of a child with special needs. Yet it is critical for single parents to be able to depend on their friends and relatives for support. Sociologists William Feigelman and Arnold R. Silverman found that like married couples, single adoptive parents feel that the adjustment period is smoother and attachment develops more quickly when they have support from friends and relatives.

Despite the responsiblity, single persons find it possible to be successful adoptive parents if they have adequate human, financial, and psychological resources. In setting up a support system, single parents should examine what they have in common with other single parents, other adoptive parents, and other parents of children like theirs, since it is likely that their children will be disabled, emotionally troubled, or of a different race or ethnic background. Though its primary emphasis is helping single persons overcome the obstacles to adoption, the Committee for Single Adoptive Parents and its publication *The Handbook for Single Adoptive Parents,* edited by Hope Marindin, are useful resources.

Financial Resources

Single parents need jobs or supervisors flexible enough to allow them to deal with the inevitable crises of parenthood. In addition, they need health insurance policies that will allow them to add their children.

Both for the obvious practical reasons as well as for peace of mind, single parents should have disability insurance or an emergency fund so they can continue to provide for themselves and their children if they become temporarily or permanently disabled, as well as adequate life insurance to provide for their children in case of their death (see the appendixes for information on child-rearing leave, insurance, and wills).

These considerations are not much different from those a biological parent should have. They are, however, more critical for the single adoptive parent, for in many cases single parents adopt children with special needs that require additional medical expenses, therapy, and special education or day care arrangements. In addition, the demands of raising a child with medical or emotional problems increase the likelihood that a parent will need to take time off from work for appointments with professionals or to care for a medical or behavioral crisis.

Emotional and Human Resources

Like many of us who have adopted, single parents often feel they must be "superparents." Having decided to become parents despite the obstacles and resistance they meet, and often having adopted children with special needs, they may have difficulty acknowledging their feelings of discontent or failure. While an adoptive parents support group is helpful in providing the support they need, single parents often find more assistance from a single parents group, such as Parents Without Partners, whose members can understand the particular difficulties of raising a child alone.

But single parents need more than emotional support. They need human resources, such as satisfactory child care (which can be difficult to find for a disabled child or one with behavioral problems) and friends or relatives close by who can provide emergency child care and other kinds of physical assistance, particularly with a disabled child. One single adoptive mother said she didn't need someone to commiserate with her nearly as much as she needed someone to help her children with cerebral palsy get dressed each morning.

Taking Care of Oneself

During a home study, an adoption worker often questions a single applicant about the effect a child will have on her social life. In general, the social worker is more concerned about this effect than the applicant. Fully committed to raising children, the single parent is attracted to people with similar values who can understand her decision to adopt or to adopt a child with special needs. In fact, the single parent often is so committed to her role that she may not take enough time for herself. Single parents are usually working parents and therefore are subject to the same demands of all parents who hold jobs and try to compensate for the time we are at work by spending our free time with our children. And after overcoming the difficulties facing single adoptive applicants, it may be hard for the single parent to admit there are times when she wants to be away from her child. For the first year after Mary Ellen adopted her son, she insisted he be included in all social activities, taking the attitude that she didn't want to spend time with anyone who didn't want the child along. Eventually, she realized it was important for her to have time for herself and spend time with her friends without her child and that it was important for the child to learn that her mother had an adult social life as well as an adult work life.

Attitudes of Others

Single adoptive parents receive conflicting messages from people outside their support systems, alternately being told how wonderful they are for taking on such a big responsibility and being given unsolicited advice on how to raise children. Single adoptive fathers, in particular, may be treated as incompetent care-givers, while being extolled as models for other men. One single father said that teachers sent notes home from school with his children with condescending pieces of advice.

Single adoptive parents sometimes have difficulty convincing the professionals who care for their children that some of their children's behavioral problems may be the result of trauma or experiences prior to adoption. The professionals may ignore evidence demonstrating that a child's behavioral problems were present before her placement and focus on the lack of a second parent in the home as the cause of the child's problems.

There is little we can do about people with such attitudes except try to differentiate between when they are a nuisance and when they are actually interfering with the child's well-being. For example, a teacher who blames a child's behavioral problems on her single-parent home needs to be educated about the child's history; a therapist with the same attitude should be replaced with one who is more sensitive to adoption issues. But when the attitudes of others are merely annoying, we should ignore them and call in our support system of people who care and understand.

Gay and Lesbian Adoptive Parents

Although some states ban the adoption of children by gay or lesbian parents and public opinion is generally against the practice, gay and lesbian parents are adopting, often with the awareness and support of the adoption agencies who make the placements. In these families, as in other adoptive families, adoption provides another layer of issues that parents and children must face. Adoptive parents often feel they have to be exceptional to prove their suitability to adopt or to prove wrong those who questioned the idea of adopting. Gay and lesbian adoptive parents may feel they have to be "superparents" both to prove their suitability to those opposed to gay and lesbian adoption and to compensate to the child for whatever pain their lifestyle may bring to her. Children who are teased because of their parent's lifestyle may have additional resentment, feeling that their parents adopted them without taking into consideration how their peers might react.

However, there are strengths to gay and lesbian adoption. Because gay and lesbian parents may have never envisioned parenthood in their future, they seldom have the emotional baggage of infertility and do not view adoption as a compromise. In addition, because they already have experienced having a nontraditional lifestyle, being an adoptive family may not require as much adjustment. Gay or lesbian parents' experiences with discrimination may give them the empathy to help their children when they feel "second best" because they were adopted or because they are members of a minority group.

Divorce in Adoptive Families

Not all single parents applied for adoption as single parents. Some have become single since the adoption through death or divorce. Although many people have wondered if adoptees' history of "losing" their parents makes adoptees more emotionally vulnerable than nonadopted children when parents divorce, researchers at Rutgers University found that was not the case. David Brodzinsky and his colleagues found that adopted and nonadopted children were similarly affected by the separation and divorce of their parents. Evidently, the divorce of parents is traumatic enough to make every child feel vulnerable, regardless of whether they felt vulnerable already as a result of being adopted. All the children in the Rutgers study were of elementary school age. It isn't known whether the impact of divorce on adopted children in the preschool or adolescent years is different. But we do know young children are concrete thinkers who believe they are the center of the universe. They think if something happens, they caused it. One boy thought the reason his adoptive father didn't send child support was because the boy wasn't his father's biological child. Parents who are divorcing are suffering themselves, but they must remember to allow their children to grieve, too, and consider that the children's grief may be affected by their past losses.

Cassandra and Bob told their child, as most divorcing parents do, that although they were no longer living together, they would still be the child's parents. "You can divorce a husband or a wife, but you can't divorce a child," they said. The parents realized immediately how hollow those words might sound to a child whose connection to her birth parents was legally terminated. Fortunately, their child seemed to accept the explanation. Perhaps she needed to be reassured and was willing to accept the explanation, ignoring the holes in logic or did not make the connection between the two legal proceedings. But parents may need to reassure their children that divorce does not affect adoption.

In some cases, the noncustodial parent does not have contact with the child after the divorce. Under such circumstances, the adoptee is most likely to feel that if she was the parent's biological child, the parent would stay in touch. The parent with custody should make it clear to the child that the other parent is not living up to his responsibilities—that it is the adult's problem, not the child's.

Divorce usually is not precipitated by an adoption unless there already were marital problems. In most cases, if it comes to a choice between their marriage and the child, a couple will disrupt the adoption rather than divorce. But whatever actually causes the divorce, some parents may associate their conflicts with stress connected to adoption and blame the child for the divorce. Obviously, a parent with these feelings needs counseling because children should not feel responsible for their parents' marital problems.

A common reaction to divorce in an adoptive home may be guilt. Parents who believe a stable marriage was a prerequisite to their approval as adoptive parents may feel they obtained a child under false pretenses. If the child was born to an unmarried woman, the feeling of obligation to provide a two-parent home may be a particular burden. As a result, the parents' sense of entitlement may be shaken, and they may doubt their suitability as parents. But it is critical for parents to overcome their guilt and retain a strong sense of entitlement so they can continue to be effective as parents during a difficult time.

Adoptive parents who have open adoptions sometimes are reluctant to let their children's birth parents know they are divorcing. Not only do they feel they have failed to live up to any general expectations that adoptive parents have to provide children with a stable, two-parent family, but the birth mother may have told them that's why she chose them. They may feel guilty that they didn't live up to her expectations and worry that she will think they misrepresented themselves. For this reason, it isn't unusual for adoptive parents to pull away from the birth parents during separation or divorce. One adoptive mother experienced a sharp drop in income after her divorce and was having trouble making ends meet. Because she had an open adoption, she knew the birth mother had married an older, financially successful man. The reversal of fortunes caused the adoptive mother to question the premise of the adoption. Eventually, she realized that the birth mother's decision to place her child with them was not conditional on the adoptive parents remaining married or the birth mother remaining in a situation in which she could not parent. It was an unalterable decision made thoughtfully, but with the knowledge that no one could see into the future. When the adoptive mother finally told the birth mother about the divorce, the birth mother was supportive. Although the birth mother was sad for the adoptive family and her child, she had been worried that the adoptive mother's lack of communication meant that the open adoption was faltering. She was glad to be back in touch with the adoptive family.

The Very Large Family

The logistics of the large adoptive family are staggering—washing dirty clothes, preparing meals, and finding ways to distinguish one toothbrush from twelve others, to name a few. And the majority of large adoptive families are integrating children who are considered to have special needs—older children, many with behavioral problems; children of different racial backgrounds; and children with mental or physical disabilities—as well as taking care of biological children. It is hardly surprising that some people do not understand the motives of those who adopt many children. In fact, parents of large adoptive families probably do not have different motives for adopting, but they do have different expectations from those with small families. They can take great joy and satisfaction in little successes—in knowing they have made some difference in a child's life.

Maintaining Order

Some large families are highly structured, well organized, and efficient. Others rely on flexibility. How people respond to the problems of cooking, cleaning, laundry, and shopping depends on their own organizational styles. Among the large adoptive families surveyed by Barbara Tremitiere, nearly half the parents had come from families with five or more children and very likely drew on their own childhood experiences for help in working out the logistics of their large families. Some parents use work charts to assign chores, while others say they can't afford the repair bills if their children use the washing machine or dishwasher. Most parents of large families find it helpful to have contact with similar families, not only for emotional support, but for ideas on solving daily household maintenance problems.

One mother of twenty-one children cautions parents not to be so concerned with maintaining order in the family that they fail to notice when some aspect of the household is functioning smoothly. When many people are living together, any one aspect that is out of order can have a cascading effect on the rest of the household. Consequently, there is a temptation to focus on what needs to be "fixed." Parents need to reflect often on what is working well.

Maintaining Individuality

It is not necessary for every child to have the same things or participate in the same activities. Indeed, it isn't fair, for example, to deny ballet lessons to one talented child just because the family cannot afford special lessons for all the children. Neither does everyone have to participate in Boy Scouts just because it's easier for the parents to transport five children to the same place than to five different places.

Getting outsiders to understand this is a major task. Parents should let friends and relatives know they are not required to invite all the children in the family swimming just because they are inviting some. One mother was delighted when her friend returned from a trip with thoughtful gifts for two of her seventeen children. Had the friend felt compelled to buy souvenirs for all seventeen, it is likely that she wouldn't have bought any. As it was, two of the children received gifts this time; the others would receive something from someone else another time. Of course, young children, in particular, do not look at the large picture, but see only their sibling receiving a treat they didn't get. Parents can deal with envious feelings by validating natural reactions, saying, for example, "I know it doesn't seem fair to you" or "It would be nice if we all had received new shirts. Amy is really lucky. I can see why you might feel jealous, but we shouldn't deny Amy the fun of getting a new shirt just because we all didn't get them."

With many children in a family, some or all of whom may be adopted, it is possible that there will be more than one child of the same age. When there is, the parents should treat them, and encourage others to treat them, as the unique people they are. Depending on their backgrounds, the children may not be performing academically at the same grade level. As a result, children of different ages may be in the same grade, or an older child may be in a grade below that of a younger child. These situations require a great deal of tact. If possible, siblings should not be in the same classroom; there is enough competition at home. The children in the family should understand why one child is in a grade below the one appropriate for her age in a way that doesn't place the blame on the child. For example, the parents can say, "In some of the other places Gina lived, the parents didn't know how to make sure Gina went to school every day, so she didn't do all the work she should have last year. Now she is getting another chance to do well in the fifth grade, and we want to help her as much as we can." The parents should make it clear that teasing a child because she is repeating a grade will not be tolerated.

Depending on the circumstances, some children in the family may have more knowledge of their birth parents than others, and perhaps more contact with them. The jealousy this evokes may be difficult to deal with. Parents should attend to each child's desire for information, providing her with as many details about her birth parents as is appropriate, and allow her to express her feelings of sadness or anger when her siblings have more information.

In an effort to give each child enough attention, privacy, and special treats, some adoptive families have been able to enlist the aid of individuals who act as "godparents" or honorary aunts and uncles to their children. This way each child has a special person who may take her out for dinner occasionally, provide a place where she can go when the family is overwhelming, or even provide money for special activities that would otherwise be unaffordable with so many children. This arrangement solves the problem of a friend or relative who wants to be involved with the family, but thinks she can't manage all the children and doesn't want to "play favorites." By letting them know it is all right to be a special friend to a particular child, the honorary aunts and uncles are able to have the active involvement they want, at a level they can handle; the child benefits from the individual attention; and the parents can get time away from the family.

The diversity of the large adoptive family is one of its greatest strengths. While parents sometimes wonder if they are being fair to other children in the family—especially to their biological children—by adopting a large number of children who require additional care, they often find that it is an enriching experience for their children as well as for themselves. Children who might otherwise be sheltered learn about different values and experiences.

Family Subgroups

Although members of a large family generally develop strong attachments, children naturally like some siblings more than others and often divide themselves into natural subgroups. Parents should not expect the children in the family to like one another equally—

there are bound to be preferences and personality conflicts. Indeed, one advantage of living with many children from different backgrounds is that children learn how to get along with people they do not always like.

Parents should not try to break up subgroups in an attempt to integrate the family better. As one experienced mother put it, raising a large adoptive family is not like *The Sound of Music*—the children are not going to sing together in harmony. But when parents observe a member of one subgroup going to the aid of someone in another group or the children acting as a unit in defense of the family, they know that underneath the daily routines, arguments, and jealousies, they have a family.

The Sibling Group

Although not every family who adopts a sibling group is classified as a large family, small families sometimes become large ones with the placement of a group of three or four siblings. How this addition affects the family depends, to some extent, on whether the siblings were together before their adoptive placement. If they were in separate foster homes, they will need to get to know one another and develop a sense of biological identity, as well as become integrated into the adoptive family. If the children do not have life books, these books can be started as a way to show the threads of their shared lives and perhaps explain why they have not always been together.

Siblings who have lived together in previous families may feel particularly close to one another because of the loss or trauma they have shared. This attachment can help them during the adjustment period; even though they have experienced losses, they have a sense of continuity from having lived together.

The parents should respect that the siblings have biological ties to one another, as well as emotional ties to the rest of the family. Their relationship to their adoptive siblings is not the same as their relationship to one another because they share a history with their biological siblings that they do not share with the rest of the family. Respecting this history does not mean endorsing the idea that the biological relationship is better than the adoptive relationship; it just recognizes that those children share something the rest of the family will never be part of.

At the same time, Joan and Bernard McNamara point out in their book *Adoption and the Sexually Abused Child* that siblings who have shared a dysfunctional family are likely to bring those patterns with them into their adoptive family. Therefore, the parents must be ready not only to help their children deal with the aftermath of a dysfunctional family upbringing, but find ways to recognize and deal with the behavior in one child that may trigger abusive, destructive, or pathological behavior in another child.

In *A Child's Journey Through Placement,* Vera Fahlberg points out that one child in a sibling group sometimes takes responsibility for parenting the other children. Once in an adoptive family, this "parentified" child may be reluctant to give up her authority, resulting in conflict with the adoptive parents. The parentified child may even foster dependence in her siblings to maintain her role. In her book, Fahlberg describes how one parentified child was encouraged to accept dependence from her foster parents and allow her sibling to become more autonomous. The foster parent acknowledged that the parentified child knew her sibling very well and expressed appreciation for the insight she could give her. But she also told the child that she deserved to have a childhood, too, and offered to show her how, thus building an alliance.

Sometimes children are more receptive to disquieting information about their pasts when it is provided by a sibling rather than by a parent or other adult. Older siblings who remember the circumstances in their biological family or foster families may be able to verify the parents' explanation of why they were placed for adoption.

Recognizing their biological heritage will help the sibling group with some of the identity questions they may have as adolescents. By observing the ways they are alike and different from their biological siblings, they may be able to develop a better sense of their genetic heritage than may other adoptees.

Maintaining Normalcy

The large adoptive family, particularly if it includes disabled children and children of different races, is highly visible in the community. Children often are embarrassed by this visibility, particularly when they reach adolescence. The parents should remember that the reaction they get to being a large family is often different from the reaction the children get. Whereas the parents may be complimented for their courage, tenacity, and altruism, the children may gain a group reputation that is based on the actions of the child with the worst behavior. The parents are known by name, while the children are asked, "Now, which one are you?" In one family, the children complained that whenever they went to a restaurant, a large table was set for them, making them stand out. To alleviate their children's embarrassment, the parents allowed the children to enter the restaurant in groups, be seated at tables set for four to six people, and be given a limit on how much to spend. One father found himself resisting an obvious solution to the growing size of his family— the purchase of a bus. As long as the family could travel together by van, he did not feel conspicuous.

Children sometimes feel less unusual when they have contact with other large adoptive families. But parents should remember that unless the children from both families happen to be close friends, the children are likely to prefer friendships of their own making.

Financial Considerations

Raising a large family is expensive, and though there are subsidies for many children with special needs, subsidies don't cover all the costs involved in raising them. Parents do not have to be rich to raise a large family, but they do have to be good money managers. They will have different ideas about allowances, what kinds of expenses children should pay for with income from part-time jobs, and other financial questions. But parents should not become so preoccupied with staying within their budget that the children become financially insecure. Barbara Tremitiere found that children in large adoptive families were remarkably aware of the financial strains on their families. While it is healthy for children to have a sense of economic reality, children should not worry about whether there is enough money to last the month.

Some parents find it is important to spend money on an occasional extravagance as a way of maintaining a sense of normalcy. Taking the family to a circus, fair, or other special event may cost one hundred dollars or more but parents sometimes believe that their children should not miss out on normal childhood activities just because their parents decided to adopt eighteen children. Family conferences, which many people believe are essential in a large family, can be used to decide whether an activity or purchase is important and what sacrifices the family is willing to make to accommodate it.

Sarah, a mother of sixteen, was frustrated by the number of boxes of unwearable used clothing that people dropped at her house. Though she was grateful to the people who made useful contributions to the family, she thought that some were making themselves feel good about giving to a "needy family," while she had to wash, mend, and dispose of tattered, dirty garments. She also was concerned about her children "looking like orphans." Sarah finally decided not to accept used clothing from any but a few friends who were thoughtful enough to pass along only wearable clothing. Other families are concerned about the emotional implications of wearing hand-me-downs—the children may feel they have to wear cast-off clothing because they are "cast-off" children—and try not to depend on second-hand clothes.

The Family with Biological and Adopted Children

When one child in the family was adopted and one was born into the family, the parents are sometimes uneasy. They are concerned that their adopted child will feel less a part of the family if everyone else is connected biologically. They worry that their birth child will feel slighted by all the hoopla surrounding adoption. Most of all, they worry that one or the other child will feel that the parents are playing favorites: that the biological child will think the adoptee is loved more because their parents went to extraordinary lengths to get her or that the adoptee will think the biological child is favored because there is a biological connection. Deep down, parents worry that they may actually feel differently about their children. After adopting our first child, I encountered a woman who responded to my news by saying, *I think what you're doing is wonderful. I could never love someone else's child.* I, of course, replied that my love for my daughter was every bit as deep as if I had given birth to her. *But you don't really know, do you?* the other woman responded.

The Benchmark Adoption Survey of public attitudes towards adoption revealed that while most people say they support adoption and think adoptive parents and their children love each other as much as parents and children who are connected biologically, only about half the public thinks that adopting is *as good as* having a biological child. They can't explain why, but people intrinsically feel there is something better about having a biological child. It's no wonder that adoptive parents and adoptees sometimes feel a twinge of doubt about whether adoptive relationships adequately compare to biological ones or immediately think that adoption is the cause of any conflict.

On the other hand, adoptees may carry the mantle of "precious child." These are the children who were longed for and waited for. These are the children for whom parents endured emotional highs and lows, bureaucratic red tape, extended international travel, extraordinary expense, or intrusive questioning. These may be the children who fulfilled the seemingly unattainable dream their parents had of having a family. It's no wonder that adoptive parents frequently talk about adoption as magical or miraculous.

Furthermore, because adoption is a different way of forming a family that is not always understood, many adoptive parents make an extra effort to educate themselves about adoption, to associate with other adoptive families, and to advocate in the community for better understanding of adoption.

Finally, even if they also have children by birth, they are *adoptive* families. Sometimes that label characterizes their identity in the community, including their children's identities at school. It's no wonder that adoptive parents feel vulnerable to accusations from their birth child that the adoptee gets more attention or is loved more because she was wanted more (especially if the birth child was unexpected).

Parents with both biological and adopted children who were interviewed on this subject said that the way their children entered their families has made no difference in the intensity or quality of love they feel for them. One mother, who adopted three children before becoming pregnant unexpectedly at the age of forty, said that before she gave birth, she felt she loved her adopted children as deeply as a mother could love a child. It was only after giving birth that she was certain. "If I hadn't been fortunate enough to conceive and bear a child, I would always wonder if there was some further dimension to parental love that I simply couldn't experience," she said. Now she knows there isn't. Nonetheless, some parents acknowledge that while they love their children the same, they sometimes like them differently. This may or may not have anything to do with adoption. One mother whose adopted daughter had a history of abuse and neglect said it is difficult to feel close to her daughter because her emotional problems interfere with relationships. She loves her daughter deeply, but time spent with her is often stormy and unpredictable. She finds it much easier to relax when she spends time with her biological children. She recognizes that it is normal for her to gravitate to situations that are more comfortable, though she knows that she needs to spend time with her adopted daughter too.

Another mother said that her extended family openly accuses her of favoring her second child—the first of two adopted children in the family. She acknowledges that there is a special relationship between her and this child, but not because she was the first child to be adopted. It simply happened that with this child she had an adequate amount of time and energy to prepare for her arrival. "I was ready for her," she said. In addition, it happened that she spent more time at home with this child when she first arrived than she did with her other two children. Furthermore, their personalities just seem to mesh. She doesn't love her more deeply than her other two children, but she realizes theirs is a special relationship.

Sometimes a parent does seem to "connect" better with one child than with another, perhaps because of physical or temperamental similarities between them that have a genetic basis. For example, a father who was a basketball star in high school may relate better to his biological daughter with basketball ability than to his adopted son who enjoys less active pursuits. But it is also important to realize that similarities can be a source of conflict in families, such as when the strong-willed parent meets the strong-willed child.

Of course, parents whose children were all born to them may like them differently or relate to them differently. One mother, who had adopted, foster, and biological children, said it was a tremendous relief when a friend with all biological children confided that she didn't like all her children the same.

However, while there are many reasons that the quality of relationships between parents and their children may be different, it is sometimes easier to associate those differences with adoption than with more subtle causes.

There are a variety of ways in which children adopted into the family and children born into the family may be different. Adopted children may have an "adoption day" that the family celebrates. Those in open adoptions may have birth relatives who give them gifts. A family may incorporate the culture of another ethnic group into their family life if they adopted transracially. Birth children have similarities to their parents based on biology, including physical traits, intelligence, and temperament. Their physical passage of birth and genetic makeup leave no question that they belong in the family, while the adoptee's membership is created artificially. Sometimes these differences are exacerbated by the fact that the child is the only one in the family in that situation—the only adoptee, the only birth child, the only Korean, the only white child. Whatever the differences, children are bound to zero in on them and evaluate their meaning.

One of the tasks of children during the elementary school years is to learn to recognize differences and determine which differences matter. That's one reason why children in the early elementary school years are such merciless teases—they are honing in on differences and trying to provoke a response. If a playground taunt doesn't get a response, the child learns it isn't an important difference. But if the child who is teased bursts into tears, the message is sent that this difference matters. Furthermore, children this age are also trying to determine their place in their families. To determine their value to their parents, they look for signs that one or the other sibling is more privileged, gets more recognition, or gets more love. If they perceive such differences, it's only natural to try to determine the unique characteristic in the sibling that might have resulted in such favoritism. Just as they do on the playground, they may try out their hypotheses with their parents or siblings: *Sam never has to do this; you let him get away with everything. I wish I'd been adopted.* And as on the playground, children will determine whether they are correct in their interpretation on the basis of their parents' reaction. However, because parents may be uncertain about whether they are truly impartial, they may overreact to such accusations, unwittingly confirming the children's feelings.

Sometimes parents try so hard to be fair to avoid accusations of partiality that the result is actually unfairness. More precisely, they may try so hard to treat their children the same that by doing so, they fail to meet the needs of one child. For example, the parents may be worried that their adopted child will feel hurt if they talk about how excited they were when they were expecting their biological child. If this becomes a taboo subject to protect the adoptee, they deny their birth child the opportunity to hear how wanted she was. Children are quick to pick up cues that their parents are over-compensating, and may interpret their parents' treatment of this subject as meaning that there really is a deficit that needs to be compensated for. Furthermore, the parents may be wrong about how the adoptee will react. For example, it may actually be good for adoptees to hear that some parents are thrilled at the news of pregnancy, since their own conception was likely viewed as a problem. In one family, the birth of a child was a positive turning point in the relationship between an adopted girl and her mother. A child who had been abused and neglected by her own birth mother, the adoptee learned to trust her adoptive mother as she watched her care for her new infant without hurting or neglecting her. She was able to absorb a lot of the mothering that she didn't get as an infant just by being with her mother as she mothered the new baby.

A parent who is accused of favoritism or who thinks she may be treating her children differently may want to do a "reality check," monitoring her own behavior or asking a spouse or trusted confidante. One mother discovered in this way that she was less supportive of her adopted son's interests than her biological daughter's because she shared her daughter's interests and didn't share her son's. Was it because there was some biological basis for the interests? It's hard to say, but her son was interpreting her behavior that way, and she vowed to find ways to be more supportive of his activities. A parent can also suggest that a child do a reality check, for example, keeping track of chores required and neglected chores forgiven, if the accusation is that one child has to do more work than the other. If there is a disparity, it can be explained or corrected.

However, parents need to keep in mind that our job as parents is not necessarily to dole out equal amounts of time, energy, or attention to our children, but to meet their needs. One child may have more needs or more pressing needs than another. That doesn't mean parents ignore the other child's needs; indeed, to do so will probably result in that child's needs suddenly become pressing. However, it does mean that as parents, we have to keep the "big picture" in mind. Children have a narrow perspective, which often includes only this very moment. It is up to the parents to make sure that, over time, all their children's needs are met.

Postadoption Pregnancy

Five percent of people with untreated infertility problems conceive after adopting—the same percentage of infertile couples who conceive but do not adopt. Yet the myth persists that one sure way to get pregnant is to adopt. Some people assume that a supposedly infertile couple who conceives after adopting regrets not having tried a little longer to achieve a pregnancy before turning to adoption. One of those with that assumption may be the adoptee.

Gail and her husband had a three-year-old adopted daughter and were getting ready to apply for a second adoption when Gail discovered she was pregnant. "See," she was told by more than one person, "you didn't have to adopt after all." Adoptive parents who are expecting the birth of a child should anticipate some insensitive remarks but consider that such remarks are usually thoughtless, rather than intentionally hurtful.

It is more difficult to deal with the issue when the adopted child is the one questioning whether the parents still want her or wondering if they only wanted her because they didn't think they could have a child any other way. The adoptee may not verbalize this question, but adoptive parents should assume it is there and reassure the child that she is an integral part of the family. When telling her about her adoption, the parents could say, "We tried for many years to have a baby, and we didn't want to wait to be parents anymore," implying, quite correctly, that the motivation to adopt was a desire to be a parent at that time, not a failure to conceive. But while the adoptee may have doubts from time to time, the parents' sincere love for her will be the best reassurance.

Since a pregnancy usually arouses curiosity in a child, the child who has not been told where babies come from and how adoption is different from being born into a family is likely to ask the appropriate questions when a new baby is on the way. Parents who explain that a baby is growing inside mommy should expect the adoptee to ask, "Did I grow inside you, too?" Several books for young children are now available that explain not only conception and birth, but donor insemination, in vitro fertilization, surrogacy, and adoption. Parents should look for a book that explains that every child grows inside a woman, but that there are now a variety of ways that conception can be accomplished and that after birth, some children join another family through adoption.

If possible, the adoptee should learn about conception and how adoption differs from being born into a family before she learns that a new baby is expected. While not crucial, it probably will help her feel better about her status in the family if she does not hear about adoption first as something that sets her apart from her sibling.

While the issue may be more apparent in the family with both biological and adopted children, all children adopted by infertile couples may at some point think that their parents would have preferred to conceive. Their parents should reassure them that while adoption may have been a second choice, it was not a second-best choice.

Adopting a Second Child

Parents adopting a second child are often more confident than they were the first time around. A process that once seemed mysterious and forbidding is now familiar. Doubts, such as whether they could love a child not born to them, have been allayed. And having been approved by an agency or selected by birth parents once, parents have reason to believe they will again be successful. Perhaps what is most important is that the alternative if they are not successful—to parent one child rather than two—seems decidedly more bearable than the alternative if they are unsuccessful adopting the first time. But that doesn't mean parents adopting a second time have it easy.

Although second-time adoptive parents tend to be more relaxed about the process because it is familiar to them and they've been successful at it, this familiarity often leads to expectations that the second adoption will proceed much like the first. The parents expect to wait, but not any longer than they waited the first time. They expect the "magic" of the first adoption to be repeated. For parents to have expectations based on personal experience is normal, but those who are adopting a second time should remind themselves that if their adoption does not proceed the way they expect it to, that's normal, too.

In addition to all the factors they considered the first time, they now have to think about how the child and the way she joins the family will affect the first child. The question is not only can they accept a minority child, a child with a disability, or a child who has contact with her birth parents, but how these factors will affect the child who is already in their family. And if the adoption falls through or the birth parents reclaim the child after placement, the parents know they will have to deal not only with their own grief, but the grief and possible insecurity of their other child.

Parents of more than one child often want their children's lives be as similar as possible. For example, if one child has contact with her birth parents and the other doesn't, they may worry about how they will cope with questions that situation raises in the family or the feelings of the child who doesn't have what her sibling has. The parents should not be overly concerned about these differences, since they are simply another example of how life is not equal for siblings in a family. Furthermore, even when adoptions appear to be similar, each child will have her own unique experience with adoption. When the differences bring up questions or feelings, the parents can look on them as opportunities to discuss issues that were present in the child's life anyway, but may have been brought into the open by the sibling's experience.

Parents who first adopted transracially or internationally often feel that by adopting another child of a similar racial heritage, their child will not feel as different as she would if she were the only minority person in the family. While diversity in the family can be helpful to the minority child, there are more important considerations for helping the transracially adopted child deal with issues of racial identity than the racial makeup of her siblings (see Chapter 9).

Some social workers believe that when faced with the possibility that their second adoption will be significantly different from their first, parents are inclined to resolve the issue in a way that protects the child they already have. They do not want the second child to have something—status based on race or presents from birth parents—that the first child doesn't have. This makes sense, since parents already know and love that child, while the second child is still unreal to them.

In their concern to protect their first child, adoptive parents also wonder when they should begin preparing their first child for the unpredictable arrival of a sibling and how it will affect their child if the birth mother reclaims the child after the placement. Parents shouldn't introduce the idea of a sibling too early. Young children are impatient and have a different sense of time than do adults. The parents can simply say to them, *We hope we're going to have another child some day.* In *The Open Adoption Experience,*

Sharon Kaplan Roszia and I point out that while young children have difficulty with long waits, they do need preparation for major changes, as well as an explanation for the tension and excitement that may be building in the family. When plans are still tentative, the parents can tell the child that there is a woman who is going to have a baby and that she may ask them to take care of her baby while she decides whether she is able to parent her. The readiness for the nursery can be explained in the same way—that this is where the baby will stay while the birth mother decides whether she can raise her baby. The parents can add that they hope the baby will become part of their family, but that they don't know what will happen. If the placement is explained as a pending decision and any reclaim as a final decision, rather than a change of heart, the parents will worry less that the previously adopted child will think her birth mother could come back for her, too. The difference is that one birth mother made a plan to place her child for adoption, while another birth mother decided, after thinking about it for a long time, not to.

Nonetheless, if the birth mother does reclaim the child, the parents need to realize that the other child in the family will still have feelings about the baby. These feelings may be mixed, for the child may have been jealous of the new baby and wished it would go away. Then when the baby did go away, they child may have felt responsible for her parents' sadness. The parents should make sure the child knows she was not responsible for the reclaim and give her a chance to express her feelings. A reentrustment ritual, similar to the entrustment ritual described in Chapter 1, can help both the parents and the first child at this difficult time.

Adoptive parents are sometimes surprised to find that friends and relatives may be more inclined to voice their reservations about adoption with a second child than they were with the first. They may have expected resistance when adoption was a new idea, but believed that the resistance had been overcome when people saw how satisfactory the experience was and grew to love the child.

However, they are sometimes confronted by people who say the equivalent of *Why don't you quit while you're ahead?* Because of stories in the news media about violent or troubled adoptees, some people believe that adoption is risky and that a satisfactory adoption is the exception. They may keep quiet about their reservations with the first adoption because they understand why a childless couple may be willing to take the risk, but they think a second adoption is "looking for trouble." For parents who have experienced adoption and found it to be a wonderful experience, this reaction hurts. They don't understand why people can't see what a great family they are. Adoption support groups are not just for first-time adoptive parents. They are organizations of people who have had similar family experiences and understand the emotions of the adoptive parents, even when their close friends and family members do not.

Siblings in Adoptive Families

One of the questions that has always perplexed me as the mother of two children is, *Are they really brother and sister?* Of course, I know that people are asking whether my two children are biologically related to each other, but I always wonder why people want to know that. Do they think that siblings who are not biologically related feel differently about each other, the way some people think about parents and children who are not biologically related? In her book, *Are Those Kids Yours?* Cheri Register says that when people ask her whether her children are *really* brother and sister, she responds, *Well, they fight in the backseat of the car.*

The study of sibling relationships is relatively young, but experts in the field echo Register's experience. Siblings develop a close relationship because they are raised together. They share time, space, schools, friends, family history—and the backseat of the car. When children are adopted as infants, they develop their relationship long before they understand how each came into the family. It is doubtful that their relationship would change simply because they learn they are not biologically related.

One of the most important functions of siblings is contributing to the formation of personal identity, and this is true in adoptive families as well as in biological families. A child notes the attributes and characteristics in herself and her siblings that are considered desirable and undesirable by society, and particularly by their parents. Furthermore, siblings often understand each other because they have seen each other's true selves, not just the personae that are presented to the world. In healthy families, this understanding leads to deep trust among siblings.

However, it is not always easy for siblings in adoptive families. They may not be close in age and therefore may have not the shared experience that leads to a close sibling relationship. Some children may not like the visibility that comes with the adoption of children of color or children with special needs. Alex, who is ten, sometimes denies that he's related to his nine-year-old sister, born in Chile. It's not that he's ashamed of her, but he sometimes tires of the involved questions that automatically follow when he says they are related. *Is That Your Sister?* by Sherry Bunin and Catherine Bunin, is a children's book that addresses this issue.

Because siblings of minority and special needs children are often thrust into the role of educating their peers on adoption, we should be sure they understand what adoption means and why we have chosen to adopt a particular child. We should also discuss with our children how much information about their siblings it is appropriate to share with people outside the family.

One clear benefit of having minority children in a white family is that the white children are exposed to racial and cultural differences that broaden their outlook on life. As a natural outgrowth of this exposure, sociologist Rita Simon found, they seem to overcome the idea of white superiority.

Although there has been little research on adoptive siblings, Judith Schaffer, coauthor of *How to Raise an Adopted Child* and former director of a counseling center for adoptive families, says that therapists at the center found it was somewhat easier for adoptees to have siblings, regardless of whether the siblings were adopted or born into the family.

Siblings often become particularly important to each other after their parents die. For adoptees, especially those who have not had contact with their birth families, a relationship with siblings after the deaths of their adoptive parents can be even more precious. Without siblings, the adult adoptees may feel truly alone in the world.

Other Kinds of Adoptions

An adoptive family is one that has added a child through the legal process of adoption. Increasingly, however, we are finding parents and children who are legally related without being biologically related or having gone through the legal process of adoption. A woman who conceives a child through donor insemination does not have to adopt the child, nor does her husband. A couple who gives birth through in vitro fertilization with a donor egg or donor sperm does not have to adopt the child. Yet those children share many of the same issues with children who were adopted in a more traditional way. Like adoptees, they have a right to know their heritage. They will have questions about why their biological parents made the contribution they did and whether they have ever wondered about the outcome. They will have identity issues that raise questions about their origins. There is often less openness with children conceived through assisted reproductive technology than with traditional adoption. When the mother has given birth to the child, both parents may believe that the child does not even have to be told the truth. The child does have a right to the truth and often senses that there is something about her origins that her parents are concealing from her. Parents who do not tell the child the truth risk a serious breach of trust with her when she does learn the facts.

The same is true for children who were adopted by stepparents. These children may have been adopted so early in life that they grew up believing that their stepparents are their biological parents. While the justification for not telling them the truth is that the stepparents have fulfilled the role that the biological parents relinquished, that does not address each individual's need to know who she is. Parents must be honest with children about their origins, even though in doing so they open the child to feelings of rejection or abandonment. Keep in mind that our role as parents is not to create an artificial environment for our children or protect them from the real world. Our job is to help our children develop into competent, confident adults who have the skills to deal with the real world.

Appendixes

Appendix A: Child-rearing Leave and Adoption Benefits

Working parents are sometimes surprised to discover that they may not be entitled to paid leave when they adopt a child, even though their employer may offer "maternity leave." Legally, employers who are covered by Title VII of the Civil Rights Act of 1964 must treat the time women are unable to work because of having given birth exactly like any other temporary disability. An employer does not have to provide maternity leave if the employer does not provide disability benefits for any other type of health condition. Consequently, because there is no physical disability for an adoptive parent, employers are not required to provide the same coverage to them as they do employees who have given birth.

However, employers with more than fifty employees are required, under the Family and Medical Leave Act of 1993, to provide eligible employees with up to twelve weeks of unpaid, job-protected leave for certain family and medical reasons, including the care of a child after an adoptive or foster placement. During the leave, the employer must maintain the employee's health coverage under any group health plan that exists. Upon their return from leaves, employees must be restored to their original positions or equivalent positions with equivalent pay and benefits.

Employers who are not covered by the Family and Medical Leave Act, but who provide "child-rearing leave," rather than or in addition to "maternity leave," must provide it to fathers as well as mothers and adoptive parents as well as biological parents.

The Double-Bind

We are understandably angry when we discover we are not entitled to the same maternity benefits we would have received had our child been born to us. Many employers will pay for up to six weeks of maternity leave, even though it usually takes no more than two weeks to heal any trauma to a woman's body caused by a vaginal delivery. The remainder of the maternity leave is needed because women are tired from caring for their newborns and want to spend time with the babies—requirements that adoptive parents share. Those who adopt older children point out their need to spend time getting to know their children, to get them established in their new schools, and to be there when they grieve for the people they were separated from and adjust to their new families.

Some adoptive parents have been criticized for wanting maternity leaves rather than quitting their jobs. Because there are so many couples waiting for babies, some people question whether the few babies who are available should be placed in families in which both parents intend to work. One adoptive mother was told that a mother had just given up a child into her care, and she should feel lucky just to have a baby. Another mother was told, "Instead of worrying about leave, you should be thrilled just to have her." These kinds of comments reflect a double standard. Adoptive mothers have the same right to choose a career and a family as any other mother. Just because a woman wants to be a mother so much that she is willing to wait years for the placement of an infant doesn't mean that she wants to be exclusively a mother. No woman is less committed to being a parent because she also wants to work.

Furthermore, the reality is that not only are two paychecks necessary for many families today, but adoptive parents have the additional expenses of the adoptions themselves. Adoptive parents are often angry when they realize that had they given birth, their employer-sponsored health plans would have paid for their maternity care, as well as provided them with paid maternity leave. In contrast, the adoptive parents may have paid for the maternity care of the birth mother out of their own pockets, in addition to other adoption expenses, and then been offered only an unpaid leave when the child finally arrived.

Fortunately, some employers are providing adoption benefits to their workers, and parents who adopt can get a tax credit for some adoption expenses. In 1990, a survey conducted by Hewitt Associates found that 12 percent of major U.S. employers offered their employees some form of adoption assistance, such as reimbursement for expenses related to the adoption of a child or child-rearing leave. Parents should check with the human resources offices of their companies to see if such benefits are provided. If they are not, they can suggest that their companies consider providing some. Since few workers utilize the benefits, the cost to the companies is low, but companies who do provide these benefits receive goodwill and positive publicity and possibly greater loyalty from their employees. More important, children and families receive the necessary support that, in some cases, can make a difference between children having permanent families or not. For more information, phone the National Adoption Center at 1-800-TO-ADOPT.

A tax credit of up to $5,000 is allowed for adoption expenses of a child adopted in the United States or internationally or $6,000 for the adoption of a U.S. child with special needs. The full amount is allowed for families with annual incomes under $75,000, while those with higher incomes receive a partial tax credit.

Families who receive assistance from their employers for adoption expenses receive tax exemptions in the same amount; the tax credit and tax exemption may be combined, but not for the same expenses. Both the tax credit and exemption apply to the taxable year in which the adoption is finalized, regardless of when the expenses were incurred. However, only those expenses incurred after January 1, 1997, are allowed, and the tax benefits will end on December 21, 2001, for all but adoptions of children with special needs. Allowable expenses include "reasonable and necessary fees, court costs, attorney fees, and other qualified expenses" that are directly related to the legal adoption of an eligible child by the taxpayer. The list of eligible costs for special needs adoptions includes renovations or purchases that are specifically required to meet the child's needs.

Appendix B: Health Insurance

Federal health insurance reforms in 1993 and 1996 ended years of discriminatory treatment of adopted children by health insurance providers. No longer can health insurance provided by an employer be denied to a child being adopted, even if the child has preexisting medical conditions. Furthermore, insurance is to be provided for children during the placement period and when the parents change jobs.

In 1997, federal legislation required states to provide health insurance coverage for any adopted child with special needs who has an adoption assistance agreement and who could not be placed with an adoptive family without medical assistance because of the child's need for medical, mental health, or rehabilitative care. Coverage must include medical and mental health benefits that are equivalent to those provided by Medicaid.

Appendix C: Wills and Life Insurance

Despite the recent trend for states to pass laws making it easier for an adopted person to inherit from her adoptive family and more difficult to inherit from her birth parents, families should be explicit about the inheritance and beneficiary rights of adoptees in the family. In the past, if a person who placed a child for adoption died leaving no will or a will that did not distinguish between that child and children she later bore, the courts frequently recognized that the child placed for adoption had a claim to her estate. Increasingly, though, states have passed legislation cutting off an adoptee's right to inherit from her birth family in the absence of a will clearly stating that as the deceased person's intent. The new statutes reflect society's greater acceptance of adoption and its diminished emphasis on a blood relationship for inheritance. They support the concept that the adoption process legally replaces the person's birth family with her adoptive family.

Even though most states now treat adoptees as heirs of their adoptive relatives, attorneys recommend that the families of adoptees be clear in their wills and life insurance policies by stating that adopted persons are to be treated as heirs. They can say: "When I use the term 'child,' 'issue,' or 'lineal descendent,' it is meant to include adopted persons," or "persons adopted before the age of twenty-one." This wording ensures that there will be no problem about the inheritance should the relative die in a state that has not modernized its inheritance laws relative to adoption. (The law of the state in which the person dies governs the distribution of the estate.) It also prevents legal challenges on the basis of adoption.

Not all attorneys are sensitive to the adoption issue, so parents may have to address the subject when preparing or updating their wills.

Consistent with the legal concept that the adoptive family supplants the birth family, if an adoptee dies leaving no will, the adoptive parents, not the birth parents, are presumed to be the heirs.

Appendix D: Children Adopted Internationally

The adoption of a child in a court in another country is legally acceptable in the United States in most cases. However, in the United States, a state court is not required to recognize a foreign adoption decree automatically, which means that the status of the child could always be challenged in a state court. For this reason, many adoption practitioners recommend that children who were adopted abroad be readopted in a court in their state of residence in the United States. Following this readoption, parents can request that the issuance of state birth certificates that will be recognized in all other U.S. states. There are certain situations in which the readoption of the child would be required, such as if both adoptive parents did not see the child prior to or during the full adoption proceedings abroad. It is advisable to contact the state social services agency or the agency facilitating the adoption for specific advice on the readoption of a child adopted abroad and to contact the state office of vital statistics for information on how and when to apply for a birth certificate.

Appendix E: Naturalization

United States citizenship is required to vote, obtain a passport, and hold public office (although a naturalized citizen cannot be president of the United States). Male citizens are also eligible for military service.

An adopted child can become a naturalized citizen of the United States as soon as his adoption is final. Most parents proceed with this step unquestioningly, but some wonder if they should allow the child to keep his citizenship in his country of birth. Dual citizenship is not recognized by the U.S. government, but it is recognized by some countries, although not by Korea. Allowing the child to remain a citizen of his country of birth is one way to communicate that his origins are important, but parents should remember that citizenship may require the child to serve in that country's military. Parents who would like their child to remain a citizen of his country of birth, in addition to becoming a naturalized U.S. citizen, should do the following:

- Check with the country's consulate in the United States to see if the government recognizes dual citizenship
- Notify their adoption agency that they intend to allow their child to retain citizenship in his country of birth, so the agency does not automatically cancel the child's citizenship when it receives notification that the child has been naturalized.

Most agencies who place children from foreign countries provide up-to-date information on the procedure for applying for naturalized citizenship. This information can be obtained from the local office of the U.S. Department of Justice's Immigration and Naturalization Service.

Children probably won't understand what naturalization means until they are about seven years old and understand both adoption and abstract concepts like political boundaries. Children younger than seven or eight can be told that they weren't born where they are now living; they were born in a place "far away" or "across the ocean." They can be told that the naturalization ceremony is "a special way that we say we are glad that we live here" and that after the ceremony the child will "belong in the United States." Most children like flags, and though young children do not understand how a flag represents a country, parents can explain that becoming a citizen means that the flag belongs to them, too. In general, it's easier for children to understand the idea of "belonging" than the concept of geographic boundaries.

Older children may be concerned that giving up their citizenship in the country of their birth is somehow disloyal and may resist becoming U.S. citizens for this reason. Their parents can explain the difference between nationality and membership in an ethnic group—that becoming a naturalized citizen does not mean that the child will no longer be Korean or Chilean. It may help the child to attend a naturalization ceremony where he can see that many adults born in other countries want to be U.S. citizens. An opportunity to talk with some naturalized adults can also help him understand that becoming a citizen is not a rejection of the land of his birth, but an opportunity to participate in the government that affects him.

Selected References and Resources

General Adoption

A few books have so changed adoption practices or thinking that they have become essential reading. At the top of the list are H. David Kirk's two books, *Shared Fate: A Theory and Method of Adoptive Relationships*, rev. ed. (Ben-Simon Publications, P.O. Box 318, Brentwood Bay, B.C., Canada V0S 1A0, 1984) and *Adoptive Kinship: A Modern Institution in Need of Reform*, rev. ed. (Brentwood Bay: Ben-Simon Publications, 1985) in which he explores the unique relationships in adoptive families and concludes that adoptive parents must acknowledge the differences between their families and families formed by birth.

Chosen Children: New Patterns of Adoptive Relationships, by William Feigelman and Arnold S. Silverman (New York: Praeger Publishers, 1983), reports the results of excellent research into a number of current adoption issues and is particularly useful on the adjustment of adoptees, the importance of support to adoptive parents, transracial and intercountry adoption, and single parent adoption. Though a research report, it is readable and useful to adoptive parents.

Claudia L. Jewett Jarratt's *Helping Children Cope with Separation and Loss* (Harvard, Mass.: Harvard Common Press, 1994) describes the feelings of grieving children and gives concrete ways to help children resolve their losses.

The Adoption Triangle: Sealed or Open Records: How They Affect Adoptees, Birth Parents, and Adoptive Parents, rev. ed. by Arthur D. Sorosky, Annette Baran, and Reuben Pannor (Garden City, N.Y.: Anchor Press/Doubleday, 1984), is one of the most comprehensive works on the search-and-reunion issue. In exploring that topic, it discusses the effect of adoption on adoptees, adoptive parents, and birth parents.

Being Adopted: The Lifelong Search for Self, by David M. Brodzinsky, Marshall D. Schechter, and Robin Marantz Henig (New York: Doubleday, 1992) describes the lifelong impact of adoption on adoptees. It is thoroughly grounded in research and contemporary psychology theory, yet is highly readable.

A Child's Journey Through Placement, by Vera I. Fahlberg, (Indianapolis: Perspectives Press, 1991), is geared toward helping professionals understand the experience of children who come into adoption through the foster care system. However, its clear presentation of the developmental needs of children, the importance of attachment and how it is built, and the effect of separation and loss on children makes it essential reading for adoptive parents, especially those who adopt children from the foster care system.

Although there are many worthwhile publications for adoptive parents, two stand out because they emphasize postplacement issues and are directed at parents, rather than professionals:

Adopted Child newsletter, Lois R. Melina, editor and publisher (P.O. Box 9362, Moscow, Idaho 83843), contains interviews with adoption experts, psychologists, child development specialists, and other experts, as well as book reviews and reports on research on adoption issues.

Adoptive Families, published by Adoptive Families of America (see Organizations), is a respected full-color magazine covering a variety of adoption issues.

Chapter 1: The Transition to Adoptive Parenthood

The effect of adoption on the family is explored in H. David Kirk's two books *Shared Fate* and *Adoptive Kinship* (see General Adoption for the full citation.)

Advice on how to prepare for the arrival of a child being adopted is given in Lois Melina's articles, "Waiting Parents Must Prepare for Child Physically and Psychologically," *Adopted Child,* (November 1990), and "Baby Care Classes Aimed at Adoptive Parents," *Adopted Child* (April 1983). A more detailed treatment of this topic is *Launching a Baby's Adoption: Practical Strategies for Parents and Professionals,* by Patricia Irwin Johnston (Indianapolis: Perspectives Press, 1997). Personal reflections on this time can be found in *In Search of Motherhood,* by Barbara Shulgold and Lynne Sipiora (New York: Dell, 1995), and *Secret Thoughts of an Adoptive Mother,* by Jana Wolff (Kansas City, Mo.: Andrews & McMeel, 1997). For more on how journal writing can be useful in adoption, particularly during times of transition, see "Writing Helps People Develop Deeper Awareness of Themselves," by Lois Melina, *Adopted Child* (May 1995).

The Open Adoption Experience, by Lois Ruskai Melina and Sharon Kaplan Roszia (New York: HarperCollins, 1993), provides detailed advice on a variety of situations encountered in open adoption, including the importance of entrustment rituals. Rituals are also explored in "Adoption Rituals Needed to Enhance a Sense of 'Family,'" by Lois Melina, *Adopted Child* (March 1990), and "Entrustment Ceremonies Provide Benefits to Birth Parents and Adoptive Parents," by Lois Melina, *Adopted Child* (April 1997). Mary Martin Mason's book, *Designing Rituals of Adoption for the Religious and Secular Community* (Resources for Adoptive Parents, 3381 Gorham Avenue, Minneapolis, MN 55426, 1995) provides specific examples of entrustment rituals and other rituals for adoptive families.

The study identifying perceived similarity as a significant factor in satisfaction with adoption was published as *The Adopted Child Comes of Age,* by Lois Raynor (London: George Allen & Unwin, 1980). The report of the study that investigated the accuracy of those perceptions is "Perceived and Actual Similarities in Biological and Adoptive Families: Does Perceived Similarity Bias Genetic Inferences?" by Sandra Scarr, Elizabeth Scarf, and Richard A. Weinberg, *Behavior Genetics* 10 (September 1980): 445–458.

The concept that entitlement is essential to successful adoptive parenting is developed in *How They Fared in Adoption: A Follow-up Study,* by Benson Jaffee and David Fanshel (New York: Columbia University Press, 1970). Other ways that infertility affects adoptive parents are described in Jerome Smith and Franklin I. Miroff, *You're Our Child: A Social/Psychological Approach to Adoption* (Washington, D.C.: University Press of America, 1981), which was revised by Smith in 1987 and published by Madison Books, then updated again by Smith in *The Realities of Adoption* (New York: Madison Books, 1997). Ruth McRoy, Harold Grotevant, and Susan Ayers-Lopez present their findings on adoptive parents' comfort with open adoption in *Changing Practices in Adoption* (Austin, Tex.: Hogg Foundation for Mental Health, 1994). Patricia Irwin Johnston's booklet *An Adoptor's Advocate* (Indianapolis: Perspectives Press, 1984) is no longer available, but Johnston incorporated many of the ideas in her book *Adopting After Infertility* (Indianapolis: Perspectives Press, 1992), which presents an overview of adoption issues from the perspective of infertile couples who are considering adoption for the first time. Ellen Sarasohn Glazer's book, *The Long-Awaited Stork: A Guide to Parenting After Infertility* (San Francisco: Jossey-Bass, 1998), is an excellent discussion of the long-term impact of infertility on parents. The subtle losses of adoptive parenting are described by Sharon Kaplan (now Roszia) and Deborah Silverstein in Lois Melina's article, "Fertile, Infertile Adoptive Parents Experience Similar Losses," *Adopted Child* (September 1990). Melina's ideas on the adoptive parent's sense of authenticity were first published in "Birth and Adoptive Parents Both Have Authenticity for Adoptee," *Adopted Child* (April 1995).

Information about changing an adoptee's name is found in Joyce S. Kaser and R. Kent Boesdorfer, "What Should We Name This Child? The Difficulties of Naming Older Adopted Children," *Children Today* 10 (November–December, 1981): 7–8, and in "Don't Rename Even a Young Child," *Adopted Child* (July 1982), by Lois Melina, which is based on an interview with pediatrician Vera Fahlberg. "The Special Student," a collection of essays compiled by Gloria Petersen for the Illinois Council on Adoptable Children that discusses how a recently adopted older child may face confusion at school over his surname, is no longer in print.

Chapter 2: Adjustment of the Family

For a basic understanding of grief, any of Elisabeth Kübler-Ross's books on death and dying is valuable, including *Death: The Final Stage of*

Growth (Englewood Cliffs, N.J.: Prentice-Hall, 1975). John Bowlby's three-volume series *Attachment and Loss* is the classic work on the ways children respond to the loss of their mothers (New York: Basic Books, 1969, 1973, 1980). Among those professionals dealing with adoption, Claudia L. Jewett Jarratt is recognized as an expert on the ways children grieve for the birth parents and foster parents they have lost and how they can be helped to resolve that grief so they can form new attachments to adoptive parents. Many of the workshops she has presented since 1977 have dealt with these topics, as does her book *Helping Children Cope with Separation and Loss* (cited in General Adoption). The technique in which adoptive parents learn the child's routine from the foster parents and therapeutic play techniques for helping children resolve grief are outlined in "Adopted Children Need More than Love," *Adopted Child* (December 1981), by Lois Melina, based on an interview with Claudia Jewett (now Jarratt).

Carol Williams has also made major contributions to understanding the adjustments children must make when they are moved from one caretaker to another, chiefly through her workshops. Her views on how infants react to being moved from one home and caretaker to another were the basis for "Even Babies Can Have Adjustment Problems," by Lois Melina, *Adopted Child* (June 1984). One of the few published articles on this topic is Justin D. Call's, "Helping Infants Cope with Change," *Early Child Development and Care* 3 (January 1974): 229–247. *Toddler Adoption: The Weaver's Craft*, by Mary Hopkins-Best (Indianapolis: Perspectives Press, 1997), gives parents good advice about the adjustment of toddlers, while Vera Fahlberg's book, *A Child's Journey Through Placement* (see General Adoption for the complete citation), describes the effects of moves on older children and gives specific suggestions for easing the transition.

For information on child care customs around the world, consult *PACT BookSource* or a catalog prepared by Adoptive Families of America (see Organizations).

The information on the adjustment of infants who were prenatally exposed to drugs or alcohol was obtained from Ira J. Chasnoff, M.D., and Dan Griffith, Ph.D., through personal interviews, conference presentations, and published papers. For more information, see "Cocaine and Alcohol Affect Unborn Babies," by Lois Melina, *Adopted Child* (November 1988); "Guidelines for Adopting Drug-Exposed Infants and Children," by Chasnoff (NAPARE, 200 North Michigan Avenue, Suite 300, Chicago, IL 60601, 1992); and "Researchers Are Optimistic about Drug-Exposed Children; Prospective Parents Are Apprehensive," by Melina, *Adopted Child* (November 1997), which was based on presentations at the conference *Adoption and Prenatal Alcohol Exposure: The Research, Policy, and Practice Challenges*, October 24–25, 1997, in Alexandria, Virginia, sponsored by the Evan B. Donaldson Adoption Institute. Research papers on the topic include "Prenatal Drug Exposure: Effects on Neonatal and Infant Growth and Development," by Chasnoff et al., *Neurobehavioral Toxicology and Teratology* 8 (1986): 357–362; "Cocaine Abuse in Pregnancy: Effects on the Fetus and Newborn," by Lynn Ryan et al., *Neurotoxicology and Teratology* 9 (1987): 295–299; "Newborn Infants with Drug Withdrawal Symptoms," by Chasnoff, *Pediatrics in Review* 9 (March 1988): 273–277. (For references on the long-term outcome of prenatal drug and alcohol exposure, see citations in Chapter 6.)

Guidelines for helping an adoptee adjust to a new school are found in "The Special Student," a collection of essays compiled by Gloria Pererson for the Illinois Council on Adoptable Children, now out of print, and in "Parents: Do Homework before Sending Non-English-Speaking Child to School," by Lois Melina, *Adopted Child* (August 1989).

Material on the adjustment of children from orphanages, particularly in Eastern Europe, was obtained from personal interviews with Sharon Cermak, Ed.D.; Victor Groze, Ph.D.; and Sandra Kaler, R.N., Ph.D., and was published in "Institutionalized Children Have Problems, Show Progress after Adoption," by Lois Melina, *Adopted Child* (November 1995). More references on children from Eastern Europe are listed in Chapter 10.

The section in this book on how siblings react to adoption was based on interviews with Laurie Flynn, Vera Fahlberg, Claire Berman, and Barbara Roberts and several siblings of adoptees, which became a series of articles on siblings published in *Adopted Child:* "Youth Talk about Adopted Siblings" (November 1983), "Kids Already in Home React to New Sibling" (November 1983), "Siblings Need Help When Older Child Arrives" (December 1983), and "Bio Children May Not Be Eager for 'International' Experiences" (April 1984), all by Lois Melina.

Information on the ways children born into a family are affected by adoption, as well as on how to prepare children already in the home for the adoption of a child who may be sexually aggressive was derived from a presentation by Jim and Kathryn Anderson at the 1985 conference sponsored by the North American Council on Adoptable Children, which was reported by Lois Melina in "Adoption Messages May Confuse Biologic Child," *Adopted Child* (November 1985).

The value of support from family and friends to the success of the adjustment is discussed in Feigelman and Silverman's book (see General Adoption for the full citation). Pat Holmes's pamphlet *Supporting an Adoption* (Wayne, Penn.: Our Child Press, 1986) helps family members and friends learn how they can be more supportive to the adoptive family. Lois Melina's audiotape, *Introduction to Adoption for Family and Friends* (P.O. Box 9362, Moscow, ID 83843, 1990) helps relatives and friends understand their own reactions to news that someone is adopting and provides advice on how to support the adoptive family.

Chapter 3: Bonding and Attachment

John Bowlby's three-volume work (see Chapter 2 for a complete citation) is still the definitive work on bonding, attachment, and separation. A more succinct and understandable discussion is found in Frank G. Bolton Jr., *When Bonding Fails: Clinical Assessment of High-Risk Families* (Beverly Hills, Calif: Sage Publications, 1983). An excellent explanation of what attachment is believed to be and how it develops can be found in *Becoming Attached: The Character of Parental Love and Its Legacy in Later Life,* by Robert Karen (New York: Oxford University Press, 1998). Karen, Charles Zeanah, and Alan Sroufe were all interviewed by Lois Melina for the article "Attachment Theorists Believe Parent-Infant Experiences Determine Later Behavior," *Adopted Child* (May 1997).

The best research on the success of attachment between mothers and their adopted infants was done by researchers at Rutgers and Yeshiva universities—Leslie M. Singer, David M. Brodzinsky, Douglas Ramsey, Mary Steir, and Everett Waters—and was reported in "Mother-Infant Attachment in Adoptive Families," *Child Development* 56 (December 1985): 1543–1551.

The attachment of parents and children adopted at an older age was discussed by Terrence J. Koller in "Older Child Adoptions: A New Developmental Intervention Program," a paper presented at the annual meeting of the American Psychological Association, Los Angeles, 1981, and in "Attachment to Older Child Has Some Twists, by Lois Melina, *Adopted Child* (January 1985). Vera Fahlberg's booklet, *Attachment and Separation* (Lansing: Michigan Department of Social Services, 1979), is a workbook for social workers that provides a general discussion of attachment, a theory about the attachment of older children, and guidelines for assessing the failure to attach. Much of this material is also contained in *A Child's Journey Through Placement* (see General Adoption for the full citation). Ways to identify failure to attach, as well as techniques to facilitate attachment with an unattached child, were discussed by Josephine Anderson (known to many as Josephine Braden) at the 1984 conference sponsored by the North American Council on Adoptable Children, which was reported on by Lois Melina in "Unattached Child: Going through Life Not Caring," *Adopted Child* (February 1985). Numerous experts in the field of attachment were interviewed by Melina for her article on attachment disorders and treatments, "Variety of Attachment Disorders Need Variety of Treatment Options," *Adopted Child* (May 1994).

Information about breastfeeding the adopted baby is contained in both technical articles and a helpful guide. Kathleen G. Auerbach and Jimmie Lynne Avery, "Induced Lactation: A Study of Adoptive Nursing by 240 Women," *American Journal of Diseases of Children* 135 (April 1981): 340–343, discusses the reasons adoptive women choose to breastfeed and the quantities of milk produced through relactation. Ronald Kleinman, Linda Jacobson, Elizabeth Hormann, and W. Allan Walker reported that the first milk of adoptive mothers does not contain colostrum in "Protein Values of Milk Samples from Mothers without Biologic Pregnancies," *Journal of Pediatrics* 97 (October 1980): 612–615. *Nursing Your Adopted Baby,* by Kathryn Anderson (Franklin Park, Ill.: La Leche League International, 1986) is a guide for relactation as are "Nursing the Adopted Baby," by Teresa Kovarik, available from Gerber Products (1-800-595-0324), and *Breastfeeding the Adopted Baby,* by Debra Stewart Peterson (San Antonio: Corona Publishing, 1994). *The Nursing*

Mother's Companion, 3rd rev. ed., by Kathleen Huggins (Boston: Harvard Common Press, 1995), also contains information about breast-feeding and adoption. Elizabeth Hormann outlines a schedule for breast-feeding the adopted baby in "Breastfeeding: Goal Is Emotional, not Nutritional Benefit," by Lois Melina, *Adopted Child* (March 1983). Individual support and help for the adoptive mother who is trying to induce lactation can be provided by members of La Leche League International (1400 North Meacham Road, Schaumberg, IL 60173-4048; phone: 847-519-7730, url: www.lalecheleague.org).

The Supplemental Nutritional System (Medela, P.O. Box 660, McHenry, IL 60050; phone: 1-800-435-8316; url: www.medela.com) and Lact-Aid Nursing Trainer (Lact-Aid International, P.O. Box 1066, Athens, TN 37371-1066; phone: 1-423-744-9090; url: www.Lact-Aid.com) can be purchased directly from the manufacture, pharmacies, and home health care suppliers or from Body Profile Clinic (phone: 1-801-392-9074). Geddes Productions (P.O. Box 41761, Los Angeles, CA 90041-0761; phone: 818-951-2809; url: www.gedespro.com) offers the video *Supplemental Nursing Systems* and *Breastfeeding Pocket Guide*, a handy reference for adoptive mothers who plan to breastfeed.

Chapter 4: Talking About Adoption

Thorough discussions of what children want to know about their adoption and what they can understand at different developmental stages can be found in *Making Sense of Adoption*, by Lois Ruskai Melina (New York: Harper & Row, 1989), and *Being Adopted* (see General Adoption for the full citation). Information on the difference between secrecy and privacy in disclosing adoption information can be found in Melina's article, "Even Well Adjusted Parents Can Be Uneasy Disclosing Adoption," *Adopted Child* (January 1991), and the corresponding audiotape, *Who Should Know? Secrecy, Privacy, and Openness in Adoption* (Lois Melina, 1993), while general information about the harmful effects of secrecy can be found in *The Dance of Deception* by Harriet Goldhor Lerner (New York: HarperCollins, 1994). Guidelines for what to tell teachers can be found in "Teachers Need to Be More Sensitive to Adoption Issues," by Melina *Adopted Child* (August 1990), while suggestions for explaining adoption to nonadopted children are contained in "Guidelines for Explaining Adoption to Children Outside the Family," by Melina, *Adopted Child* (December 1991).

Reports and research on how adoptees feel about what they have been told about their adoption are found in Lois Raynor's "The Adopted Child Comes of Age," (cited in Chapter 1), *and* John Triseliotis's *In Search of Origins,* and Betty Jean Lifton's *Lost and Found* (cited in Chapter 5).

The theory that it is traumatic to tell a child of her adoption too early is put forth in Herbert Wieder's article "On Being Told of Adoption," *Psychoanalytic Quarterly* 46 (January 1977): 1–22. A child's need to know the circumstances of his birth is explained by Marshall Schechter in "Child Needs to Know Birth Story, by Lois Melina, *Adopted Child* (September 1982).

One of the most illuminating reports in recent years shows how children's understanding about adoption changes with their developmental age: "Children's Understanding of Adoption," *Child Development* 55 (June 1984): 869–878, by David M. Brodzinsky, Leslie M. Singer, and Anne M. Braff of Rutgers University. Children's reluctance to discuss adoption is explored in "Children's Reluctance to Discuss Adoption May Hide Real Interest," by Lois Melina, *Adopted Child* (August 1991).

Numerous books published for children describe the adoption process or tell the story of a child's adoption. Everyone has his or her own favorite. Two of the most popular are *Tell Me Again About the Night I Was Born,* by Jamie Lee Curtis (New York: HarperCollins, 1996), and *The Day We Met You,* by Phoebe Koehler (New York: Simon & Schuster, 1990). For more titles, consult the Tapestry Book catalog, the Perspectives Press catalog, or the *PACT BookSource,* all listed in Sources of Books and Merchandise on page 358.

For more on how to explain difficult information to children, consult *Making Sense of Adoption* by Lois Ruskai Melina (cited earlier in Chapter 4). Discussions of the abandonment of children can be found in Melina's articles, "Parents Advised of Ways to Explain Abandonment to Children" and "Understanding China's Policies Leading to Abandonment of Girls," *Adopted Child* (February 1996), which are based on interviews with Kay Johnson, and "Abandonment' in Korea Sometimes a Pretense," *Adopted Child* (February 1986). More about the adoption of children with HIV/AIDS is presented in "Adoption of Children with HIV/AIDS Is Unique Challenge," by Melina, *Adopted Child* (October 1991), and the topic of children conceived through rape is addressed in "Avoid False Stereotypes in Explaining Birthfathers Who Raped," by Melina, *Adopted Child* (April 1992).

The importance of life books and how to make them can be found in *A Child's Journey Through Placement* (see General Adoption for the full citation) and *Making Sense of Adoption* by Melina.

The role of forgiveness was described in Lois Melina's article, "The Wounds of Adoption Can Be Healed; *Forgiveness*—Justice and Mercy—Is the key," *Adopted Child* (August 1997), which was based on interviews with Michael E. McCullough, Ph.D., coauthor with Steven J. Sandage and Everett L. Worthington of *To Forgive Is Human: How to Put your Past in the Past* (Downers Grove, Ill.: InterVarsity Press, 1997), and Harold Kushner, author of *How Good Do We Have to Be? A New Understanding of Guilt and Forgiveness* (Boston: Little, Brown, 1996), as well as *Forgiveness: A Bold Choice for a Peaceful Heart,* by Robin Casarjian (New York: Bantam Doubleday Dell, 1992).

Chapter 5: How Adoption Affects the Family

Not as much attention has been given to the impact of infertility and adoption on parents as is needed. Ellen Glazer's book *The Long-Awaited Stork* (see Chapter 1 for the full citation), and Elinor Rosenberg's book *The Adoption Lifecycle: The Children and Their Families Through the Years* (New York: Free Press, 1992) are among the few that address the topic. David Brodzinsky deals with the topic in "Infertility and Adoption Adjustment: Considerations and Clinical Issues," in *Infertility: Psychological Issues and Counseling Strategies,* edited by Sandra R. Leiblum (New York: John Wiley, 1996). The impact of religion on the self-esteem of adoptive parents is developed by Michael Gold in *And Hanna Wept: Infertility, Adoption, and the Jewish Couple* (New York: Jewish Publication Society, 1988). Lois Melina addressed this topic in "Clergy Need to Understand Infertility, Adoption Issues," *Adopted Child* (August 1988).

Claudia Jewett Jarratt's book *Helping Children Cope with Separation and Loss* (see General Adoption for the complete citation) contains detailed information on how to explain unpleasant facts to a child. Carol Williams explains in her workshops how to talk to children about why they were placed for adoption and how to answer other questions they may have. One of these excellent presentations formed the basis for three articles in *Adopted Child:* "Child's Adoption Queries Tied to Age" (July 1982), "Help Your Child Make a Scrapbook" (May 1982), and "Talking to Children About Their Unpleasant Past" (June 1985).

The effect of unrealistic expectations on parents is described in *Parent Burnout,* by Joseph Procaccini and Mark W. Kiefaber (Garden City, N.Y.: Doubleday, 1983). These ideas were adapted to the adoptive parents' situation by Procaccini and Jean Oser in "Burn-out: Infertility, Home Study Can Lead Adoptive Parents to Expect too Much, by Lois Melina, *Adopted Child* (October 1983).

Claudia Jewett (now Jarratt) talks about the emphasis that adoptive parents place on environmental influences in *Adopting the Older Child* (Boston: Harvard Common Press, 1979). *Secret Thoughts of an Adoptive Mother* is cited in Chapter 1. *Being Adopted* is undoubtedly the best description of the impact of adoption on the adoptee (see General Adoption for the full citation).

In Jill Krementz's book *How It Feels to Be Adopted* (New York: Knopf, 1982), nineteen adopted children tell in their own words what it is like to be adopted. The impact of adoption on the adoptee is often found in books that deal with adoptees' desire to search for information about their biological origins, such as *The Adoption Triangle* (see General Adoption for the complete citation), and *In Search of Origins: The Experiences of Adopted People* (Boston: Routledge & Kegan Paul, 1973), John Triseliotis's report on seventy adoptees who requested information about their biological origins in Edinburgh, Scotland.

The first-person accounts of adoptees, such as Betty Jean Lifton's *Twice Born: Memoirs of an Adopted Daughter* (New York: McGraw-Hill, 1975), give insights into the experiences of adoptees, as does Lifton's book *Lost and Found: The Adoption Experience* (New York: Dial Press, 1979), which is based on her own experiences as well as interviews with other adoptees. How some adoptees feel about their extended families is explored by John Triseliotis in *In Search of Origins* and by Lifton in "Adoptees May Question Membership in 'Clan,'" by Lois Melina,

Adopted Child (August 1985). More recent accounts include *A Man and His Mother,* by Tim Green (New York: HarperCollins, 1997).

Family romance fantasies are discussed by Sorosky, Baran, and Pannor in *The Adoption Triangle* (see General Adoption for the complete citation) and by Herbert Wieder, "The Family Romance Fantasies of Adopted Children," *Psychoanalytic Quarterly 46* (April 1977): 185–200.

For references on grief, see Chapter 2. Information on the ways holidays can be difficult for people with unresolved grief is contained in *Birthmark,* by Lorraine Dusky (New York: M. Evans 1979), and "Adoption May Affect Holidays and Other Occasions in Subtle Ways," by Lois Melina, *Adopted Child* (November 1993). Suggestions for celebrating adoption anniversaries can be found in "Adoption Day Ritual Acknowledges Significant Day for Child, Family," by Melina, *Adopted Child* (December 1995). The full citation for *Designing Rituals for Adoption* is in Chapter 1. John McCutcheon's song "Happy Adoption Day" can be found on his audio tape, *Family Garden* (1993), and was published as a children's picture book (Boston: Little, Brown, 1996).

The full citations for the books of H. David Kirk are in General Adoption. Kirk's most recent essay, is which he discusses the difference between sociologists' and psychologists' approaches to adoption, is "Search and Rescue: A Belated Critique of 'Growing Up Adopted,'" in *Families and Adoption,* ed. by Harriet E. Gross and Marvin B. Sussman (Binghamton, NY: Haworth Press, 1997), also published in *Marriage & Family Review* 25 (1997).

Among the many excellent books on child development are *Your Three Year Old: Friend or Enemy* and *Your Four Year Old: Wild and Wonderful* by Louise Bates Ames and Frances L. Ilg (New York: Dell Publishing Co., 1976), and *The Hurried Child* and *All Grown Up and No Place to Go* by David Elkind (Reading, Mass.: Addison-Wesley, 1981, 1984).

Chapter 6: Are Adoptees at Risk?

The controversy over the long-term effects of adoption on adoptees began with the publication of "Observations on Adopted Children," *Archives of General Psychiatry 3* (July 1960): 45/21–56/32, by Marshall D. Schechter, who concluded that adopted children were represented in his psychiatric practice a hundred times more than could be expected from the general population. H. David Kirk, Kurt Jonassohn, and Ann D. Fish, in "Are Adopted Children Especially Vulnerable to Stress?" *Archives of General Psychiatry 14* (March 1966): 291–298, question Schechter's statistics and report that in their study, adopted children were not over-represented in psychiatric populations.

More recently, Paul M. Brinich and Evelin B. Brinich looked at the representation of adoptees at a psychiatric institute from 1969 to 1978 and found a higher percentage of adoptees than expected among the children, but a lower rate among adults. Their findings are reported in "Adoption and Adaptation," *Journal of Nervous and Mental Disease 170* (August 1982): 489–493.

One of the best studies of a nonclinic population was undertaken in Great Britain, where 16,000 children who were born during one week of 1958 were followed for growth, academic performance, and social adjustment. Two books report on those in the sample who were adopt-ed: Jean Seglow, Mia Kellmer Pringle, and Peter Wedge, *Growing Up Adopted* (Windsor, England: National Foundation for Educational Research in England and Wales, 1972), which looks at the sample at age seven, and Lydia Lambert and Jane Streather, *Children in Changing Families: A Study of Adoption and Illegitimacy* (London: Macmillan, 1980), which looks at them four years later.

Another important study is Alexina Mary McWhinnie's *Adopted Children: How They Grow Up* (London: Routledge & Kegan Paul, 1967/New York: Humanities Press), in which the author interviewed fifty-eight adult adoptees and looked at their long-term adjustment, as well as factors that might have influenced their adjustment, such as the level of communication in the adoptive home about the subject of adoption.

Benson Jaffee and David Fanshel's *How They Fared in Adoption: A Fol-low-up Study* (see Chapter 1 for the complete citation) reports on one hun-dred families who adopted children from 1931 to 1940 and evaluates their child-rearing practices, how the parents told the children they were adopt-ed, the parents satisfaction with adoption, and the adoptees' adjustment.

Janet L. Hoopes found that adoptive parents were more protective and less authoritarian than biological parents and that adopted children had lower self-esteem and less self-confidence than nonadopted children in her examination of 260 adoptive families, which is reported in *Prediction in Child Development: A Longitudinal Study of Adoptive and Nonadoptive Families* (New York: Child Welfare League of America, 1982).

In a retrospective study, *The Adopted Child Comes of Age* (London: George Allen & Unwin, 1980), Lois Raynor found that adoptees and their parents were more satisfied with the adoption when they perceived themselves as similar in some way. Adoptees were also more satisfied when their parents gave them freedom to pursue their own interests.

Although the methodology they used has been questioned, Kathlyn S. Marquis and Richard A. Detweiler reported in "Does Adopted Mean Different? An Attributional Analysis," *Journal of Personality and Social Psychology* 48 (April 1985): 1054–1066, that the adoptees they studied were more confident than the nonadoptees and viewed their parents as more nurturing, comforting, helpful, and protectively concerned than biological parents.

A major look at the academic achievements of adopted children is provided by the Collaborative Perinatal Project, which studied the pregnancies of women at fifteen hospitals throughout the United States, beginning in 1959, and followed children born to the women until 1974. Among them were 243 children who were adopted as infants. The results were published in *Early Correlates of Speech, Language, and Hearing: The Collaborative Perinatal Project of the National Institute of Neurological and Communicative Disorders and Stroke*, edited by Frank M. Lassman, Paul J. LaBenz, and Elaine S. LaBenz (Littleton, Mass.: Wright-PSG, 1980).

The adjustment and academic performance of adoptees and nonadopted children ages six to eleven, who were matched closely for age, sex, race, socioeconomic status, family structure, and number of siblings, were evaluated by the Rutgers University team of David M. Brodzinsky, Dianne E. Schechter, Anne M. Braff, and Leslie M. Singer in "Psychological and Academic Adjustment in Adopted Children," *Journal of Consulting and Clinical Psychology* 52 (August 1984): 582–590.

A review of the literature on this subject would not be complete without mentioning Michael Bohman's *Adopted Children and their Families* (Stockholm: Proprius, 1970); Michael Bohman and Sören Sigvardsson's "A Prospective, Longitudinal Study of Children Registered for Adoptions: A 15-Year Follow-up," *Acta Psychiatrica Scandinavica* 61 (April 1980): 339–355; and Barbara Tizard's *Adoption: A Second Chance* (London: Open Books, 1977).

More recently, William Feigelman analyzed data from the National Longitudinal Study of Youth and presented his findings in "Adopted Adults: Comparisons with Persons Raised in Conventional Families," in *Adoption and Families*, edited by Harriet E. Gross and Marvin B. Sussman (Binghamton, NY: Haworth Press, 1997). Feigelman's study was reported on in "Study Sheds New Light on Outcome for Adolescent, Adult Adoptees," by Lois Melina, *Adopted Child* (August 1995). A comparison of the number of patients registering for psychiatric services as children and as adults can be found in "Adoption and Adaptation," by Paul M. Brinich and Evelin B. Brinich, *Journal of Nervous and Mental Disease* 170 (August 1982): 489–493. Ruth McRoy's research was published as *Emotional Disturbance in Adopted Adolescents: Origins and Development*, by McRoy, Harold D. Grotevant, and Louis A. Zurcher Jr. (New York: Praeger, 1988), and was reported on in "Causes of Adoptees' Emotional Problems Probed," by Lois Melina, *Adopted Child* (September 1987). David Brodzinsky suggests that children may be distracted or overwhelmed by adoption issues in *Being Adopted* (see General Adoption for the full citation).

Related to the issue of the long-term effects of adoption on the adoptee are studies of identity conflict during adolescence, and investigations of why some adoptees search for information about their biological parents and why others do not. For these sources, see Chapter 8.

Evidence of a greater risk among adoptees for certain behavioral problems associated with learning disabilities is detailed in "Overrepresentaton of Adoptees in Children with the Attention Deficit Disorder," by Curtis K. Deutsch, James M. Swanson, Jan H. Bruell, Dennis P. Cantwell, Fred Weinberg, and Martin Baren, *Behavior Genetics* 12 (March 1982): 231–238; *Minimal Brain Dysfunction: A Prospective Study*, by Paul L. Nichols and Ta-Chuan Chen (Hillsdale, N.J.: Lawrence Erlbaum Associates, 1981); and "Adoption and Foster Care Rates in Pediatric Disorders," by J. Thomas Dalby, Sharon L. Fox, and Robert H. A. Haslam, *Developmental and Behavioral Pediatrics* 3 (June 1982): 61–64.

There are a number of good references for parents of children with attention deficit disorder, including *Raising a Hyperactive Child,* by Mark A. Stewart and Sally W. Olds (New York: Harper & Row, 1973), and the books by Edward M. Hallowell and John J. Ratey: *Driven to Distraction: Recognizing and Coping with Attention Deficit Disorder from Childhood Through Adulthood* (New York: Pantheon Books, 1994) and *Answers to Distraction* (New York: Pantheon Books, 1995). "Pseudo-ADHD" is described in Hallowell's book *When You Worry About the Child You Love* (New York: Simon & Schuster, 1996). Good resources on learning disabilities include Betty B. Osman's book, *Learning Disabilities: A Family Affair* (New York: Random House, 1979), and *No One to Play With: The Social Side of Learning Disabilities,* by Osman in association with Henrietta Blinder (New York: Random House, 1982).

The long-term effects of prenatal drug exposure are described in "Three-Year Outcome of Children Exposed Prenatally to Drugs," by Dan R. Griffith, Scott D. Azuma, and Ira J. Chasnoff, *Journal of the American Academy of Child and Adolescent Psychiatry* 33 (January 1994): 20–27, and "Outcomes for Drug-Exposed Children Four Years Post-Adoption," by Richard P. Barth and Barbara Needell, *Children and Youth Services Review* 18 (1995): 37–56, and was the topic of a two-day conference, *Adoption and Prenatal Alcohol and Drug Exposure: The Research, Policy and Practice Challenges,* October 24–25, 1997, Alexandria, Virginia, sponsored by the Evan B. Donaldson Adoption Institute. These materials formed the basis for two reports by Lois Melina in *Adopted Child:* "Prenatal Drug Exposure Affects School-Age Child's Behavior" (January 1996) and "Researchers Optimistic about Drug-Exposed Children; Prospective Parents Are Apprehensive" (November 1997). For a complete bibliography on the topic, contact the Evan B. Donaldson Adoption Institute (see Organizations). *Fetal Alcohol Syndrome* by Ann Streissguth, Ph.D., is an excellent resource for families with children prenatally exposed to alcohol.

For more on resiliency in children, see *The Invulnerable Child,* edited by E. James Anthony and Bertram J. Cohler (New York: Guilford Press, 1987); *Vulnerable But Invincible: A Longitudinal Study of Resilient Children and Youth,* by Emmy E. Werner and Ruth S. Smith (New York: McGraw-Hill, 1982); and "The Role of Self-understanding in Resilient

Individuals: The Development of a Perspective," by William A. Beardslee, *American Journal of Orthopsychiatry* 59 (April 1989): 266–278. These sources were the basis of Lois Melina's article "Some Children Better Able to Develop Resiliency to Adversity," *Adopted Child* (April 1991).

Adoptees' thoughts on the ways in which adoption provides adoptees with opportunities for growth is explored in "Adoption Experience May Cultivate Traits, Life Directions, in Adoptees," by Lois Melina, *Adopted Child* (September 1995).

Information on David Kirschner's theory of the adopted child syndrome was obtained in personal communications with the author and reported in "'Adopted Child Syndrome' Gives Mistaken Impression of Adoption," by Lois Melina, *Adopted Child* (February 1992).

Chapter 7: The Important Family History

Genes, Brain, and Behavior, edited by Paul P. McHugh and Victor A. McKusick (New York: Raven Press, 1991), and *Genetics and Mental Illness,* edited by Laura Lee Hall (New York: Plenum, 1996), were consulted for information about the role of genetics in behavior, along with the article "Born Happy?" by Sharon Begley, *Newsweek* (October 14, 1996): 78–80. Another interesting discussion of the subject is found in *Not in Our Genes* by R. C. Lewontin, Steven Rose, and Leon J. Kamin (New York: Pantheon Books, 1984). For a look at heredity, environment, and adoption and how attitudes toward genetics have changed over the years, see "Stronger Role for Genetics gaining Support in Adoption," by Lois Melina, *Adopted Child* (September 1989).

Further information on the medical risks of children born of incestuous relationships can be found in "Children of Incest," by Patricia A. Baird and Barbara McGillivray, *Journal of Pediatrics* 101 (November 1982): 854–857.

Chapter 8: Contact with Biological Relatives

For more on open adoption, see *The Open Adoption Experience,* by Lois Ruskai Melina and Sharon Kaplan Roszia (New York: HarperCollins,

1993), and *The Spirit of Open Adoption,* by James L. Gritter (Washington, D.C.: Child Welfare League of America, 1997). For a report on research on open adoption, conducted by researchers at the University of Texas and the University of Minnesota, see *Openness in Adoption: New Practices, New Issues,* by Ruth McRoy, Harold D. Grotevant, and Kerry L. White (New York: Praeger, 1998), and *Changing Practices in Adoption,* by McRoy, Grotevant, and Susan Ayers-Lopez (cited in Chapter 1). Public attitudes toward open adoption were surveyed by Princeton Survey Research Associates for the Benchmark Adoption Survey, conducted for the Evan B. Donaldson Adoption Institute (see Organizations) in 1997. Publication of the findings had not been finalized as this book went to press.

There is considerable overlap in accounts of identity conflicts in adoptees, the reasons some adoptees search, and descriptions of the long-term adjustment of adoptees. John Triseliotis (see Chapter 5 for the complete citation) found that adoptees more likely to search for their biological parents, rather than for information, when information about their adoption was revealed in a hostile or evasive way or when their lives were unsatisfactory. Triseliotis also describes the significant events that often precipitate a search. As the definitive work on this subject, *The Adoption Triangle* (cited in General Adoption) explores the reasons adoptees search, as well as the outcome of reunions.

Though not a report of scientific research, Betty Jean Lifton's *Lost and Found* (See Chapter 5 for the complete citation) provides insights into the search-and-reunion issue, as do the first-person accounts of birth mothers who have searched: *Birthmark,* by Lorraine Dusky, (New York: M. Evans, 1979), and *I Would Have Searched Forever,* by Sandra Kay Musser (distributed by Haven Books, a division of Logos International, Plainfield, N.J., 1979). A more recent account of search and reunion is *Adoption Reunions,* by Michelle McColm (Second Story Press, 760 Bathurst Street, Toronto, Ontario, Canada, M5S 2R6, 1993). Carol Demuth's thoughts on the role of adoptive parents when adoptees are searching are described in "Adoptive Parents Need Support When Son or Daughter Searches," by Lois Melina, *Adopted Child* (February 1994), and are explored in more detail in Demuth's book, *Courageous Blessing: Adoptive Parents and the Search* (Aries Center, 1437 Meandering,

Garland, TX 75040, 1993). Another good resource is *Birthbond: Reunions Between Birthparents and Adoptees,* by Judith S. Gediman and Linda P. Brown (Far Hills, N.J.: New Horizon Press, 1989).

Chapter 9: Ethnic and Cultural Identity

The self-esteem of transracially adopted children was examined by Owen Gill and Barbara Jackson in *Adoption and Race: Black, Asian and Mixed Race Children in White Families* (New York: St. Martin's Press/London: Batsford Academic and Educational, 1983), a follow-up study of children in the British Adoption Project. No differences in self-esteem or self-concept between black children adopted by white parents and black children adopted by black parents or differences between black adoptees and white, nonadopted adolescents were found by Ruth G. McRoy and Louis A. Zurcher Jr. in *Transracial and Inracial Adoptees: The Adolescent Years* (Springfield, Ill.: Charles C. Thomas, 1983). The book also describes the experiences of blacks adopted transracially, including dating and friends, siblings, school, and extended family members.

Dong Soo Kim, in his doctoral dissertation, "Intercountry Adoptions: A Study of Adolescent Self Concept Formation of Korean Children Who Were Adopted by American Families" (University of Chicago, August 1976), found that the Korean adoptees' self-concepts were similar to those of the Americans in his control group.

The results of a longitudinal study of transracial adoption were reported in the following books by Rita J. Simon and Howard Altstein: *Transracial Adoption* (New York: John Wiley, 1977), *Transracial Adoption: A Follow-Up* (Lexington, Mass.: Lexington Books, 1981), *Transracial Adoptees and Their Families: A Study of Identity and Commitment* (New York: Praeger, 1987), and *Adoption, Race, and Identity: From Infancy Through Adolescence* (New York: Praeger, 1992). Information on friendship and dating patterns among transracially adopted teenagers can be found in the studies by McRoy and her colleagues, as well as the study by Simon and Altstein.

Although Judith Porter did not study adoptive families, her book *Black Child, White Child: The Development of Racial Attitudes* (Cambridge, Mass.: Harvard University Press, 1971) is a helpful look at children's awareness of their racial identity. Interviews with Rita Simon and Judith Porter were used for the articles "Racial Identity Forms in Preschool Years" and "Transracial Homes Foster Positive Images," by Lois Melina, *Adopted Child* (July 1983).

William Feigelman and Arnold S. Silverman's book *Chosen Children* (cited in General Adoption) is a source of much of the information about the support that interracial families need and the extent to which they receive it, the association between positive racial identity and adjustment, and the development of racial identity among black, Colombian, and Korean adoptees Guidelines for the appropriate use of ethnic dolls are given by Karen Zelan in Lois Melina's article, "Ethnic Dolls: Too Much of a Good Thing?" *Adopted Child* (December 1982).

Information about ethnic identity can be found in *Ethnic Groups and Boundaries: The Social Organization,* by Fredrik Barth (Boston: Little Brown, 1969); *Creating Ethnicity: The Process of Ethnogenesis,* by Eugeen E. Roosens (Newbury Park, Calif.: Sage Publications, 1989); *Children's Ethnic Socialization: Pluralism & Development,* by Jean S. Phinney and Mary Jane Rotheram (Newbury Park, Calif.: Sage Publications, 1987); *Ethnic Identity: Creation, Conflict and Accommodation,* edited by George de Vos and Lola Romanucci-Ross (Walnut Creek, Calif.: Altamira Press, 1995); *Shades of Black: Diversity in African-American Identity,* by William Cross Jr. (Philadelphia: Temple University Press, 1992); *Psychological Storms: The African American Struggle for Identity* (Chicago: African American Images, 1993); "Ethnicity, Ethnic Identity, and Competence Formation: Adolescent Transition and Cultural Transformation," *Journal of Negro Education* 60 (1991): 366–387; *Black and White Racial Identity: Theory, Research, and Practice,* by Janet E. Helms (New York: Praeger, 1993); *A Race Is a Nice Thing to Have: A Guide to Being a White Person or Understanding the White Persons in Your Life,* by Janet E. Helms (Topeka, Kans.: Content Communications, 1993); *Latino Ethnic Consciousness: The Case of Mexican Americans and Puerto Ricans in Chicago* by Felix Padilla (South Bend, Ind.: University of Notre Dame Press, 1985); *Ethnic Labels, Latino Lives: Identity and the Politics of Representation in the U.S.,* by Suzanne Oboler (Minneapolis: University of Minnesota Press, 1995); and *The Hispanic Condition,* by Ilan Stavans (New York: HarperCollins, 1995). These materials, along with interviews with several of the authors and with Joseph Crumbley and James Mahoney, formed the basis for the following articles by Lois Melina in *Adopted Child:* "Ethnic Identity Includes Ancestry, but Is Shaped by Experience" (September 1996), "Latino Adoptees Share Ethnicity Issues with Other Latinos in America" (August 1996), and "Black Identity Serves to Protect Ego, Give Purpose, and Bridge Cultures" (January 1995). For a videotape containing many of Joseph Crumbley's suggestions, see *Parenting Tasks in Transracial Adoption* (Philadelphia: Action Duplication, 1995), which can be obtained from Crumbley (5500 Wissahickon Ave., Suite 102A, Philadelphia PA, 19144, 215-843-5987).

Chapter 10: International Adoption

An excellent book about international adoption is *Are Those Kids Yours?* by Cheri Register (New York: Free Press, 1991). Research on international adoption can be found in *Chosen Children* (see General Adoption for the full citation) and *Intercountry Adoption: A Multinational Perspective,* by Howard Altstein and Rita J. Simon (New York: Praeger, 1991). Hei Sook Park Wilkinson discusses being Korean in a white society in *Birth Is More Than Once: The Inner World of Adopted Korean Children* (Sunrise Ventures, 708 Parkman Drive, Bloomfield Hills MI 48013, 1985).

Jim Cummins's excellent booklet, *Bilingualism and Minority-Language Children* (Toronto: Ontario Institute for Studies in Education, 1981), is out of print. Both Cummins and Wallace Lambert of McGill University were interviewed for "Bilingualism Benefits Foreign-born" and "Foreign Children Easily Forget Native Tongue," both by Lois Melina, *Adopted Child* (October 1982).

The value of culture camps is described in "Advice Given on Starting a Successful Culture Camp for Adoptees," by Lois Melina, *Adopted Child* (March 1995). The article "Trip to Korea Triggers Many Feelings for Adoptees," by Lois Melina, *Adopted Child* (October 1987), describes some of the issues related to adoptees visiting their homelands, and the articles "Children Need Help Facing Negative Images of Countries of Origin" and "Adoptees May Worry about Birth Family; Feel Guilty Leaving Country," both by Lois Melina, *Adopted Child* (February 1990), explain other issues that internationally adopted children face, including "survivor guilt." These articles were based on interviews with a number of people, including therapist Holly van Gulden and psychiatrist Robert Jay Lifton.

Attitudes toward international adoption were surveyed in the Benchmark Adoption Survey (see Chapter 8 for the full citation).

Information about health issues for internationally adopted children was obtained from "Health Care of the Internationally Adopted Child Part 1: Before and at Arrival into the Adoptive Home," by Marie A. Sills Mitchell and Jerri Ann Jenista, *Journal of Pediatric Health Care* (March–April 1997): 51–59, and "Health Care of the Internationally Adopted Child Part 2: Chronic Care and Long-term Medical Issues," *Journal of Pediatric Health Care,* (May–June 1997): 117–125, as well as in a number of articles by Jenista in *Adoption/Medical News* (Adoption Advocates Press, 1921 Ohio Street, NE, Palm Bay, FL 32907; phone 407-724-0815): "Chronic Hepatitis B: Diagnosis" (October 1995), "Pre-Adoption Testing: Bane or Boon?" (April 1996), "Iodine and Adopted Chinese Children" (June 1996), "Ethnic Orthodontics: Race Can Make a Difference" (February 1997), and "Rickets in the 1990's" (June 1997).

Research on the reversibility of malnutrition was published in "Malnutrition and Environmental Enrichment by Early Adoption," by Myron Winick, Knarig Katchadurian Meyer, and Ruth C. Harris, *Science* 190 (December 19, 1975): 1173–1175; "Malnutrition and Mental Development," by Myron Winick, in *Human Nutrition—A Comprehensive Treatise, Vol. 1: Nutrition—Pre and Postnatal Development,* edited by Myron Winick (New York: Plenum Press, 1979); and "Malnutrition and Adoption: Two Variables in Child Development," by Marcos Cusminsky, Luis Garcia Azzarini, Zulema Dopchiz, Maria C. Alonso, Graciela Narduzzi, and Monica Berisso, *Early Child Development and Care* 15 (April 1984): 45–56. Guidelines for measuring growth in internationally adopted children were presented by George Sterne and Robert Bilenker in "Height and Weight: North American Growth Charts Can Be Used for All Children," by Lois Melina, *Adopted Child* (December 1984).

Though no longer available, Joyce Kaser's article, "Parenting the Ageless Child," was helpful in understanding the issues for children of indeterminate ages. Jerri Ann Jenista's article on the same topic, "Estimating an Unknown Age of a Child," *Adoption/Medical News* (January

1996) is an excellent, up-to-date source of information.

Linda Massey and Harold Lubin provided details on lactose intolerance for Lois Melina's article, "Milk: Your Child May not Have to Give It Up," *Adopted Child* (February 1982).

Information about children from orphanages, particularly those in Romania, can be found in *The Development of Romanian Orphanage Children Adopted to Canada: Final Report* by Elinor W. Ames et al. (to obtain a copy, phone the Adoptive Parents Association of British Columbia at 604-588-7300); "A Follow-Up Study of Adopted Children from Romania," by Victor Groze and Daniela Ileana, *Child & Adolescent Social Work Journal* 13 (December 1996): 541–565, a version of which was presented at the twenty-first annual conference of the North American Council for Adoptable Children, Norfolk, Virginia, August 3–6, 1995; "Attachment Security and Indiscriminately Friendly Behavior in Children Adopted from Romanian Orphanages," by Kim Chisholm et al., *Development and Psychopathology* 7 (1995): 283–294; "The Health of Children Adopted from Romania," by Dana E. Johnson et al., *Journal of the American Medical Association* 268 (December 23–30, 1992): 3446–3451; and personal communication with Dana Johnson, M.D. Some of this information first appeared in the article "Institutionalized Children Have Problems, Show Progress after Adoption," by Lois Melina, *Adopted Child* (November 1995).

With Eyes Wide Open: A Workbook for Parents Adopting International Children Over Age One is available from the Children's Home Society of Minnesota (2230 Como Avenue, St. Paul, MN 55108; phone 612-646-6393).

Chapter 11: Serious Behavioral Problems

In compiling the information on children with serious behavioral problems for the first edition of this book. I depended heavily on several people whose knowledge of this subject is extensive: Claudia Jewett Jarratt, Barbara Tremitiere, Kathryn S. Donley Ziegler, Linda Katz, James Mahoney, Josephine Anderson, and John Boyne. Since most of these people use training workshops and conferences to communicate their ideas, much of the information has not been published. Jarratt's workshop at the 1985 conference of the North American Council on Adoptable children touched on how parents can deal with children who have serious behavioral problems. Tremitiere travels throughout the United States speaking with authority about the large adoptive family and raising children with serious behavioral problems. Some of her ideas were reported in "Tough Stance Taken with Difficult Teenagers," by Lois Melina, *Adopted Child* (November 1982). She later expanded on this topic in a personal interview for this book. Her research on the large adoptive family was presented at the 1985 conference of the North American Council on Adoptable Children, and her research on disruption at the 1984 conference of the council. Many of the ideas that Ziegler has presented at workshops and seminars have been compiled into *Helping Placements Survive: Minimizing the Chance of a Disruption*, by Bonnie C. Bedics and Kathryn S. Donley (Social Work Department, University of West Florida, Pensacola, FL 32514). This work also summarizes studies of the causes of disruption. Linda Katz's ideas on the parental characteristics that enhance the success of the adoption of a child with behavioral problems were presented at the 1984 conference of the North American Council on Adoptable Children and reported by Lois Melina in "Disturbed Children: Child's Behavior Not Only Factor in Success of Placement," *Adopted Child* (November 1984). Mahoney presented a workshop on task-oriented therapy and how to choose a therapist at the 1985 conference of the North American Council on Adoptable Children. The importance of a therapist who is sensitive to adoption issues was discussed by Jacqueline Hornor Plumez and Alan Long in "Child Therapy: When Is It Indicated?" by Lois Melina *Adopted Child* (April 1983). Boyne's thoughts on the risk of child abuse in adoptive homes were shared at the 1984 conference of the North American Council on Adoptable Children and reported in Lois Melina's article "Adoptive Homes Not Immune to Child Abuse," *Adopted Child* (September 1984).

Suggestions for dealing with children who are the same age or close in age came from "Kids Close in Age Need Individuality," by Lois Melina *Adopted Child* (January 1983).

Joyce S. Cohen's research on disruption, "Adoption Breakdown with Older Children," was included in *Adoption: Current Issues and Trends*, edited by Paul Sachdev (Toronto: Butterworth's, 1984).

More recently published books that are useful for parents of children with severe behavioral problems include *Adoption and the Sexually Abused Child*, edited by Joan McNamara and Bernard H. McNamara (Portland: University of Southern Maine, 1990); *Successful Adoptive Families: A Longitudinal Study of Special Needs Adoptions*, by Victor Groza (New York: Praeger, 1996); *A Child's Journey Through Placement* (see General Adoption for the full citation): *Residential Treatment: A Tapestry of Many Therapies*, by Vera Fahlberg (Indianapolis: Perspectives Press, 1990); *Adoption Policy and Special Needs Children*, edited by Rosemary J. Avery (Westport, Conn.: Auburn House, 1997); *Adoption and Disruption: Rates, Risks and Responses*, by Richard P. Barth and Marianne Berry (New York: Aldine DeGruyter, 1988); *Parenting with Love and Logic: Teaching Children Responsibility* by Foster Cline and Jim Fay (Austin, Tex. Navpress, 1990) and *Parenting with Love and Logic: Preparing Adolescents for Responsible Adulthood*, also by Cline and Fay (Austin, Tex.: Navpress, 1993). Material on the effect on the family when a child goes into residential treatment was published in Lois Melina's article, "Families Have Mixed Feelings When Child Goes into Residential Care," *Adopted Child* (April 1990), based on an interview with Vera Fahlberg, M.D.

Chapter 12: Special Situations in Adoption

Information on the general effect a disabled child has on parents and siblings appears in *Families of Children with Special Needs: Early Intervention Techniques for the Practitioner*, by Allen A. Mori (Rockville, Md.: Aspen Systems, 1983), and *Severely Handicapped Young Children and Their Families: Research in Review*, edited by Jan Blacher (New York: Academic Press, 1984).

Lois Melina wrote about the adoption of children with HIV/AIDS in "Adoption of Children with HIV/AIDS Is Unique Challenge," *Adopted Child* (October 1991).

A general guide for parents of disabled children on such subjects as getting the right diagnosis, finding schools and programs, and organizing support services is *The Special Child Handbook* by Joan McNamara and Bernard McNamara (New York: Hawthorn Books 1977), which contains a chapter on adoption of the special needs child. Two booklets published by the North American Council on Adoptable Children but now out of print are: *Adopting the Child with Special Needs*, by Joan McNamara (1982), and *Adopting the Child with Special Needs: A Sequel* by Linda Dunn (1983). Reflections on the adoption of children with special needs; details on specific disabilities; and practical information, such as the use of computers by children with disabilities, are found in *Commitment: The Reality of Adoption*, by Grace Sandness (Mini-World Publications, 9965 Quaker Lane, Maple Grove, MN 55369, 1984). J. P. Blank's *Nineteen Steps Up the Mountain: The Story of the DeBolt Family* (Philadelphia: J. B. Lippincott, 1976) is the story of the adoption of special needs children by Dorothy and Robert DeBolt.

Opinions on the effect of divorce on adopted children were given by Judith Schaffer, Claire Berman, Claudia Jewett, and Judith S. Wallerstein in "Effect of Divorce on Adopted Children not Known" and "Adoptive Parents Feel Guilty over Divorce, by Lois Melina, *Adopted Child* (August 1984). The findings of David Brodzinsky, Jennifer Clarke Hitt, and Daniel Smith were published in their article, "Impact of Parental Separation and Divorce on Adopted and Nonadopted Children," *American Journal of Orthopsychiatry* 63 (3) (July 1993): 451–461. The topic was also addressed in "Parents Wonder If Adoptees Have Stronger Reactions to Divorce," by Lois Melina, *Adopted Child* (March 1994). The effect of a parent's death on an adopted child was discussed in "A parent's Death: Each Time a Unique Sorrow," in a special introductory issue of *Adopted Child* in 1981.

Research on single adoptive parents can be found in *Chosen Children* by Feigelman and Silverman (see General Adoption for the complete citation); "Single-Parent Adoptions," by Benjamin Schlesinger, in *Adoption: Current Issues and Trends*, edited by Paul Sachdev (cited fully in Chapter 11); and "Single Persons as Adoptive Parents," by Joan F. Shireman and Penny R. Johnson, *Social Service Review* 50 (March 1976): 103–116. *The Handbook for Single Adoptive Parents* (1997), edited by Hope Marindin and available from the Committee for Single Adoptive Parents (see Organizations for address), is also helpful. The experiences of single adoptive parents were described in presentations by Donna Naclerio and Cathie Thomas at the 1985 conference of the North American Council on Adoptable Children and by Barbara Jirik and Barbara Young at the council's 1984 conference.

Issues for gay and lesbian adoptive parents were addressed in "Gay Adoption Case Raises Questions about Parents, Children's Rights," by

Lois Melina, *Adopted Child* (April 1994). *The Lesbian and Gay Parenting Handbook,* by April Martin (New York: Harper Collins, 1993) also addresses adoption issues.

The ways siblings help each other during the adjustment period are described in *Large Sibling Groups: Adoption Experiences,* by Dorothy W. Le Pere, Lloyd E. Davis, Janus Couve, and Mona McDonald (San Antonio: Texas Department of Human Resources, 1985) and *The Sibling Bond,* by Stephen P. Bank and Michael D. Kahn (New York: Basic Books, 1982).

The full citation for *Adoption and the Sexually Abused Child* is in Chapter 11, and the full citation for *A Child's Journey Through Placement* is in General Adoption. The Benchmark Adoption Survey was cited in Chapter 8. *"Are Those Kids Yours?"* was cited in Chapter 10, and *The Open Adoption Experience* was cited in Chapter 1. *How To Raise an Adopted Child: A Guide to Help Your Child Flourish from Infancy through Adolescence,* by Judith Schaffer and Christiana Lindsrom (New York: E. P. Dutton, 1994), contains information about families with biological and adopted children, as does Ellen Glazer's book, *The Long-Awaited Stork* (see Chapter 1 for the full citation). Lois Melina described issues in families with biological and adopted children in "Parents with Biologic and Adopted Children May Worry about Partiality," *Adopted Child* (March 1996), and explored adopting a second child in "Parents Want Similar Adoption Experience the Second Time Around," *Adopted Child* (October 1994), using interviews with Ronny Diamond, Mona McDonald, and Marlene Piasecki. *Is That Your Sister?* by Sherry Bunin and Catherine Bunin (New York: Pantheon Books, 1976) gives a six year old's view of what it is like to have a sister of a different race than the rest of the family.

The unique issues of stepparent adoption are described in "Caution Urged in Adopting Stepchild," by Lois Melina, *Adopted Child* (January 1986). The similarities between donor insemination, donor egg, and surrogacy are described in Lois Ruskai Melina's *Making Sense of Adoption* (see Chapter 4 for the full citation). Children's books that address conception through assisted reproductive technology include *Let Me Explain: A Story About Donor Insemination,* by Jane T. Schnitter (Indianapolis: Perspectives Press, 1995); *Mommy, Did I Grow in Your Tummy? Where Some Babies Come From* by Elaine R. Gordon (E. M. Greenburg

Press, 1460 7th Street, Santa Monica, CA 90401, 1992); and *How Babies and Families Are Made (There is More Than One Way!)*, by Patricia Schaffer (Berkeley, CA: Tabor Sarah Books, 1988).

Appendixes

Guidelines for covering adoptees in health insurance policies and naming them as beneficiaries in wills and life insurance policies are outlined in "Check Your Health Insurance Before Adopting," by Lois Melina, Adopted Child, special introductory issue, and "Mention Adoption in Will, Lawyers Say," by Lois Melina, Adopted Child (March 1982).

What young children understand about the naturalization process was the topic of "'Citizenship' difficult concept for child" by Lois Melina, *Adopted Child* (May 1983), featuring Albert J. Solnit.

Organizations

Adoptive Families of America (2309 Como Avenue, St. Paul, MN 55108; phone: 612-645-9955), is a nonprofit adoptive parent support organization with chapters throughout the United States.

Committee for Single Parents (P.O. Box 15084, Chevy Chase, MD 20815) provides information and support to single persons who want to adopt.

The Evan B. Donaldson Adoption Institute (phone: 212-360-0280; E-mail: geninfo@adoptioninstitute.org) is a not-for-profit nationally focused organization whose mission is to improve the quality of information about adoption, enhance the understanding and perception of adoption, and advance adoption policy and practice. It sponsors a biennial conference and publishes mongraphs. An extensive database of adoption-related articles is available on its website: www.adoptioninstitute.org.

International Soundex Reunion Registry (P.O. Box 2312, Carson City, NV 28702) lists birth parents, siblings, and adoptees who are willing to exchange information or meet each other and has a medical information registry that encourages adoption agencies to notify birth families or adoptees when critical genetic information is discovered. Enclose a self-addressed, stamped envelope when you write for information.

The National Adoption Information Clearinghouse (P.O. Box 1182, Washington, DC 20013-1182; phone: 703-352-3488, 888-251-0075; E-mail: naic@calib.com; url:www.calib.com/naic) has a variety of informative resources.

The National Organization on Fetal Alcohol Syndrome (1819 H Street NW, Suite 750, Washington, DC 20006; phone: 202-758-4585; url: www.nofas.org; E-mail: nofas@erols.com) is a good source of information for parents of children with FAS or FAE.

North American Council on Adoptable Children (970 Raymond Avenue, Suite 106, St. Paul, MN 55114; phone: 612-644-3036; http://members.aol.com/nacac; E-mail: nacac@aol.com) is a nonprofit organization that advocates the adoption of children with special needs.

Resolve, Inc. 1310 Broadway, Somerville, MA 02144-1779; phone: 617-623-1156; E-mail: resolveinc@aol.com; url:www.resolve.org) is an information, advocacy, and support group for infertile couples.

Sources of Books and Merchandise

Adoptive Families of America has an excellent catalog of adoption books; adoption announcements; and other merchandise.

PACT BookSource is an annotated catalog of books on adoption and race. It is available from Pact (3450 Sacramento Street, Suite 239, San Francisco, CA 94118; phone: 415-221-6957; E-mail: info@pact-adopt.org; url:www.pactadopt.org).

Perspectives Press (P.O. Box 90318, Indianapolis, IN 46290-0318; phone: 317-872-3055; E-mail: ppress@iquest.net; url:www.perspectives-press.com) publishes books on infertility and adoption.

Tapestry Books (P.O. Box 359, Ringoes, NJ 08551-0359; phone 800-765-2367; E-mail: info@tapestrybooks.com; url:www.tapestrybooks.com) is a mail order catalog of books on adoption and special parenting issues.

Internet Resources

There are a variety of adoption resources available on the Internet—far too many to list here. Two good comprehensive sites are www.adopting.org and www.adoption.com.

A general listserv on adoption is listserv@MAELSTROM.STJOHNS.EDU. To subscribe, send a message "subscribe adoption."

Resources from Lois Melina

Lois Melina has a variety of resources, including her monthly newsletter *Adopted Child,* collections of back issues of the newsletter, and audiotapes of her presentations to adoptive parents and adoption professionals. This revised edition of *Raising Adopted Children,* along with *Making Sense of Adoption* and *The Open Adoption Experience,* can also be ordered from her. Quantity disacounts are available. For a catalog of her materials, contact her at P.O. Box 9362, Moscow, ID 83843; phone 1-888-882-1794; E-mail: Lmelina@moscow.com; url: www.raisingadopted-children.com.

Index

20909515R00242

Made in the USA
San Bernardino, CA
29 April 2015